Entrepreneurship and Economic Development

ELGAR IMPACT OF ENTREPRENEURSHIP RESEARCH

Series Editors: Maija Renko, *University of Illinois at Chicago*, Norris Krueger, *University of Phoenix, US* and Friederike Welter, *IfM Bonn and University of Siegen, Germany*

More so than many other disciplines, entrepreneurship is expected to have immediate relevance for practitioners, policy makers, and students. At the same time, the increasingly uniform incentive systems at business schools around the world reward those scholars who publish their research in lofty academic 'A' journals. Entrepreneurship scholars at various career stages struggle with different facets of the same question: How do I make my scholarship relevant and impactful, and to whom? And what does relevance mean?

This series comprises books that engage readers in a critical discussion on the relevance, measurement and impact of entrepreneurship scholarship and leave them with actionable suggestions to increase the relevance of their research.

Titles in the series include:

How to Make Your Doctoral Research Relevant
Insights and Strategies for the Modern Research Environment
Edited by Friederike Welter and David Urbano

The Truth about Entrepreneurship
Policy Making and Business Creation
Paul D. Reynolds

Entrepreneurship and Economic Development
The Global Scope of Business Creation
Paul D. Reynolds

Entrepreneurship and Economic Development

The Global Scope of Business Creation

Paul D. Reynolds

Honorary Professor in Entrepreneurship, Aston Business School, Birmingham, UK and Founding Coordinating Principal Investigator, Global Entrepreneurship Monitor Program

ELGAR IMPACT OF ENTREPRENEURSHIP RESEARCH

Edward Elgar
PUBLISHING

Cheltenham, UK • Northampton, MA, USA

Published by
Edward Elgar Publishing Limited
The Lypiatts
15 Lansdown Road
Cheltenham
Glos GL50 2JA
UK

Edward Elgar Publishing, Inc.
William Pratt House
9 Dewey Court
Northampton
Massachusetts 01060
USA

A catalogue record for this book
is available from the British Library

Library of Congress Control Number: 2022931715

This book is available electronically in the **Elgar**online
Business subject collection
http://dx.doi.org/10.4337/9781802206746

ISBN 978 1 80220 673 9 (cased)
ISBN 978 1 80220 674 6 (eBook)

Printed and bound by CPI Group (UK) Ltd, Croydon, CR0 4YY

Contents

Preface

In the early 2000s at a press conference announcing the latest Global Entrepreneurship Monitor (GEM) cross-national comparisons emphasizing the high levels of business creation in less developed countries a reporter asked, "Can there be too much entrepreneurship?" This seemed like an important question then—and now. The expansion of the GEM project now provides harmonized data for the entire range of national economic development. These data can be used to consider the role of business creation in economies at all stages of development.

This monograph provides an answer to this important question. It starts with a description of business creation and its contributions in six distinct stages of economic and societal development. These range from subsistence or indigenous cultures to the most highly developed knowledge-service economies. The overview of subsistence cultures is based on impressions from hundreds of field observers that have reported on indigenous societies over the past century, usefully organized in the Human Relations Area Files at Yale University.

Data from diverse sources on the latter five stages of development have been assembled to provide descriptions of business creation activity. Some descriptions are based on a subset of countries at a development stage and all countries are included in some later development stages. Some descriptions are based on calculations that are not straightforward but details of all procedures are provided in endnotes and appendices. The amount and nature of business creation makes different contributions at different stages of development.

The result is a clear answer to "Can there be too much entrepreneurship?" The answer is NO. Business creation reflects the efforts of volunteers responding to their context to create new firms. Firms that will provide diverse types of contributions at different stages of economic development. All ventures that persist, usually because the revenue exceeds costs, make economic and social contributions. The continuous churning (firm births and deaths) in the business population adjusts the level of activity to match the demand for goods and services in each sector. This reflects continuous bottom-up adjustments to economic conditions. Government agencies may be able to track, after the fact, these adjustments, but top-down strategies to promote business creation are unlikely to provide an optimal economic structure in most economies.

This does not mean that governments do not have a role in facilitating business creation and economic adaptation. Adjustments in the institutional context and preparation of the young for participating in the economy can minimize the social costs of the disruptions associated with business creation. Disruptions associated with economic adaptation are often referred to as "creative destruction." The most appropriate public policies, however, will depend on the stage of economic development. There are no universal "best practices."

This monograph was completed during the coronavirus lockdown in a Colorado mountain ranching and resort community. While the result contributes to understanding the importance of business creation, completion has served to minimize the strain of extreme social distancing and isolation.

Paul Reynolds
Steamboat Springs, Colorado
U.S.A.
February 2022

1.   Business creation: A global phenomenon

Basil, a young Ojibwa in northern Ontario in Canada, describes his efforts at business creation in the 1940s.

> Before launching my timbering (firewood) operation, I conducted a mental market-research survey ... There were Pulch, Meeks, Shabow, Bee Dee, Kitchi-Flossie, Chick, Kitchi-Susan, Shawnee, Kitchi-Low See, Christine Keeshig, Maggie, Eezup, Pollock, and many, many more. ... Then I realized that many of my potential customers cut their own wood, and that I would be in direct competition with my uncle Stanley. There wasn't as much revenue in cutting wood as I thought.
>
> I needed advice. I went to my Uncle Stanley, who was expert in survival. He suggested that I go into the fur industry, at the primary level, trapping or harvesting raccoons. And he showed me a price list issued by one of the fur buyers on Spadina Avenue in Toronto to illustrate how profitable the racoon industry was: up to twenty-four dollars for a prime pelt. I panted and drooled. Uncle was willing to share his expertise and his resources. There were more raccoons than my uncle and I together could harvest. All I needed was to kill one fat raccoon every day and I'd be in business. Uncle was generous. He conceded to me ... my own hunting territory ... One of the advantages of this kind of enterprise is that little capital investment is required. My total capital equipment consisted of two enthusiastic but inexperienced dogs and an axe. But that was all that was required for this kind of business.[1]

Ingvar's initial business creation efforts were also modest, but the results, many decades later, were quite different.

> As a schoolboy in the late 1930s in one of the poorest areas of Sweden, Ingvar Kamprad traveled the neighborhood on his bicycle selling door-to-door small items such as matches and Christmas ornaments. His father's cash reward for school success in 1943 led him to register a new firm at 17 called "IKEA, Ingvar Kamprad." His one-man firm sold fish, vegetable seeds, and magazines, delivered by bicycle or by milkmen. After four years he expanded to produce a mail-order catalogue in 1947 and added furniture and home furnishings in 1950. Six years later, after the purchase of a small furniture factory, a showroom was opened where customers could order furniture. IKEA furniture was very popular at furniture shows in Stockholm. Other Swedish manufacturers, as a protest of low prices, tried to organize a boycott of IKEA. The response was to create an in-house design unit and source products from Denmark and Poland. Efforts to reduce shipping costs and retail prices led to flat-packed furniture, easy to carry home to be assembled by customers. Growing demand led to the first large scale IKEA outlet near Stockholm

in 1958. Expansion, slow and deliberate, relied on retained earnings and did not require funding from creditors or stockholders. It was five more years before a store was opened outside of Sweden, and another ten years before a store opened outside the Nordic countries in Switzerland. Most expansion was in continental Europe until the 1980s, when stores were established in the United States and the United Kingdom. By 2019, 76 years after incorporation, the IKEA conglomerate managed 433 stores with 219,000 employees across 52 countries attracting annual sales of US$44.6 billion.[2]

Two young men in quite different settings. Basil actively involved in a tribal culture with multiple social relationships works to find a business that will not disrupt existing economic activity. This Subsistence economy is embedded in, and dependent upon, the Canadian economy. Ingvar is operating in an advanced market economy where he begins trading under the assumption that good prices and products will attract customers. There is not much concern over the effects on competitors.

These examples reflect radically different cultural and economic settings for business creation. One emerges in an indigenous culture and the other in an advanced formalized economy. One, beaver trapping, is designed from the start as a small-scale initiative that will allow one person to participate in two economic systems, the informal Ojibwas and the money economy of Canada. The second, serving retail customers with a variety of products, undergoes continuous adaptation and expansion until IKEA becomes a global hub of a network of suppliers and customers.

Both activities, despite different trajectories, provide benefits to the founders and the greater community. The nature of business creation and the resulting benefits, however, can vary depending on the context or stage of economic development.

GLOBAL SCOPE

Worldwide, about 750 million are involved in business creation in 185 countries. As shown in Figure 1.1, one-fifth are in 36 Agricultural (low human development) economies, one-quarter in 35 Agricultural-Industrial (medium human development) economies, almost half in 54 Service-Industrial (high human development) economies, and one-tenth in 34 Progressive Service-Industrial and 26 Knowledge-Service (together considered very high human development) economies.[3] This does not include activity among the 400 million in 4,000 indigenous cultures.

Participation, presented in Figure 1.1, is three times higher in Agricultural economies compared to Knowledge-Service economies, 27 per 100 versus 8 per 100 adults. Countries in the early stages of human development have more

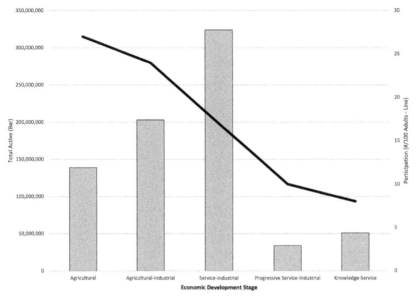

Note: Details in Appendix Table B.6.

Figure 1.1   *Business creation by economic development: participation
              and prevalence*

business creation; economic development is accompanied by a decrease in
activity.

While all who pursue business creation confront the same basic challenges,
the nature of the process may vary with economic development, including
adjustments in:

• The backgrounds of individuals participating in business creation.
• The composition of the business creator community.
• Motivations for participation.
• The economic contributions of new ventures.
• The economic sectors emphasized by business creators.
• Challenges that lead to business terminations.

If major features of the business creation process shift with economic development, the most effective public policies will be different for different stages of
economic development. It is unlikely that one set of "best practices" will have
universal application.

Task specialization and small-scale production is ubiquitous in subsistence tribes or indigenous cultures. Providing goods or services to others outside a household is the beginning of a stand-alone business. An interdependent community of such ventures—where rugs are traded for pottery—may be considered a nascent market economy. The coalescing of scattered communities into larger societies is a precondition for the emergence of nations and, eventually, advanced economies.

Business creation is a major feature in advanced economies, where a range of diverse, interdependent businesses provide a wide assortment of goods and services as well as a variety of work careers. These are countries with a mixture of established large-scale businesses, ongoing churning among Main Street businesses, and the occasional transformative Wall Street entrepreneurial venture. Such economic systems did not magically appear but reflect centuries of development of institutions and productive organizations. Business creation, or entrepreneurship, is a basic feature of this evolution. Continuous churning among the business population facilitates market innovation, improved productivity, and ongoing adaptation.[4]

Because these transformations took place over centuries, precise longitudinal descriptions of these changes are not available. On the other hand, there is considerable diversity among today's nation-states. Existing countries may be considered to represent different stages of development.

Regardless of the context, all business creators confront the same basic challenges. Perhaps most fundamental is developing something that will appeal to customers, followed by ways to locate, inform, and attract them. Producing the output involves a different set of challenges. Resources may be required for tools, equipment, and physical assets. An efficient procedure to create the output may involve technical and administrative expertise. A substantial effort could require locating, training, and organizing workers and managers. Perhaps most critical is locating, informing, and attracting customers. The new business will be part of an economic system. Relationships with other businesses as well as government institutions and agencies must be established and, in many cases, formalized. And not least is the matter of dealing with competitors, those that seek to attract the same customers, financiers, suppliers, and employees. Successful business creators will have found a balance among these challenges.

Many factors will affect the nature and extent of these challenges, particularly the technical demands of the productive process, the sector in which the new firm will compete, and the immediate social, political, and economic context. While most new ventures compete in established sectors, the small proportion that are based on a new and unique good or service have a unique advantage—they may not have any competitors. On the other hand, attracting customers involves an additional challenge of informing them of the benefits of an unfamiliar good or service.

Responses to these issues vary for countries at different stages of economic development. These are not, it should be said, different levels of cultural development. Some subsistence societies—with many centuries of history—have cultural and religious institutions that are just as sophisticated and complex as any in advanced economies.

ASSESSMENT STRATEGY

The following explores variation in business creation and new firm contributions across different stages of economic development. Precise descriptions of business creation across diverse economies are a recent development. This assessment was designed with several features.

> First, information was assembled that would describe different states of economic development, with a focus on both the economic status and overall well-being of typical citizens.
> Second, harmonized cross-national descriptions were used to identify different stages of economic development. While economic development is an ongoing, continuous process, analysis of the role of business creation is simplified if different stages can be identified and described.
> Third, examination of business creation activities was completed for countries at different stages of economic development. It turns out that some features of business creation are similar across the major stages while others vary in significant ways.

The implementation of this strategy has been useful, but there are some caveats.

Descriptions of business creation are based on harmonized data collection coordinated by the Global Entrepreneurship Monitor (GEM) program from 2000 through 2017. This reflects standardized procedures to identify those active in business creation in 891 surveys of representative samples of adults completed in 104 countries. Processing this consolidated data set began with standardized operational definitions and transformations for all 2.8 million cases. This was followed by producing descriptions for each of the 891 surveys using the appropriate case weights. The next stage was to average surveys across all available years for each country.[5] The final stage was to average data across all countries in each of the five stages of economic development. A description of the ongoing GEM program is provided in Appendix A.[6]

Identifying different stages of development is based on a comprehensive overview using standardized data to compare citizen well-being—the 185 countries included in the 2019 United Nations Human Development Report.[7] While this provides almost universal coverage, it does omit some countries, such as Kosovo and Taiwan. Relevant features of all countries were taken from this report's statistical appendix and supplemented with data from other standardized cross-national assessments. Details of the measures and sources are provided in Appendix B.

The assessment emphasizes groups of countries at different stages of development. There is some diversity within each stage; some countries are borderline and only recently improved, and others might soon join a more advanced stage of development. More problematic, except for the most advanced economies, is that some data is not available for all countries at each stage of economic development. As a result, some descriptions are based on data from convenience samples; the data does not reflect a representative sample of countries in that stage of development.[8] This is, however, the best evidence currently available.

WHAT ABOUT ENTREPRENEURSHIP?

Entrepreneurs and entrepreneurship are major topics in public discussions. The major focus is often on how to encourage more entrepreneurship. This is often associated with attention to the consequences of "creative destruction," the social costs associated with the displacement of existing firms by new businesses. While there are advantages to a broad conceptualization of entrepreneurship, there is no agreement on operational definitions for identifying an entrepreneurship. "I know it when I see it" is not a useful approach for systematic research.

On the other hand, precise criteria for identifying those actively involved in business creation have been developed, extensively replicated, and field tested in over 100 countries. Much of this business creation, however, is relatively routine as men and women create new ventures in traditional economic sectors. A very small proportion involves ventures designed for high growth that may have a major impact on traditional market sectors. The success of these initiatives is difficult to predict at the initial stages of business creation. There is substantial evidence that most high-growth firms take several decades to become a dominant feature of their sector or national economy.[9] The growth trajectory of IKEA is typical.

The primary focus of the following assessment are the hundreds of millions of individuals involved in creating businesses, from one-person self-employment to large-scale team efforts that may employ hundreds. For a small proportion, the start-up teams hope for growth and expect some market adaptation. Both the mass of small-scale efforts and the rare high growth venture provide significant contributions to economic growth.

WHAT FOLLOWS

Chapter 2 discusses six stages of economic development. The following chapters review business creation in each stage in some detail. Chapter 9 compares stages of economic development. Chapter 10 reviews implications of these differences for business creators and policy makers. The appendices provide details on the multiple data sets used in the assessment.

NOTES

1. Johnson (1988, p. 175).
2. IKEA International A/S (2020), Lewis (2019), Tikkanen (2020), and Wikipedia (2020).
3. This is a relabeling and slight revision of the United Nations Human Development Categories (United Nations, 2019b), discussed in more detail in Chapter 2.
4. Assessments of both national regions and cross-national effects finds churning is associated with economic growth (Reynolds, 1998, 2020, chapter 3).
5. While there is considerable variation in the level of business creation between countries at different stages of development, the year-to year stability for individual countries is quite high (Reynolds, 2014). Representing individual countries by the average value across annual surveys provides a more precise indicator of business creation typical for the country.
6. Details of the data collection design for the core features provided in Reynolds et al. (2005). The consolidated data set is available in a public archive (Reynolds, 2021). The project website provides the annual reports, hundreds of country reports, and—after a three-year lag—the consolidated adult population data sets for each annual assessment.
7. United Nations (2019b).
8. There is substantial variation by stage of development. There is no standardized data on Subsistence economies, different data sets cover different subsets of Agricultural economies, and there is almost universal coverage for the most advanced Knowledge-Service economies.
9. Reynolds (2020, pp. 129–130).

2.   Economic development: Structures and values

Descriptions of economic activities in the early stages of human development—such as the Roman Empire in the time of Christ, the Islamic world of Mohammed, or India and China in the first millennium—emphasize broad patterns or important events, such as technical innovations. They do not provide detailed descriptions of the introduction and organization of productive activities. An alternative is to consider the current range of human communities, which may be considered to represent the diversity of economic development. These vary from the subsistence economies of indigenous communities to highly advanced economies. While this range of activity may not represent the most basic human communities, it does reflect a substantial diversity of contexts for business creation.

In tribal cultures some individuals focus on specific activities and develop personal expertise. Perhaps a family specializes in making clothing and exchanges this for food with a family that excels in farming or fishing. Such task specialization may improve efficiency and outcomes. The result may be more effective tools, weapons, clothing, pottery, farming, or hunting. While others benefit from the output, the task specialist may gain status, recognition, and personal satisfaction. Trade would follow the personal relationships between the specialist and others in their community. The goods or services exchanged would generally be immediately consumed or utilized. Such barter systems limit the potential to store "economic value" for future use. The exchange relationships may be systematized and well established, although formal, written agreements may not exist. Mutual trust facilitates the exchanges, and the trust is reinforced by interdependence within the community. Disagreements about exchanges may be handled informally, perhaps resolved by respected elders. Firm growth is constrained by the small size of the trading community. Accumulation of profits and wealth may be difficult without a stable store of value and discouraged by norms of equality. Such informal businesses are found in all economies but are ubiquitous in indigenous communities and tribal cultures.

Advanced economies with established institutions, including a monetary system, provide a quite different context. Individuals or teams that create a business usually trade the output for money. National institutions maintain the economic value of the currency. Money is easily traded for other economic goods or retained as a store of value. Businesses may be recognized as independent economic actors, with a legal status comparable to natural persons. While parties to the exchanges may have ongoing personal relationships, it is not a critical feature. Mutual trust facilitates these exchanges, but there may be formal institutions regulating critical features of commercial activity. Major disagreements may be resolved by an established legal system. Complementary institutional structures and a large market can facilitate business expansion and the potential for accumulation of wealth. The separation of business activities from personal life reduces the potential for resentment of success.

Most people in today's world, however, do not live and work in the extremes—in either subsistence cultures or highly advanced economies. Among the 8 billion world citizens four in five are in economies that provide an intermediate context. About one in 20, 400 million, are members of indigenous groups that are embedded in established nation-states. The ratio of the informal, interdependent communities to formalized, institutionally maintained economic activity varies with economic development.

Significant changes occur as subsistence cultures coalesce into nations. Personal security and well-being in self-sufficient tribal communities is based on a range of interdependent relationships among family, kin, and tribal members. This mutual support is a source of economic security, health care, retirement support, and, when needed, justice. As nations emerged, many of these functions became the responsibility of formalized government institutions.

National development, or modernization, changes the context for business creation. As economic activity becomes more complex and specialized, political, economic, and legal institutions emerge that provide a predictable, formalized context. Informal task specialization begins to share economic activity with formalized, registered firms. The proportion of activity in unregistered or informal sectors declines, but never disappears.

DEFINING STAGES OF DEVELOPMENT

Exploring the contextual effects on business creation across national development is a challenge. Most development takes place over many generations, and it is not possible to retroactively assemble harmonized data across several hundred years for a single country. This is complicated by the shifting of national boundaries. It is useful, however, to consider the situation of current economies at six stages of development.

- *Subsistence cultures*: Mutually interdependent tribal cultures (or indigenous groups), such as the Lapps in northern Scandinavia, the Navajo in the southwestern United States (U.S.), and the Suku in southwestern Congo.
- *Agricultural*: National economies where the majority of employment is in farming, forestry, hunting, and fishing, as in Afghanistan, Ethiopia, Nigeria, and Papua New Guinea.
- *Agricultural-Industrial*: National economies with most of the employment in agricultural and industrial sectors, as in Cameroon, Honduras, India, and Viet Nam.
- *Service-Industrial*: National economies with more than half of employment in industrial and customer-oriented sectors, as in Bolivia, China, Egypt, Mexico, and the Philippines.
- *Progressive Service-Industrial*: National economies where the majority of employment is in industrial and customer-oriented sectors and where progressive values dominate, as in Argentina, Croatia, Portugal, and Slovenia.
- *Knowledge-Service*: National economies with most of the employment is in sectors oriented to consumers or where advanced training and education are required and progressive values are widespread, as in Australia, Finland, South Korea, Switzerland, the United Kingdom, and the United States.

These are, of course, different stages along a continuum, and not discrete, mutually exclusive categories. There is diversity among economies in each category and as communities and nations develop, they gradually change from one category to another. Subsistence cultures can be considered the origin of all economic development, but there is little precise data on their characteristics. Chapter 3 provides a more detailed description.

Comparisons of the other five stages are facilitated by a wealth of harmonized data gathered by a range of international organizations and projects, details of which are in Appendix B. The major differences are presented in Table 2.1. The primary basis for the classification is the United Nations Human Development (UNHD) Index developed for 185 countries. There is, however, one adjustment. The UNHD Index "very highly developed" category has been divided into two groups. The 34 Progressive Service-Industrial nations where 19% of adults have post-secondary education is separated from the 26 Knowledge-Service countries where 39% of adults have post-secondary education. This would include vocational and technical training, university, college, graduate, or professional educational experiences. Knowledge-Service

Table 2.1   *Economic development: selected features*

	Agricultural	Agricultural-Industrial	Service-Industrial	Progressive Service-Industrial	Knowledge-Service
Number of countries (n = 185)[1]	36	35	54	34	26
Total population: 2018, millions	923	2,240	2,486	593	939
Global population share (total = 7,539)[2]	12%	30%	38%	8%	13%
UNHD Index	0.48	0.62	0.74	0.84	0.92
Major UNHD Index components[3]					
Life expectancy at birth (years): 2018	62.2	68.5	74.0	77.3	82.0
Adult mean years of education	9.2	11.5	13.6	15.4	17.3
GNIPC: 2011 ($1,000, PPP)	$2.0	$5.8	$12.6	$33.9	$46.5
Economic structure (proportion jobs)[2]					
Agricultural	51%	38%	20%	6%	3%
Industrial	12%	18%	22%	28%	19%
Consumer oriented	28%	30%	35%	35%	35%
Knowledge based	9%	14%	23%	31%	43%
Total	100%	100%	100%	100%	100%
Educational attainment[4]					
Adults with post-secondary education Force w/ Secondary, Adv Educ	3%	6%	16%	19%	37%

Entrepreneurship and economic development

National value structure	Agricultural	Agricultural-Industrial	Service-Industrial	Progressive Service-Industrial	Knowledge-Service
Contextual: secular-rational	9%	14%	25%	50%	57%
Contextual: intermediate	35%	39%	35%	33%	29%
Contextual: traditional	56%	47%	40%	17%	14%
Total	100%	100%	100%	100%	100%
Individual: self-expressive	18%	15%	20%	31%	63%
Individual: intermediate	41%	37%	38%	35%	25%
Individual: survival	41%	48%	42%	34%	13%
Total	100%	100%	100%	100%	101%

Note: The five categories are based on the four levels of human development presented in the 2019 UNHD report (United Nations, 2019b, table 1). The labels are changed to reflect the major focus of the economic structure. In the report they are labeled as low, medium, high, and very high human development. The very high category is bifurcated by identifying very high economies where over 70% of employment is considered service (not agricultural or industrial) and more than 20% of the adult population had post-secondary (vocational, trade, college, graduate, professional, etc.) educational experience in 2015 (Barro and Lee, 2016). [1] Country counts are reduced for some characteristics reflecting missing data. [2] United Nations (2019b), table 7. [3] United Nations (2019b), table 1; GNIPC = gross national income per capita, which includes income from overseas operations from domestic businesses; PPP = purchasing power parity. [4] United Nations (2019b), tables 5 and 9.

countries have, in addition, 78% or more of employment in consumer-oriented or knowledge-based sectors.

The magnitude of the differences for citizens in these different countries is more apparent in a graphic comparison. The UNHD Index and its major components are presented in Figure 2.1. To facilitate comparisons, the four measures have been converted to standardized indices.[1] It makes clear that all three components of the index—life expectancy, educational attainment, and annual income—vary across the five stages. Life expectance at birth (represented by the bar with cross-hatching) is 62 years for Agricultural economies and 20 years later, at 82 years, in Knowledge-Service economies. Average adult educational attainment (represented by the white bar) is nine years for Agricultural economies and almost twice that level, at 17 years, in Knowledge-Service economies. Annual income per person (represented by the grey bar) shows the greatest difference, at $2,000 per year in Agricultural economies and over 20 times greater, at $46,500 per year in Knowledge-Service economies. Life is quite different for those living in different stages of economic development.

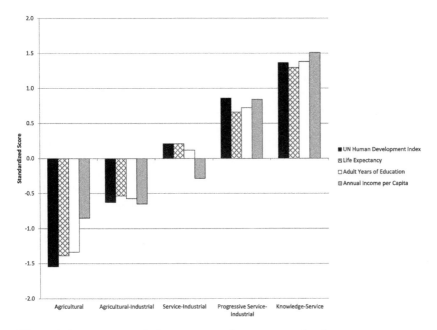

Figure 2.1   *National characteristics by economic development*

There are two features of economic and human life that vary across these five stages. There are major differences in the productive activities, reflected in the sectors in which people work. There are also major differences in the national values emphasized by the citizens.

DIVERSITY IN ECONOMIC EMPHASIS

Differences in the economic structure is represented by the proportion of employment in four major economic sectors:[2]

- Agriculture, which includes farming, forestry, fishing, and hunting.
- Industrial, which includes mining and quarrying, manufacturing, utilities, and construction.
- Consumer-oriented, which includes trade (wholesale, retail, and motor vehicle related), transportation and communication (including media), lodging, food service and bars, and miscellaneous (recreation, entertainment, religious, and other services).
- Knowledge-based, which includes finance and insurance, real estate, business and administrative services, public administration, education, and health and social services.

The creation of a knowledge-based category, which includes sectors that require post-secondary school training, complements the focus on identifying the most advanced economies based on adult educational attainment.

The distribution of work across these four sectors, illustrated in Figure 2.2, shows a clear shift across the five categories of economic development. Over half (51% on average) of employment in Agricultural economies is in farming, forestry, hunting, and fishing. There is less agricultural work in Agricultural-Industrial economies, but 56% of work is in either the agricultural or industrial sectors. Agricultural work is less prominent in Service-Industrial economies, where 57% of work is in industrial or consumer-oriented sectors. There is a further reduction in agricultural work in Progressive Service-Industrial economies, where 63% of jobs are in industrial or consumer-oriented sectors. In Knowledge-Service economies three in four jobs, or 77%, are in consumer-oriented or knowledge-based sectors. Most work in knowledge-based sectors requires post-secondary education.

The major differences across different stages of development are related to emphasis on the agricultural and knowledge-based sectors. From Agricultural to Knowledge-Service economies, agriculture work varies from 51% to 3% of all employment. But across all countries agricultural work varies from over 70% in the Agricultural economies of Chad and the Central African Republic to less than 1% in the Knowledge-Service economy of Singapore. This is offset by increasing proportions of work in knowledge-based sectors, where the average increases from 9% to 43%. But knowledge-sector employment is

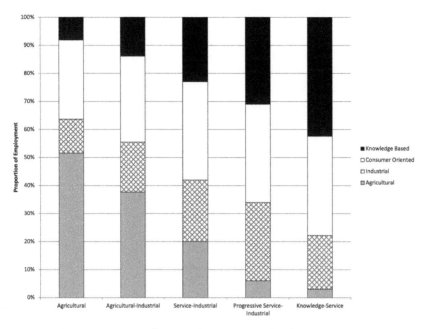

Figure 2.2   Sector employment by economic development

less than 4% in the Agricultural economies of Somalia and Niger and greater than 50% in the Knowledge-Service economies of Sweden and Luxembourg.

There is much less variation across stages of development in the proportion of work in industrial or consumer-oriented sectors. The proportion of industrial jobs varies from 12% to 19%. The least variation occurs in consumer-oriented sectors, which varies from 28% to 35% across the five stages.

DIVERSITY IN NATIONAL VALUES

It is useful to characterize national values on two dimensions. One is attitudes toward authority, an individual's perspective toward their political and economic context. The extremes reflect a contrast between traditional versus secular-rational values. The second is an orientation toward individual well-being, reflecting immediate personal goals. This is characterized by contrasting an emphasis on survival, often day to day, versus a desire for self-expression or personal fulfilment. These two orientations, which are largely unrelated, not only shift across stages of development but are associated with business creation. They are reflected in multi-item indices, based on responses by representative samples of adults in different countries.[3] The relationship of each value dimension to a wide range of items is summarized in Table 2A.1 for orientation to authority, and Table 2A.2 for individual well-being. Indices for both orientations reflect a continuum.

A traditional authority orientation emphasizes patriotism, the importance of work, commitment to God and religion, households dominated by the husband, families with more children, greater respect for authority, a conservative political emphasis but reduced personal political activity. There is some diversity regarding the relationship between the economy and government action. Maintaining order is seen as very important, but there is a range of views about income equality and government ownership of productive enterprises. Both market competition and individual freedoms are seen as positive.

Those with a secular-rational authority orientation are less nationalistic and do not value work as highly. The significance of God and religion is much reduced. While family life is seen as important, the emphasis is reduced. There is greater tolerance of equality between spouses, a preference for fewer children, and an acceptance that parents might pursue interests that do not involve children. There is less automatic acceptance of authority, more progressive or liberal orientations, and a greater tendency to participate in politics. Maintaining order is emphasized and rapid market reforms that may disrupt stability are a concern. There is less emphasis on income disparity and reduced concern about private versus government ownership of productive enterprises, business competition, and individual freedom.

Those with a survival individual well-being emphasis are less satisfied and not as happy, less likely to feel good about an accomplishment, unlikely to trust others and do not expect fair treatment, are concerned about their financial situation and work security, consider work important but are less satisfied with their job, consider good pay and security important in a job, value obedience in children, are less likely to think they have freedom of choice and control, emphasize material advances associated with economic growth, and consider obedience and religious faith important.

A self-expressive individual well-being emphasis is associated with greater life satisfaction, more happiness, and a sense of accomplishment. They are more likely to trust others and expect to be treated fairly. They are more satisfied with their financial situation and less worried about job security. There is a greater emphasis on leisure and more job satisfaction. While a good job should provide pay and security, it should also present opportunities for personal initiative. Adults feel it is important that children become independent, imaginative, and show determination and perseverance; child obedience is seen as less significant. They are more likely to emphasize post-materialism national objectives, such as the environment and citizen input, rather than economic growth. Independence, determination, and perseverance are considered more important than obedience and religious faith.

All economies—all countries—have citizens that emphasize a wide range of values. But different stages of economic development are associated with shifts in the proportion of adults with different value orientations, as shown in Fig 2.3. The emphasis on authority values is presented on the left and on individual well-being values on the right.

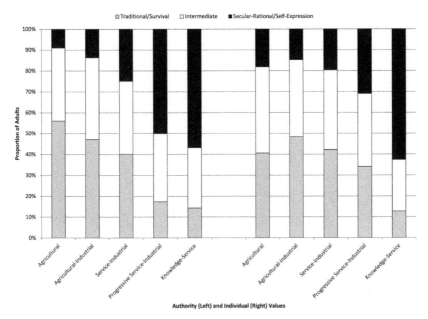

Figure 2.3   National values by economic development

Most of those (40% to 55%) in Agricultural, Agricultural-Industrial, and Service-Industrial economies emphasize traditional authority and survival well-being. But in more developed economies increasing proportions emphasize secular-rational and self-expressive values. Twice as many of those in Progressive Service-Industrial economies emphasize secular-rational values (50% versus 25%) and half again as many (30% versus 20%) self-expression values compared to those in Service-Industrial economies. The difference is even greater for Knowledge-Service economies, where three in five emphasize secular-rational and self-expression values.

There is no question that the typical value orientations are different at each stage of national economic development. While it is not possible to determine causality, greater national wealth has probably led to an expansion of government institutions that support all citizens, particularly the disadvantaged.

This would lead to greater confidence that improvements in personal health, education, and financial well-being will be sustained.

Regardless of the stage of economic development, there is a relationship between national values and the prevalence of business creation. Figure 2.4[4] shows the joint impact of authority and well-being values on the level of activity. Participation in business creation is the lowest (7 per 100 adults) in countries emphasizing secular-rational and self-expressive values, represented by the bar in the front-right corner of Figure 2.4. Participation is three times higher (21 per 100 adults) in countries emphasizing traditional and survival values, represented by the bar in the back-right side of Figure 2.4.

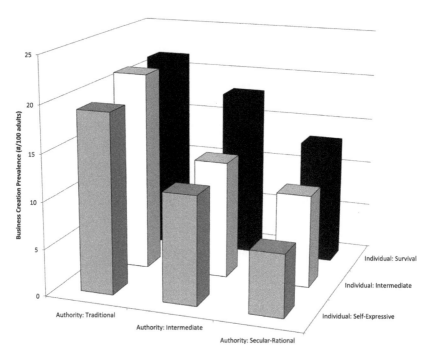

Figure 2.4   National values and participation in business creation

This reflects the confluence of four national characteristics among the 13 countries such as Algeria, Pakistan, and Uganda in the traditional/survival values category. The emphasis on traditional authority and survival individual well-being is associated with a very low gross domestic product (GDP) per capita and high levels of business creation. All these economies are Agricultural, Agricultural-Industrial, or Service-Industrial. These values are present in countries where business creation is widely accepted as an appropriate career choice.

The 12 countries in the secular-rational/self-expressive category such as France, Japan, and Sweden are almost the exact opposite, with a focus on secular-rational authority and self-expressive individual well-being, a high GDP per capita, and low levels of business creation. These are all Progressive Service-Industrial or Knowledge-Service economies.

GLOBAL DISTRIBUTION

Countries in different stages of development tend to be clustered in different regions of the world. The proportion of 185 countries in eight global categories is presented in Figure 2.5. Countries in six regions are contiguous, such as Western Europe and Sub-Saharan Africa.[5] There are two exceptions, both dominated by Knowledge-Service economies. These are the highly developed Asian countries (Hong Kong, Japan, Singapore, and South Korea)[6] and four countries in North America and Oceania (Australia, Canada, New Zealand, and the U.S.). These Anglo economies inherited the values and institutional structures of the U.K.

Almost all countries in Western Europe are Knowledge-Service countries, with four (Austria, Italy, Malta, and Portugal) identified as Progressive Service-Industrial. Two-thirds of Central and Eastern European countries are Progressive Service-Industrial, with Latvia considered Knowledge-Service and Bosnia and Herzegovina, Georgia, Moldova, North Macedonia, Serbia, and Ukraine considered Service-Industrial. Most Middle Eastern, North African (MENA) economies are Service-Industrial, with Iraq and Morocco considered Agricultural-Industrial and Syria and Yemen considered Agricultural. Countries in Latin America and the Caribbean cover the entire range of intermediate stages, with one, Haiti, considered Agricultural. Developing Asian countries, including the small island countries in Oceania, are mostly in the Agricultural-Industrial and Service-Industrial stages, the exceptions being the Progressive Service-Industrial economies of Brunei Darussalam, Malaysia, and Palau and the Agricultural economies of Afghanistan and Papua New Guinea. Over 60% of the African Sub-Saharan countries are in the Agricultural stage and, except for the Progressive Service-Industrial Seychelles, the others are in the Agricultural-Industrial and Service-Industrial stages.

The global distribution by stage of economic development reflects ongoing progress in different parts of the world. Except for Western and Central Europe indigenous or tribal cultures, representing the Subsistence stage of development, are embedded in economies in all regions of the world.

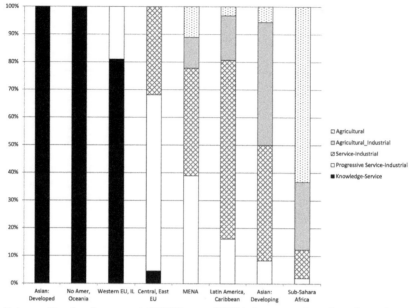

Note: Based on the aggregated UNDP report (2019b), the presentation reflects four Asian: developed (excluding Taiwan), four North American and Oceanian, 21 Western European (including Israel), 22 Central and Eastern European, 18 Middle Eastern, North African, 31 Latin American, Caribbean, 36 Asian developing, and 49 Sub-Saharan African countries.

Figure 2.5   Global distribution of economies by stage of development

BUSINESS CREATION

About one in ten of the world population, 751 million individuals, are involved in the early stages of business creation. There is dramatic variation across the stages of economic development. As shown in Figure 2.6, the prevalence of business creation is over three times greater, at 27 per 100 adults, in Agricultural economies compared to Knowledge-Service economies, at 8 per 100 adults. This prevalence is based on counting those in two stages of the process. Nascent entrepreneurs involved in the early start-up or pre-profit phase are represented by the black segments of the bars. Those identified as owner-managers of a new firm that has been profitable for up to 42 months are represented by the white segments of the bars. There are usually more nascent entrepreneurs than new firm owners, reflecting the fact that most start-ups do not become profitable businesses and many that reach profitability only operate for a few years. Even so, discouraged entrepreneurs tend to be more satisfied with their work than those with traditional jobs.[7]

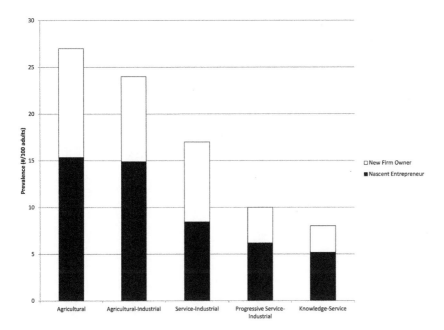

Figure 2.6   Participation in business creation by economic development

Most global activity is found in the earlier stages of national economic development, as shown in Table 2.2. Almost one-fifth (18%) of all business creators are active in Agricultural economies, home to 12% of the world population. In contrast, Knowledge-Service economies are the context for 13% of the population but 7% of all business creators.

A small proportion of business creators are planning for growth, expecting ten or more employees in five years, and expect to have an innovative impact on their markets in which they will compete. These efforts are more consistent with the typical conception of entrepreneurship. The prevalence varies from 1 in 108 adults for Agricultural economies to 1 in 416 in Knowledge-Service economies; it is about 1 in 230 in the three intermediate stages of economic development. As will be seen, most contributions from business creation reflect activity in established sectors, not the impact of rare high-potential initiatives.

Women are active in business creation at all stages of economic development, although they are more involved in countries in the earlier stages of economic development. While men in Agricultural economies are three times as involved as men in Knowledge-Service economies, 30 per 100 compared to 10 per 100, women are four times as likely to be involved, 24 per 100 compared to

Table 2.2   *Economic development and business creation*

	Agricultural	Agricultural-Industrial	Service-Industrial	Progressive Service-Industrial	Knowledge-Service
Business creation (#/100)	27	24	17	10	8
Nascent entrepreneur	79,000	126,000	161,000	21,000	33,000
New business owner-manager	60,000	77,000	163,000	13,000	18,000
Total business creation active	139,000	203,000	324,000	34,000	51,000
Proportion of global total (751,000,000)	18%	27%	43%	5%	7%
Business creation: opportunity (#/100)	18	15	11	7	6
Business creation: best choice (#/100)	8	8	5	2	1
High-potential business creation (#/100)	0.92	0.41	0.43	0.46	0.24
Male business creation (#/100)	30	27	19	13	10
Female business creation (#/100)	24	21	14	8	6

Note: Mean values for 9 Agricultural economies, 13 Agricultural-Industrial, 32 Service-Industrial, 25 Progressive Service-Industrial, and 26 Knowledge-Service. These 105 countries represent a human population of 6.6 billion as of 2018; 87% of the total population of 7.6 billion.
Source: Reynolds (2021).

6 per 100. While women are about one-third of business creators in advanced economies, they are almost half of those involved in Agricultural economies.

Global regions with a larger proportion of developing economies have higher levels of business creation, as shown in Figure 2.7. With two exceptions, there is a very high correspondence between the proportion of Agricultural, Agricultural-Industrial, and Service-Industrial economies and high levels of business creation, presented in Figure 2.7. The first exception is the four countries in North America and Oceania. Australia, Canada, New Zealand, and the U.S. all have Knowledge-Service economies but much higher levels of business creation than their development peers in Western Europe and Asia. This probably reflects a somewhat different history, as all four reflect the Anglo institutions and culture of the U.K. and were created by overwhelming the original subsistence communities.

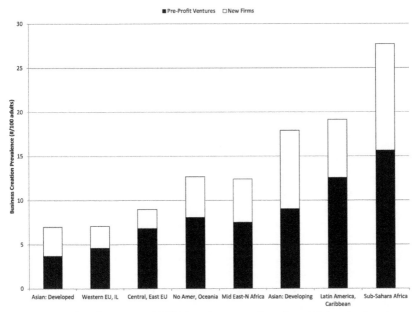

Note: Based on the aggregated GEM data, the presentation reflects 5 Asian: developed (including Taiwan), 21 Western European (including Israel), 19 Central and Eastern European, 4 North American and Oceanian, 15 Middle Eastern and North African, 21 Asian: developing, 20 Latin American and Caribbean, and 15 Sub-Saharan African countries.

Figure 2.7   Global regions and business creation

The other exception is the countries in the MENA region. In this case, the level of business creation is somewhat less than regions with a similar level of development. This reflects the lower level of participation by women in economic affairs in many Islamic countries, although there is considerable variation within and among countries in this regard.[8]

Comparisons among regions illustrates the impact of differences associated with levels of development. The majority of business creation is occurring in developing Asian, Latin American and Caribbean, and Sub-Saharan African countries. The remaining assessment, however, emphasizes all stages of economic development.

CHALLENGE FOR ANALYSIS

Business creation is ubiquitous—common in societies or economies at all stages of development. There is considerable evidence that successful business creation has positive outcomes for both the participants and the greater society. The assessments of each stage of economic development focus on several issues:

• The sources of variation in participation in business creation in different contexts.
• The effect of context on the business creation process.
• Contributions of new firms to national economies.

The results have implications for those pursuing business creation as well as policy makers concerned with promoting its contributions.

The following chapters review business creation at each stage of economic development. Chapter 3 provides an impressionistic review of wide-scale activity in Subsistence economies. The following five chapters are based on harmonized data sets that represent countries in each stage of development. In some cases, the descriptions represent subsamples of convenience and in others there is useful data on all countries. The subsamples of convenience, however, are large enough to provide confidence that the most important features are accurately represented. Chapter 9 provides a review of the major similarities and differences across the different stages. Chapter 10 discusses implications for public policy.

NOTES

1. Across all countries the measures have been converted so the average value is 0 and the standardization is 1.0. Technically this is the creation of Z-scores for the four measures.
2. These four categories are based on a consolidation of 14 sectors as defined by the United Nations Standard Industrial Classification codes and used by the International Labour Organization (2020) for tracking employment by economic sector.
3. The World Values Survey (Inglehart et al., 2020) has coordinated surveys of adult populations across diverse countries in seven multi-year waves of data collection in 1981, 1989, 1994, 1999, 2005, 2010, and 2017. As each national survey involved from 1,000 to 1,500 respondents, the total number of completed interviews is over 400,000 in 92 countries. This has facilitated the creation of reliable multi-item indices that reflect variation in the values associated with contextual and individual orientations. Each reflects a cluster of interrelated attitudes and perspectives.
4. The distribution of average national contextual and individual values was coded into three equal groups. The number of countries in each cell is provided in the table below. The prevalence of business creators precedes the slash. The number of countries is reduced as only those with GEM-based estimates of participation in business creation and World Value Surveys were included. The percentage of Progressive Service-Industrial or Knowledge-Service economies are in parentheses.

Well-being values	Authority values			Total
	Traditional	**Intermediate**	**Secular-rational**	
Survival	19%/13 (0%)	18%/10 (20%)	13%/7 (57%)	18%/30 (20%)
Intermediate	21%/11 (9%)	13%/10 (50%)	10%/10 (56%)	15%/30 (37%)
Self-expressive	22%/4 (0%)	12%/12 (92%)	7%/12 (100%)	11%/28 (82%)
Total	21%/28 (4%)	14%/32 (56%)	9%/28 (68%)	15%/88 (45%)

Countries in each cell are as follows:

Well-being values	Authority values		
	Traditional	Intermediate	Secular-rational
Survival	Algeria, Bangladesh, Ghana, Iraq, Jordan, Libya, Morocco, Nigeria, Pakistan, Rwanda, Uganda, Yemen, and Zimbabwe	Armenia, Azerbaijan, Georgia, Indonesia, Kazakhstan, Kyrgyzstan, Lebanon, Romania, Tunisia, and Zambia	Albania, Belarus, Lithuania, Moldova, Montenegro, Russia, and Ukraine
Intermediate	Brazil, Burkina Faso, Ecuador, Egypt, Guatemala, Mali, Peru, Philippines, Tanzania, Trinidad and Tobago, and Turkey	Chile, Cyprus, Ethiopia, India, Malaysia, Poland, Singapore, South Africa, Thailand, and Viet Nam	Bosnia and Herzegovina, Bulgaria, China, Estonia, Hungary, Korea (South), Latvia, Macedonia (North), Serbia, and Taiwan
Self-expressive	Columbia, Dominican Republic, Mexico, and Venezuela	Argentina, Australia, Canada, Finland, Haiti, Israel, Italy, New Zealand, Spain, United Kingdom, United States, and Uruguay	Croatia, Czechia, France, Germany, Hong Kong, Japan, Netherlands, Norway, Slovakia, Slovenia, Sweden, and Switzerland

5.   As the political and economic structures of Israel are very similar to Western Europe and very unlike other MENA economies, it is included with Western Europe.
6.   Taiwan would be included in this group, but it is not listed in the UNHD assessment.
7.   Reynolds (2018, chapter 2).
8.   Reynolds (2012).

APPENDIX

Table 2A.1   *Orientation to authority values: selected aspects*

Traditional	Issue	Secular-rational
87%	Very proud of nationality	29%
78%	Willing to fight for my country	66%
77%	Work is very important in life	54%
39%	Strongly agree: Work is a duty to society	20%
39%	Strongly agree: People who do not work turn lazy	26%
35%	In the long run, hard work usually brings a better life	15%
82%	God is very important in life	15%
1%	God not at all important in life	21%
75%	Religion is very important in life	17%
37%	Belong to a religious organization	11%
95%	Family is very important in life	86%
46%	Strongly agree: Husband and wife should both work	37%
37%	Agree: Women with more income than men are a problem	22%
52%	Strongly agree: Wife must obey	41%
31%	Four or more children is the ideal family size	12%
87%	Parents' duty is to do the best for their children	65%
11%	Parents have a life of their own, apart from responsibilities to their children	29%
83%	Greater respect for authority would be a good thing	39%
29%	Having the army rule would be fairly or very good	15%
21%	Consider self to the left in politics	31%
41%	Consider self to right in politics	25%
17%	Have signed a political petition	36%
81%	Maintaining order in the nation is very important	65%
12%	Rapid market reforms are negative for national stability	28%
16%	Incomes should be made more equal	12%
21%	Larger income differences would be a good incentive	10%
16%	Private ownership of businesses should be increased	10%
16%	Government ownership of businesses should be increased	8%
37%	More competition in business is good	20%
36%	Completely agree there should be more freedom for individuals	24%

Note: The 214,175 cases from the first six waves of the World Value Survey are sorted into thirds, reflecting a traditional, intermediate, or secular-rational emphasis. Column values reflect the proportion strongly endorsing each item on a variety of different scales. All differences are statistically significant. Details on sources are in Appendix Table B.2.

Table 2A.2   Individual values: selected aspects

Survival	Issue	Self-expression
28%	Satisfied (8, 9, 10) with life	58%
68%	Feeling very, quite happy	91%
57%	Felt pleased about an accomplishment	69%
12%	Most people can be trusted	39%
66%	Most people would take advantage of me, rather than be fair	48%
18%	Satisfied (8, 9, 10) with household financial situation	37%
49%	Very much worried about losing my job or not finding work	39%
57%	Work makes life worth living, not leisure (4, 5)	41%
46%	Satisfied (8, 9, 10) with my job	60%
88%	Good pay important in a job	77%
76%	Good security important in a job	67%
43%	Opportunity for initiative important in a job	56%
41%	Important children become independent	58%
17%	Important children are imaginative	29%
33%	Important children have determination and perseverance	45%
48%	Important children are obedient	31%
39%	Considerable (8, 9, 10) freedom of choice and control	55%
53%	Materialist emphasis	16%
4%	Post-materialist emphasis	22%
65%	Country's first objective should be high economic growth	56%
32%	Country's second objective should be giving people more influence	38%
33%	Obedience/religious faith emphasis	19%
26%	Determination, perseverance/independence emphasis	44%

Note: The 204,172 cases from the first six waves of the World Value Survey are sorted into thirds, reflecting a survival, intermediate, or self-expressive emphasis. Column values reflect the proportion strongly endorsing each item on a variety of different scales. All differences are statistically significant. Details on sources are in Appendix Table B.2.

3.   Subsistence economies: Specialization and survival

Corruption is the failure to share any largess you have received with those with whom you have formed ties of dependence.[1]

All national economies emerged from subsistence cultures; collections of households constantly challenged for survival.[2] Subsistence societies emerged in a wide range of natural environments and created productive technologies suited to their unique context. While now a small proportion of the world population, indigenous (native) peoples or subsistence cultures are present in all regions of the world. These subsistence cultures provide a distinctive context for business creation.

There are about 400 million persons in almost 4,000 indigenous cultures.[3] The distribution by world region is provided in Table 3.1. The largest number, over 300 million individuals in over 2,000 different indigenous cultures, are in Asia, mostly in China and India. This is followed by Africa and Latin America, both with over 50 million indigenous peoples. The number of distinctive cultures in these regions, 800, is probably an undercount. Other world regions account for less than 10 million indigenous people in less than 1,000 distinct cultures. Except for northern Scandinavia, there are no indigenous peoples identified in Western or Central Europe.

Subsistence cultures emerged as small collections of households cooperating to obtain food and resources needed to sustain themselves. Over hundreds of generations norms, values, and a social organization emerged to facilitate collective survival. While there are many variations in tribal cultures and social organization, there are some universal features, such as the presence of a family unit.

A norm of mutual dependency emerged in subsistence cultures: an assumption that all will contribute to tribal survival and all will share burdens and successes. While the disadvantaged or those with "bad luck" will be supported by the community, those with special skills or "good luck" are expected to share their benefits. This norm of shared interdependence continues to be a feature of current subsistence societies. Although most subsistence cultures now exist within a market economy, they are a distinctive context for business creation.

There is variation in the economic emphasis of subsistence cultures. The mixture of hunting, gathering, fishing, herding (pastoralism), and agricultural

Table 3.1   *Indigenous peoples by world region*

World region	Indigenous population	Distinctive cultures
Asia	315,200,000	2,156
Africa	60,400,000	73
Latin America	50,600,000	741
North America	5,900,000	577
Oceania	2,000,000	5
Other	550,000	42
Arctic	190,000	3
Total	434,840,000	3,597

Note: In those cases where the proportion of indigenous peoples is provided, the country population for 2020 is used to determine an indigenous population count. The country overviews emphasize changes in legal status of the indigenous people and their traditional territory, much of which is coveted for commercial opportunities (mining, agricultural, tourism, etc.). A number of countries are not included (e.g. Egypt, Korea) and some regions included (e.g. Easter Island) are not countries. A similar overview for 2012 is provided in World Bank Group (2015, p. 3), with a total of 300 million. The Asia category includes Bangladesh, Cambodia, China, India, Indonesia, Japan, Laos, Malaysia, Myanmar, Nepal, Philippines, Taiwan, and Thailand; Africa includes Algeria, Botswana, Burkina Faso, Burundi, Cameroon, Central African Republic, Eritrea, Ethiopia, Gabon, Kenya, Libya, Mali, Morocco, Namibia, Niger, Republic of the Congo, Rwanda, South Africa, Tanzania, Tunisia, Uganda, and Zimbabwe; Latin America includes Argentina, Bolivia, Brazil, Chile, Columbia, Costa Rica, Ecuador, French Guiana, Guatemala, Guyana, Mexico, Nicaragua, Panama, Paraguay, Peru, Suriname, and Venezuela; North America includes Canada and the United States; Oceania includes Australia, French Polynesia, Hawaii, New Zealand, and Papua New Guinea; Other includes Israel, Palestine, and Russia; Arctic includes Canadian Inuit, Greenland, and Sapmi (Lapp communities in Finland, Norway, Russia, and Sweden).
Source: Based on country-by-country assessments from Mamo (2020).

(or horticultural) activities varies across different climates and geographies (see the Appendix at the end of this chapter). Even so, task specialization and divisions of labor are found in all subsistence tribal cultures. Perhaps most basic is a specialization by gender, with women focusing on childcare and domestic tasks, often including agriculture, and men emphasizing hunting, fishing, and construction. But beyond such gender differentiation, there are endless examples of task specialization, often with individuals or families engaged in multiple, simultaneous activities. For the community, the result is an improvement in quality or efficiency of economic output. For individual business creators, there may be a gain in respect and prestige and the ability to avoid unpleasant work assignments.

Reports from all over the world describe task specialization or rudimentary business creation in subsistence tribal cultures:

[A]ll adult males are craftsmen in a general sense, for all men can build houses, make a bow, weave a simple mat, and hammer out a crude arrowpoint. ... those knowledgeable in more specialized crafts never make them a full-time occupation, and every craftsman is also engaged in the more ordinary activities, such as hunting and fishing. (Horticulturalist Suku, southwestern Congo)[4]

She [Vestine] was involved in many businesses. She ran a "cabaret"—a bar where sorghum beer, banana beer, bottled beer and soft drinks were sold. She bought staples such as beans, sorghum, and sweet potatoes for resale. She sold a small amount of goods such as soap, detergent, candles, sugar, and tea in her shop. She also administered the land that her mother was allotted by her husband. ... She grew cash crops and rented out land to others. ... From 1983 to 1985 she ran a brick and tile-making business. (Agriculturalist-pastoralists, Rwanda)[5]

[T]he small-time criollo [of pure Spanish descent] who might be a worker or employee at the sawmill and on the side clear a few hectares of land which he works himself with the help of hired labor. (Hunter-gathering Warao Indians, Venezuela)[6]

Fishing has provided excellent opportunities, especially for the older, retired herders and the small, less active herders. ... Fishing profits also help the small herder to maintain a herding livelihood. (Pastoral Saami, northern Sweden)[7]

[T]he largest farmer in Nayon ... also owns one of the two buses serving the village. It is not clear in this case whether the farmer has a business on the side, or that he has bought a bus to ensure efficient and reliable means of transporting his products to market and only incidentally transports the goods and persons of his fellow-villagers. (Agriculturalist-pastoralist Quechua Indians, Ecuador)[8]

Like all other specialists of Chucuito (potters, shopkeepers, ayllu head men, or doctors) the magicians of the village are basically farmers and pursue their professional calling in their spare time. Visits to clients are fitted in between routine agricultural activities, and many professional calls are made after sundown. Nevertheless, although the magician is chiefly dependent on farming for his livelihood, he relies on his profession for much of his ready cash. (Horticultural Aymara, Peru)[9]

In the Sierra de Jarara and the Sierra de Macuira and in other places distant from urban centers, some old women live who are acquainted with the magic and curative properties of various plants. This knowledge is ... much sought after and remunerated in proportion to the importance of the case, its efficacy, and the prestige of the herbal expert who prescribes it, and the importance of the person who requests it. Another profession is that of midwife, who receives payment in relation to her ability and the means of whoever applies for her services. (Pastoralist Goajiro, Columbia)[10]

In 1973 Wayne Sekaquaptewa started the Hopi newspaper *Qua Toqti*. In 1976 he started a tour company, Hopiland Tours and an Indian construction company, Pueblo Builders ... His first concern in all this economic activity was to provide jobs for his people. (Intensive agricultural Hopi, Arizona)[11]

There are also multiple examples of family or household initiatives:

The Asin Fura family of Ndere reorganized itself around the butchery founded there in 1924. The butchery expanded into a shop, in the 1950s a tearoom was added, and then, in the 1970s, the family extended its activities into motor transport. (Intensive agriculture Luo, Kenya)[12]

[O]ne matrilocal extended family ... was maintained by a joint economic enterprise having real financial value, in which the old mother and her three married daughters combined to make tourist items (belts, purses, chinchorros [hammocks]) in sufficiently large volume to be sold by the *Comision Indigenista* in shops along the highway. The women pooled their resources to keep the business going and divided the profits. The daughters of the three women also assisted significantly in making and selling the product. (Pastoral Goajiro, Venezuela)[13]

Many rich reindeer-breeders who have two or more herds do keep a separate wife with each herd. Ettl'hIn, for example ... had two herds, and a wife attending to each. Ei'heli, on the Oloi River ... was the owner of four herds, with as many wives looking after them. (Pastoralist Chukchee, Siberia)[14]

Historically, an influential family was one that had its members strategically distributed throughout the most vital sectors of society, each prepared to support the others in order to ensure family prestige and family status. ... Business operations have continued to be family affairs, often large government loans for business ventures have been obtained simply because the owners were recognized as members of families with good Islamic and [Iranian] revolutionary credentials. ... Successful members were expected to assist less successful ones to get their start. Iranians have viewed this inherent nepotism as a positive value, not as a form of corruption. (Intensive agricultural Iranians, Iran)[15]

This household head spent many years in military service before returning to Valiyagramam to take over the local toddy-shop. He had previously shared a wife with his younger brother but on retirement built a separate house and took his own wife, a matriculate and diploma shorthand-typist from the eastern hilly area. Together the couple run a photocopy shop and typing institute in town. (Intensive agriculture Keralans, India)[16]

There is ... one crucial impediment to Luo wives shifting completely to the centre of Luo entrepreneurial activities in Nairobi. ... they move from town to country and back again, on average about every six months ... A husband is ... helped in this if he has two wives, who can alternate in management of a market stall. ... Luo women acquire the training need for economic independence in Nairobi, but are then required to transfer their expertise to their husband's rural home, where they may continue to trade and at the same time arrange for the flow of fish and ... other food back to the stall in Nairobi. (Intensive agricultural Luo, Kenya)[17]

It is difficult to find tribal cultures without task or work specialization. Exchanging output with those outside the family, using barter or money transactions, is an incipit form of business creation.

BUSINESS CREATION, STATUS, AND PRESTIGE

Successful business creators in many subsistence cultures gained prestige in their communities:

> Most employees seemed to have some form of entrepreneurship as their immediate goal, but only as a means of advancing themselves in the village. The schoolteachers invested their savings in cattle ... one intended to start a trading store ... The school attendance orderly had invested with his brother in a bakery ... The road boss invested part of his savings in the expansion of the trading store owned by his brother. (Horticulturalist Tonga, Zambia)[18]

> The incentives to the formation of a family business are of two sorts: (1) Large families benefit from the operation of a store because they can make their purchases wholesale. (2) Storekeeping carries prestige. (Horticulturalist Kuna, Panama)[19]

> Today only a few men have enough capital to establish large cocoa farms worked by hired labor. But by trading an astute man can become very rich. In the past there were noted traders; today the produce buyers, the building contractors, and the truck owners are the town's wealthiest men, enjoying the highest prestige. (Horticulturalist Yoruba, Nigeria)[20]

> Both Oktay and Attila buy the surpluses that small farmers produce or arrange for such crops to go to the market on their trucks. Furthermore, both Oktay and Attila extend credit in winter to poorer villagers or small producers who run short of food or cash ... Thus, Oktay and Attila are entrepreneurs or patrons who have different dyadic ties to clients (some of who are their poorer kinsmen). As patrons they use credit and their role as entrepreneurs ... to build up a following. (Commercial economy Turks, Turkey)[21]

> In some respects he [Frank Audet] was no different from a typical white entrepreneur/businessman. In spite of the fact that he had grown up in the bush living the traditional hunting, fishing, and trapping life, and even though he couldn't read or write, he'd managed to learn to speak English and had received a government small business loan. With equipment borrowed from the Northwest Territories forestry service, he started a woods bison big game hunting camp. Within four years he was financially successful ... and the forest service was borrowing equipment from him. ... Frank was interviewed by the "ace" reporter of the CBC [Canadian Broadcasting Corporation] Mackenzie radio station. He was proud of his success and celebrity. (Hunter-gathering Chipewyans, Canada)[22]

Clearly, there is substantial diversity among subsistence cultures in the rewards for those involved in business creation. In some societies economic success leads to greater status and prestige, in others, discussed below, it may conflict with values of equality or sharing. Those seen as greedy may also be seen as corrupt.

BUSINESS CREATION CHALLENGES

There are many opportunities for business creation in subsistence economies. Those seeking to improve their situation through business creation may confront several challenges:

- Land ownership.
- Limited customer base.
- Managing credit.
- Norm of equality.
- Access to capital.

There are many examples of each.

Land Ownership

Ambiguity about land ownership substantially complicates business creation. There is considerable diversity related to land ownership among subsistence cultures on two levels. First is the extent to which indigenous peoples have control of land or land-based resources, such as plants or animals. Property rights have little meaning unless recognized by the national government and the legal system. The second issue is how members are allowed to use tribal land, which varies among subsistence cultures.

In many cases, land that traditionally supported subsistence economies was not considered to have much economic value. As a low-value resource, there was little challenge to use by indigenous peoples; definitions of physical boundaries and acceptable uses were often informal or imprecise. Over time, some land is now considered to have economic value for a variety of activities (mining, timbering, advanced agriculture, tourism). As a result, in many countries the allocation of land to provide support for indigenous people versus contemporary commercial purposes is a major issue. This dilemma is complicated by the presence of considerable plant and animal biodiversity on undeveloped land. Conservation activists consider indigenous people to be more appropriate stewards of biodiversity than multinational corporations.[23] Clarifying land ownership to facilitate business creation, which would improve indigenous people's economic well-being, is not included in these discussions.

There is great diversity in how tribal cultures treat land held in common. Some facilitate ownership by individual members, others insist that all land be held in trust by the tribe.

> One [Navajo] individual began applying for a business lease in October 1966, to operate a gas station [on the reservation]. By 1970, when his lease appeared to be ready for approval, he had lost interest in pursuing the matter and had obtained a

[work] position in another area. Another [Navajo] person, returning from college, hoped to "show the world how to run a business." After five years his application had not been approved, nor had it been rejected. In the meantime, he lost his desire to be a businessman. (Agricultural-pastoralist Navajo, Arizona)[24]

[T]here is a great deal of diversity in the way village leaders reallocated land. For example, in the peri-urban village of Kyichuling, village leaders have reallocated land twice since decollectivisation—in 1994 and again in 1997. If villagers acquire salaried urban jobs, the village leaders require that they return their Household Responsibility land to the village. However, because land is not reallocated every year, the land temporarily reverts to village collective land. Until 2000 all villagers were required to work on collective land (with the amount of work determined by the amount of Household Responsibility land). Starting in 2000, however, the village leaders required families with land designated for return to the village to pay a yearly rent to the village (collective fund) until the next reallocation. (Intensive agriculturalist Tibetans, Tibet)[25]

Tribal members that cannot legally own land are at a major disadvantage in obtaining financial support, for these assets cannot be used as collateral for loans related to either the land or any related structures. Further, if tribal ownership is considered immune from judgments in the external legal system, outside financial institutions are reluctant to accept this collateral for an asset-backed loan.

There has been recent attention to the complications created by the absence of legal property rights in developing countries. In many communities this was considered so important that members developed their own property registration systems and even issued hard-copy titles to individual owners. Such systems emerged in gold mining camps in the U.S. in the 1800s. Recognized as legitimate within the community, this would encourage owners to improve assets on the property for personal or commercial uses. In many cases national governments would incorporate these emergent property rights systems into the national registration systems.[26] There are many examples where this process converted unregistered land within national boundaries into legally registered land assigned to an owner.

Limited Customer Base

Many subsistence tribal cultures are small or modest in size. Even large subsistence tribes may be composed of hundreds of small communities.

The Suku number about 80,000. They live in open rolling savanna of low population density (15–20 persons per square mile), in villages ranging in size from a score [about twenty] to two hundred persons and located at intervals of a couple of miles. (Horticulturalist Suku, Republic of the Congo)[27]

In 1861 John Ward, U.S. Indian Agent, estimated the total population at 2,500 ... divided as follows: 650 in three villages on 1st Mesa, 450 at Mishong'novi-Sipau'lovi, 600 at Shungo'povi, and 800 at Oraibi.[28] Today [1970] the population of the eleven villages is about 4,500.[29] (Intensive-agricultural Hopi, Arizona)

The Warao (people of canoes), who number about 8,000 live in the Orinoco delta, eastern Venezuela. ... The majority of the Warao are settled in about 250 villages raised on piles on the banks of the river and widely scattered, principally in the central delta and in the region near the coast. (Hunter-gathering Warao, Venezuela)[30]

Among the 566 federally recognized tribes in the U.S. in 2013, 31% have less than 500 members and 4% less than 100. Even the largest reservations consist of collections of affiliated tribes. The Navajo nation in Arizona, with close to two hundred thousand, is composed of ten different federally recognized tribes with populations from 2,500 to 40,000. (Agricultural-pastoralist Navajo, Arizona and New Mexico)[31]

Business creators in many subsistence cultures are confronted by a relatively small customer base, composed of family, relatives, and neighbors. A small potential market poses substantial limits for growth. It can also make it difficult for the businessperson to focus solely on economic transactions when they may have multiple social relationships with the "customers."

Managing Credit

One of the most common business activities in subsistence cultures is to implement a small store or trading post. These ventures, often in the home, supply goods from outside the community to tribal members. For the businessperson, this involves participating in a cash economy for merchandise, but dealing with cash-poor relatives and neighbors as customers. It frequently does not go well.

Many [indigenous] stores are remarkably short-lived, lasting no more than a few weeks or months. These tend to be owned by people who are perceived to be wealthy and, consequently, are particular targets for demand sharing. By opening a store, they attempt to protect themselves from "demands" so as to preserve their possessions. (Hunter-gathering Enxet, Paraguay)[32]

[T]he scope of entrepreneurship is limited by the involuted network of kinship and neighbourhood ties within which every Skolt [Lapp] finds himself enmeshed. These ties are grounded in a morality of generalized reciprocity in direct contradiction with the rules of commerce governing the market for goods, services, and labor. Consequently, an entrepreneur exploiting the local Skolt market must be prepared to accept the costs of a socially marginal position if the enterprise is to pay off financially ... Given the general and persistent shortage of cash in the community, he faces the alternatives of either handing out unlimited credit, with the consequent threat of bankruptcy, or of making precipitate demands for payment and risking loss of custom as a result. (Pastoral Skolt Saami, Finland)[33]

Individual enterprise is hampered by the network of economic obligations and services in which every Palauan is enmeshed. Men who attempt to set themselves up in shopkeeping, barbering, or in any other private undertaking find that they have plenty of business but little income. They do not feel that they can charge their relatives for services or goods; and their relatives either assume they should not be required to pay or are inclined to charge what they get against obligations owed them on other accounts by the struggling businessman. Consequently a man's stock and time dwindle away with no cash returns to put back in the business. (Belau, Republic of Belau)[34]

This presents a major dilemma that prevents many in subsistence tribes from creating a sustainable trading business, a complication not confronted by "outsiders" whose primary customer relationships are economic.

Norm of Equality

Norms of equality emerge in all social groups. In many work situations, some may have a talent for organizing and coordinating work. If they consider their contributions are more significant, they may—or may not—receive additional benefits.

Esteban was the first director and at the heart of the new factory. He worked extremely hard, had a business head and the enterprise went well. A conflict soon developed, however, because Esteban argued that he should receive a bonus for being the director. All eight members called a meeting. They decided unanimously to refuse Esteban's request and to reduce him to the status of an ordinary worker. Esteban left shortly afterwards. ... The business quickly started to go sour. (Agriculturalist-pastoralist Basque, Spain)[35]

Neither is the [Warao] Indian organizer ... to be envied. He is under constant pressure from the rank and file of his team to provide large quantities of food such as wheat flour, sugar, cassava bread and salted fish and meat, as well as much coveted clothing items such as shirts, pants, and cloth for dresses. If a cash profit is forthcoming, his share is strictly equal to that of all the others, no extra amount for his management services is tolerated. (Hunter-gathering Warao Indians, Venezuela)[36]

[T]here is the old Palauan custom which makes it undesirable for a man to appear prosperous. All men, by their own protests, are poor. To be otherwise is to invite all kinds of maneuvers to wheedle and coerce a man out of his money. (Belau, Republic of Belau)[37]

Despite the many examples of those with successful businesses improving their status and reputation within their communities, it does not occur in all subsistence cultures and in some cases economic success needs to be carefully managed to avoid negative reactions.

Access to Capital

Any business creation requires some capital investment, if only in basic tools and supplies. The lack of personal capital is a major problem for members of subsistence tribal economies. Most subsistence economies in the twenty-first century are involved with market economies that have a monetary system and barter is no longer common. It is relatively straightforward to track capital requirements and wealth accumulation. There are multiple examples of the constraints the lack of capital places on business creation.

> Possibilities for Skolts to set up independent enterprises ... are limited by goth [people of Germanic origins] social and economic constraints. On the economic side, Skolts lack investment capital and have nothing to offer as security for bank loans. (Pastoralist Saami, Finland)[38]

> The two restaurants are owned by Chinese who have been in this business for more than 20 years. ... The initial capital required is thus much higher; one of the two has invested more than 100,000 *baht* (UKP[39] 2,500) in the shop-house. ... To invest in a food stall, one needs not more than 1,000 *baht* (UKP 25) and, as a result, there are more than 15 food stalls within and outside the marketplace. (Intensive-agriculture Thai, Thailand)[40]

> [T]he entrepreneurs have tools to the average replacement value of $30 and equipment associated with their cash-cropping to an average replacement value of $180—an average of $210 per man. By comparison Orokaiva people of Inonda village had only about $13 and Sivepe village about $18 worth of tools and equipment per household. (Other subsistence combination Orokaiva, Papua New Guinea)[41]

> When I asked women why they went into market trading, many ... said first it was because they had only low levels of capital. (Horticulturalist Akan, Ghana)[42]

Lack of capital and lack of access to institutions that facilitate capital accumulation is a major constraint on business creation in subsistence economies. This would account for the large proportion of activity in sectors that do not involve substantial capital, such as handicrafts, personal services, or small-scale trading.

One recent solution to this problem has been the provision of micro-loans to business creators in rural villages in developing countries. Cash-poor women artisans in rural Bangladesh were not able to afford supplies without paying high interest for informal loans. A relationship with the formal financial system was developed by organizing teams of women that would be responsible for loans to individual members of the group. The group accepted responsibility for supervision of the loans to individual members and repayments to the bank; the Grameen Bank was the first micro-loan financial institution. The high repayment rates from these small sale borrowers have led to the creation of a for-profit micro-finance sector with hundreds of financial institutions and billions in loans. They have helped sponsor millions of small businesses.[43]

Commentary

While business creation is very common in subsistence cultures, there is great diversity in the context. Land and other assets may be collectively owned and managed or assigned to individuals. The size of the community may vary from hundreds to tens of thousands. Many business creators may have difficulty managing the interface between the host market economy, where money payments are required, and customers with whom they have multiple relationships and may not be able to provide cash payments for goods or services. While in some cases business success is honored and income inequality accepted, in other societies strong norms of equality can discourage aggressive business expansion. And in many poorer communities access to capital is a major problem, particularly when there are few physical assets and legal ownership may be ambiguous.

Perhaps reflecting the high level of task specialization and small business creation in subsistence economies, the members seem very aware of these challenges. Given the choice of pursuing small-scale firms within their own culture or pursuing business creation in the host economy, many pursue the latter option. The experiences of American Indians in the U.S. suggests that this can be a successful strategy.

ACCOMMODATING MARKET ECONOMIES: AMERICAN INDIANS IN THE UNITED STATES

Before there was a U.S. or Canada, American Indians developed subsistence tribal cultures in a diversity of environments including the wetlands of Florida, the woodlands of the northeast, the great plains of the Midwest, the deserts of the southwest, the rainforests of the northwest, and the Arctic tundra. Contemporary American Indian communities reflect the cultural and social organizations that emerged in these diverse settings.

American Indians in the U.S. are widely dispersed. Many live on hundreds of reservations and a large proportion are in the host society. Like other ethnic groups they appear to be more active in business creation than the White majority. A national survey completed in 1998 identified adults active as nascent entrepreneurs in the pre-profit stage of business creation. Figure 3.1 indicates that participation by American Indians is similar to African Americans and both groups are twice as active as Whites. Given that these results reflected phone interviews, it is likely that most of these self-identified American Indians are living off their reservations.

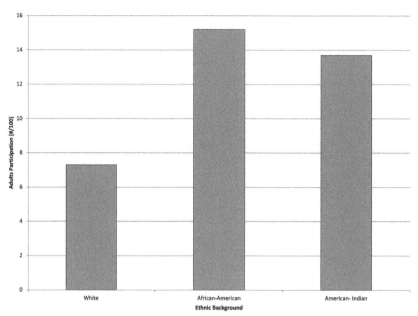

Note: Data from United States adult population sample of the Global Entrepreneurship Monitor program (Reynolds et al., 2005). Survey vendor provided data on ethnic background that included American Indian as an option. Data set from the author's archives. It involved 724 White, 82 African American and 81 American Indians. There were 20 Hispanic respondents excluded from analysis as the sub-sample was too small for a reliable estimate.

Figure 3.1   Active nascent entrepreneurs by ethnicity

More precise evidence of participation is available from a 1993 study in Wisconsin. In this case, carefully developed samples facilitate comparisons of those from different ethnic backgrounds.[44] American Indian respondents were randomly selected from six of 11 federally recognized Indian nation tribal voting rolls. The work values of a representative sample of American Indians are compared to White Wisconsinites in Table 3.2. On these six topics—ranging from an interest in making societal contributions to a chance for greater wealth—there is no statistically significant difference between the two groups.

American Indians in Wisconsin are just as active in business creation as other ethnic groups, as presented in Figure 3.2.[45] The comparisons emphasize four types of participation, pursuing new firm creation as active nascent entrepreneurs, discouraged nascent entrepreneurs that have abandoned a start-up effort, currently engaged as the owner-managers of a new firm, and those who

Table 3.2   *Work orientations: American Indians versus Whites*

Item	American Indian	White
Best work makes a contribution to society	3.2	3.0
Best work provides autonomy and independence	3.3	3.1
Best work uses special skills and abilities	3.3	3.2
Best work provides a chance for greater wealth	2.8	2.7
I will take the best work I can find	2.8	2.8
I prefer work so I can remain in the area	3.1	2.9

Note: Mean scores on a four-point scale. Comparison based on representative samples of 108 American Indians and 226 White residents of Wisconsin.

have abandoned or shut down a business. The prevalence of each activity, in number per 100, is provided for each ethnic category. Two-thirds of the American Indians are living on reservations. Because of small samples few differences are statistically significant.

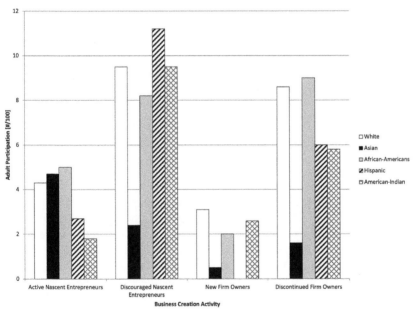

Note: This involved 226 White, 127 Asian, 107 African American, 121 Hispanic, and 108 American Indian respondents (71 living on reservations, 37 living off the reservation).
Source: Reynolds et al. (1993, table 5.1).

Figure 3.2   *Participation in business creation: American Indians and other ethnic groups*

Table 3.3   Social networks: American Indians and other ethnic groups

	White	Asian	African American	Hispanic	American Indian
Work colleagues	6.0	4.5	4.8	5.5	6.2
Family, relatives	6.1	2.8	6.1	5.7	8.3
Total social network	12.1	11.6	11.0	11.2	14.5

The level of activity reported by White and African American respondents is quite similar. American Indians and Hispanics seem to have similar patterns, with less participation than Whites or African Americans. Asian respondents seem to be active as nascent entrepreneurs but less likely to report they have abandoned a start-up, are a new firm owner-manager, or have shut down a firm.[46] Perhaps most important is that differences between American Indians and the other ethnic categories are matters of degree; they are clearly engaged in all stages of business creation.

Business creation is very much a social activity and a social network can contribute to success.[47] American Indians report larger social networks than other ethnic groups.[48] As shown in Table 3.3, the average size of the social networks for four ethnic categories is similar, from 11.0 to 12.1. But for the fifth, the American Indians, it is somewhat larger at 14.5. This difference is statistically significant. As can be seen, this reflects a much larger family social network reported by American Indians; the work colleague social networks are about the same size for all five ethnic groups. All ethnic groups consider that about one-third of these individuals provide "good" or "very good" help. As their social networks are larger, this leads to more personal assistance for American Indians.

In a longitudinal study of business creation outcomes many American Indians appear to be successful in business creation. One-fourth of American Indians report initial profits in the six years after entering the start-up process in 2004. As shown in Figure 3.3 this is slightly less than the one-third of profitable outcomes for whites, and about half of the profitable outcomes reported by African Americans and Hispanic nascent entrepreneurs. The relative lack of success for American Indians may reflect a more casual approach to creating small-scale enterprises or a lack of resources for the start-up phase.

In general, American Indian participation in business creation is like other ethnic minorities and greater than the White majority. Their work values are like the White majority, they may have a large social network for support, and many successfully create profitable new firms. Overall, regardless of diverse cultural backgrounds, American Indian business creation is a common activity in the U.S. It reflects an important career option for many and is a source of contributions to both tribal economies and the larger U.S. economy.

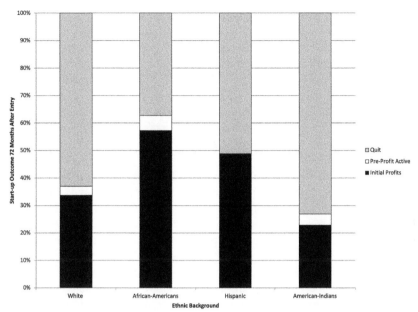

Note: Consistent with United States government surveys, the question about Hispanic background is asked separately from a single item on other ethnic categories. In this case, those responding as Hispanic and White are included with Hispanic, those responding Hispanic and American Indian are included with American Indian. As only 17 respondents were identified as Asian, they are omitted from the presentation. Based on 486 White, 110 African American, 43 Hispanic, White/Hispanic, and 46 American Indian, American Indian/Hispanic respondents.
Source: United States Panel Study in Entrepreneurial Dynamics II outcome data from Reynolds et al. (2016), with details on ethnic background from Curtin and Reynolds (2018).

Figure 3.3   Business creation outcomes by ethnic background

OVERVIEW

Business creation among the 400 million indigenous people that represent 4,000 cultures can provide individual gains and benefits to their communities. Task specialization and business creation are ubiquitous in subsistence cultures. New firm creation by indigenous peoples takes three forms, each with a different context. First are those initiatives within the subsistence economy, where inputs, business operation, and the customer base are all within the indigenous society. Second are those efforts that are based on serving as an interface between a host market economy and the tribal economy. Third is business creation by members of the indigenous tribe implemented within the host market economy.

Contexts for the first type of business creation, within the tribal culture, can be very diverse. At one extreme would be a loose confederation of those with a common cultural background. At the other extreme is a highly formalized self-governing tribal structure that regulates commercial initiatives.

Loosely affiliated cultural groups may share language, history, and cultural norms. Participation in systematic efforts to maintain a distinct cultural identity may be voluntary. The subsistence community may have limited legal control of traditional land or resources. Individuals, households, and groups representing the cultural tradition are expected to prepare for the future as they see fit. Everybody is, so to speak, on their own. Norms of cultural interdependence may be supplemented by norms of individual or family self-sufficiency.

At the other extreme are cultural groups that have organized to maintain a unique cultural identity, with systematic efforts to maintain traditional languages, social organization, and cultural values that would represent a distinctive way of life. Members may share the value of mutual interdependency, an emphasis on ensuring the well-being of all. These efforts are more effective if the subsistence community has a legal claim to territory, such as many American Indian tribes in the U.S., or access to resources, as with Suomi (Lapps) in northern Scandinavia following reindeer herds. Some tribes may discourage commercial activities considered detrimental to maintaining a distinctive cultural identity. This can take the form of careful control of tribal resources, such as land ownership or trust funds, or restriction on business activities that would compete with tribal enterprises.

Individual members may wish to pursue business creation within the tribal culture, confronting these many complications. The tribe may benefit from these initiatives, but the benefits may be constrained by tribal regulations and procedures. It may limit the range of business activity that can be developed.

For business creators, both the open collaboration and tight control can pose a challenge. In the first case there may be substantial limits to the customer base and extensive regulations may preclude implementing many types of businesses. These can lead many indigenous peoples to choose to develop a business that is at the intersection between the tribal culture and the external economy. There are many examples of the emergence of trading activities where host economy goods are provided to tribal members. The reverse is also common, where indigenous arts or crafts are provided for sale to customers from the host society, as in the following example:

> On the second Friday of every month, the Navajo (Dine) Rug Weavers Association holds a public rug auction in the Crownpoint, New Mexico elementary school. (The closest motels are 60 miles away.) Coming from a range of Navajo tribes forty to fifty weavers, almost all women, each offer two to three rugs for sale. Initiated in 1964 and now well attended by buyers and sellers, the auction provides a way

for Navajo weavers to sell their recent output directly to buyers and immediately receive a cash payment, less the 15% auction fee.[49]

This monthly event involves two types of business. There is the Navajo Weavers Association of Crownpoint that supervises the auction and the individual producers who create the rugs for sale. Sustained operation would suggest that these have been successful enterprises.

The third option for indigenous members is to pursue business creation in the host economy. These initiatives will have the same opportunities and confront the same challenges as all other business creators. This may or may not pose additional challenges. Discrimination against the tribal culture may lead to some additional complications.

COMMENTARY

Systematic, detailed descriptions of business creation in subsistence economies is not available. But a review of activity from diverse ethnographic accounts would suggest the following:

- Virtually all members are engaged in task specialization or one or more business activities, serving members outside their immediate household. In many cases it is the default career option.
- There is considerable diversity in the assistance or constraints provided by the tribal culture.
- What is considered an acceptable success varies dramatically, from strict norms of equality to celebration and status for high-growth outcomes.
- Both the size of the markets and cultural norms can constrain firm growth.
- As an ongoing activity, indigenous business creation is a major source of collective and individual economic advantage.

As business creation and task specialization are widespread among subsistence cultures, it is reasonable to assume they have contributed to the survival of indigenous peoples. Business creation has been a common activity from the earliest stages of human development.

NOTES

1. Rosen (2010).
2. Extensive use was made of the Human Relation Area Files (2020) archives in identifying relevant examples for this chapter. The effort required to locate and classify descriptions of behavior in tens of thousands of documents relevant to thousands of subsistence cultures is a unique social science resource. Examples of business creation were identified with the Outline of Cultural Materials

subject code 472 (Individual Enterprise) with variation across subsistence types and global regions.

3. These estimates are based on country estimates with substantial variation in procedures (Mamo, 2020). National governments vary in how they legally define and recognize indigenous peoples. For example, Canada has three main categories and the United States, as of 2020, recognizes 574 tribes, many reflecting the same tribal culture in different locations. Large Asian countries also reflect diversity, with India recognizing 705 indigenous cultures, Bangladesh 54, and China 55. Furthermore, many countries have indigenous peoples that have not been officially recognized. As a result, the figures in Table 3.1 should be considered as very approximate estimates.

4. Kopytoff (1965, p. 446). Field date: 1958–1959.
5. Jefremovas (1991). Field date: 1984–1985.
6. Heinen (1973, p. 610). Field date: 1966–1971.
7. Beach (1981). Field date: 1973–1977.
8. Beals (1966, p. 77). Field date: 1949.
9. Tschopik (1951, p. 285). Field date: 1940–1942.
10. Gutierrez de Pineda and Muirden (1948, p. 281). Field date: 1947.
11. Wyckoff (1986, p. 128). Field date: 1979–1980.
12. Cohen and Odhiambo (1989, p. 80). Field date: 1978–1982.
13. Watson (1968, p. 120). No field date.
14. Bogaraz-Tan (1904–1909, p. 599). No field date. The author mentions that 75–85% of the males have only one wife.
15. Hoglund (1989, p. 109). Field date: 1850–1987.
16. Osella and Osella (2000, p. 62). Field date 1989–1996. Town name Valiyagramam, a pseudonym.
17. Parkin (1978, p. 130). Field date: 1968–1969.
18. Colson (1971, p. 136). Field date: 1949, 1956–1957, 1960, 1961, 1965.
19. Holloman (1969, p. 202). Field date 1966–1967.
20. Lloyd (1965, p. 559). Field date: 1949–1959.
21. Starr (1978, p. 22). Field date: 1966–1968.
22. Smith (1995, p. 125). Field date: 1974.
23. Mamo (2020); World Bank Group (2015).
24. Gilbreath (1977, p. 49). Field date: early 1970s.
25. Yeh (2004, p. 116). Field date: 2000–2002.
26. De Soto (1989, 2000).
27. Kopytoff (1971, p. 69). Field date: 1958–1959.
28. Bradfield (1971, p. 61, Appendix 4). Field date: 1966–1970.
29. Bradfield (1973, p. 1). Field date: 1966–1980.
30. Suarez (1971, p. 58). Field date 1963–1968.
31. U.S. Department of the Interior (2014, Table 3). Counts of tribal membership are only provided for 37% (207) of 566 tribes. Several tribes are listed as having less than ten members.
32. Kidd (1999, p. 276). Field date: 1984–1996.
33. Ingold (1976, p. 110). Field date: 1971–1972.
34. Barnett (1963, p. 31). Field date: 1947–1948.
35. Heiberg (1989, p. 209). Field date: 1969–1976.
36. Heinen (1973, p. 612). Field date: 1966–1971.
37. Barnett (1963, p. 31). Field date: 1947–1948.
38. Ingold (1976, p. 110). Field date: May 1971–September 1972.

39. United Kingdom pounds.
40. Khuwinphan (1980, p. 194). Field date: 1974–1976.
41. Crocombe (1967, p. 14). Field date: 1962–1965.
42. Clark (1994, p. 172). Field date: 1978–1990.
43. Convergences (2018); Yunus (1998).
44. Reynolds et al. (1993), chapter 5 prepared by Gary Mejchar, James Murry, and Keith Tourtillott. Representative samples of Whites, Asians, African Americans, and Hispanics based on ethnic identity in Wisconsin state driver license files. Of the 108 American Indian respondents, 71 lived on or near their reservation and 37 were living off the reservation.
45. Reynolds et al. (1993), reported on the first project that used adult population surveys to identify those participating in business creation, which became known as the Panel Study in Entrepreneurial Dynamics research protocol followed by several extensive national projects in the United States and a number of other countries (Reynolds and Curtin, 2009b, 2011).
46. Asian respondents were somewhat younger and more recent immigrants to Wisconsin and, therefore, had less time to engage in business creation.
47. Reynolds (2018, chapter 5).
48. Includes only American Indians living on or near their reservation.
49. Crownpoint Rug Auction (2021), Navajo Rug Appraisal Co. (2021), and author personal observation.
50. This appendix is based on Human Relations Area Files (2020, p. 44). Frequency distribution based on counts for 316 of 331 cultures in the "AddCultures" listing with Orientation (OCM 100) material.

APPENDIX: SUBSISTENCE VARIATION

There is substantial diversity in the physical environment in which tribal cultures evolved.[50] Variations in the climate and sources of food require different technologies which, in turn, may affect the social organization and culture of surviving tribes. Estimates of the subsistence base at the origin, many generations in the past, of a sample of 316 tribal cultures are presented in Table 3A.1.

The classification represents the best judgment of well-informed ethnographers and anthropologists about the major economic focus of cultural groups:

- Hunter-gatherers (or foragers): substantial dependence (86% or more) on hunting, fishing, or gathering.
- Primarily hunter-gatherers (or foragers): major dependence (56% or more) on hunting, fishing, or gathering.
- Pastoralists: major dependence (56% or more) on following herds or maintaining livestock.
- Horticulturalists: major dependence (56% or more) on simple agriculture.
- Intensive agriculturalists: major dependence (56% or more) on intensive agriculture with some permanent fields that may involve irrigation.
- Pastoral/agricultural: pastoralism and agricultural/horticulture combined are 76% or more of the economy. (Not in any other category.)
- Other subsistence: other combinations of hunter-gathering, pastoralism, and horticulture or agriculture.
- Commercial economy: primary activity in wage and salary work, selling products, or operating a business.

Any given cultural community may change their subsistence base over time, and many have or are shifting emphasis to accommodate commercial, market economies.

These are alternative forms of economic activity and not different stages of "cultural advancement." Intensive agriculture is not a more advanced or sophisticated subsistence base than hunter-gatherers or following migratory herds. Except for those that have become involved in the surrounding commercial economy, all represent a focus on substance survival that involves hunting, gathering, fishing, herding, or farming at different levels of intensity.

Very few tribal cultures now exist in isolation. Most are embedded within established market economies—such as the Lapps in northern Scandinavia, Aborigines in Australia, or North American Indians in Canada and the U.S. In other settings, such as Sub-Saharan Africa, a variety of tribal cultures—some with centuries of brutal competition—are consolidating into nations. As these new political units adopt the structures and institutions of more advanced

Table 3.1   Indigenous cultures: subsistence categories

	Hunting, fishing, and gathering	Herding, livestock	Simple agriculture	Intense agriculture, irrigation	Wages, product sales, business ownership	Proportion of known cases
Hunter-gatherer	86–100%					17%
Primarily hunter-gatherer	56–85%					8%
Pastoralists		56–100%				6%
Horticulturalists			56–100%			17%
Intense agricultural				56–100%		23%
Agricultural/pastoral		76–100%	76–100%	76–100%		8%
Other subsistence					Not present	13%
Commercial economy					Dominate	8%
Total						100%

market economies adjustments in the social organization, values, and norms of the subsistence tribal cultures is to be expected.

The current situation of tribal cultures reflects a mixture of long-established practices and institutions that are adapting to reliance on local, national, and international market economies.

4. Agricultural economies: Exiting farming

Sarah and her sister were raised by their mother after their father abandoned the family. She left secondary school at 14 to support the two of them after their mother died. She carefully watched the proprietor of the baby clothes shop where she worked. When her sister was also hired, they were able to save money for a new business. Their small equity capital was matched with a bank loan and they opened a shoe stall in a six-booth retail location in Kampala, Uganda. By constantly searching for the lowest cost shoes, she buys 40 pairs at a time, and with two part-time employees she supports her small family. Her sister can stay in school and expects to start a business when she graduates.[1]

Ben left Nigeria for Europe in his late teens. His request for asylum was denied and after five years on the edge of society he decided to return home, where he was welcomed by family and friends. He prepared a business plan for a car parts business and received a small grant from a government program for denied asylum seekers. He found a suitable location, with affordable rent, in the Oshodi area of Lagos. While there is substantial competition, he has emphasized service and good prices and after six months is seeking a larger location. He has accepted, as a cost of business, the "membership fees" to the "Union" paid by all shop owners for "protection."[2]

About 12% of the global population live in 36 Agricultural economies, such as Ethiopia, Madagascar, Nigeria, and Uganda. One-quarter, or 140 million, among the half a billion adults in their working years are actively involved in business creation. They are working on initiatives that will provide more or new or better goods and services.

THE NATIONAL CONTEXT

Agricultural economies are very young countries, as 43% of the population are less than 16 years old and only 3% are over 64 years old. Half of the adults are literate, and about one-quarter of adults have completed secondary (high school) education. A small proportion, 3%, have gone beyond secondary school for vocational, university, graduate, or professional training. About two-thirds of those 15 and older are in the labor force, 73% of men and 58% of women. Most formal jobs, however, do not require a high level of skill and 66% of workers make less than $3.60 per day. Only 13% of retirees have a pension. While many have work, the benefits are modest.[3]

Government programs to assist the citizens in Agricultural economies are relatively undeveloped, absorbing less than one-fourth of the annual GDP, which is about \$2,100 per person. Annual government spending on health care is about \$116 per person, for education about \$73 per person, and total spending on all forms of social protection (related to sickness, disability, retirement, unemployment, and the like) is about \$8 per person. Agricultural economies are not able to provide their citizens with basic benefits.[4] About half are living on \$1.90 per day and a third are in severe poverty.[5]

Life may be improving for those in Agricultural economies. Three-fifths have confidence in the national government, are satisfied with their local community, and feel they have freedom of choice. About half trust the legal system and feel safe walking outside at night. Less than half are satisfied with their standard of living, the quality of education, and health care. Only two-fifths consider the local labor market, which is largely informal and unregistered, as good.[6] Most of the adults emphasize traditional authority and survival individual values, with less than one-fifth emphasizing secular-rational authority or self-expressive individual values.[7]

CAREER OPTIONS

Those growing up in an Agricultural economy expect to work. Career choices are, to some extent, constrained. Half or more of all work is in agriculture, with 12% in industrial sectors, 28% in consumer-oriented businesses, and a small proportion, 8%, associated with sectors requiring post-secondary education. In the non-agriculture sectors, 84% of the jobs are unregistered. Half of all work is a form of unregistered self-employment, one-third is in unregistered firms with less than ten employees, and only 7% in registered firms with more than ten employees.[8] For the majority, "getting a job" is not an option.

On the other hand, all are embedded in a culture of entrepreneurship. In some agricultural economies every fourth person is active in early-stage business creation.[9] Virtually all adults have been, are, or will be involved in some type of business creation. Those born into Agricultural economies, particularly the subsistence cultures in rural areas, grow up surrounded by adults—family, relatives, neighbors—pursuing small-scale business creation. Three-fifths know someone involved in business creation. Over four-fifths consider business creation a good career choice and new firm success a source of status. Not only do three-fifths see good business opportunities, but three-fourths think they have the skill and knowledge to start a business.[10] Cultural support and acceptance of business creation could not be greater.

In addition, as there are few established firms, a major advantage for business creation in agricultural economies is the lack of established competition. There are many promising business opportunities to be exploited by new ventures. Given the wealth of business opportunities, the lack of work in established organizations, and the absence of reliable social protection from the government, it is not a surprise that the major response of adults seeking a role in the economy is to start a business.

HOW MUCH ACTIVITY?

The amount of activity in 36 Agricultural economies is presented in Table 4.1. Many millions are involved in the largest countries, such as Afghanistan, the Democratic Republic of Congo, Ethiopia, and Nigeria. Even the smallest countries, such as Comoros and Djibouti, have over 100,000 business creators. As can be seen, men are slightly more than half, 56%, of active business creators. On the other hand, 61 million women are involved. Nigeria alone has almost 20 million women business creators.

Those visiting these countries will notice a great deal of street-level entrepreneurship, even though much activity may be hidden from view. More than half are nascent ventures in the pre-profit or initial stages of firm creation and may not have a physical presence. The remainder are new firms with initial profits. Those focusing on the consumer sectors, such as a market stall, may be the most visible, while new firms emphasizing business customers may be less obvious.

Understanding the situation confronted by business creators and their role in economic development involves attention to who gets involved, the nature of those active in business creation, the economic contributions of their ventures, and the major challenges they confront.

WHO PURSUES BUSINESS CREATION?

Age, gender, access to personal resources, and workforce activity are all related to participation in business creation. Men, at 34 per 100, are more involved than women, at 24 per 100. Men of all ages are slightly more likely to be involved than age-peer women, as shown in Figure 4.1. The gender difference is greatest among those 55 to 64 years old.

There is a high level of activity among men of all ages—those 55 to 64 years old are just as likely to be involved as those 18 to 24 years old. This may reflect the lack of stable employment in established work organizations, the short life of many new businesses, and the lack of pensions for those of retirement age. Men in Agricultural economies may find they must constantly be involved in firm creation throughout their work career. Women, in contrast, seem to be quite active from 18 to 54 years old, with some decline in activity among those 55 and older.

Table 4.1   Business creators in Agricultural economies

Country	Total population: 2018	15–64-year-old population: 2018	Total business creators	Business creators: men	Business creators: women
Afghanistan	37,172,000	20,194,000	5,397,000	3,122,000	2,275,000
Benin	11,485,000	6,236,000	1,666,000	964,000	702,000
Burkina Faso*	19,751,000	10,398,000	3,100,000	1,737,000	1,363,000
Burundi	11,175,000	5,839,000	1,561,000	903,000	658,000
Cent African Rep	4,666,000	2,468,000	660,000	382,000	278,000
Chad	15,478,000	7,800,000	2,085,000	1,206,000	879,000
Comoros	832,000	478,000	128,000	74,000	54,000
Congo (Demo Rep)	84,068,000	42,720,000	11,417,000	6,605,000	4,812,000
Cote d'Ivoire	25,069,000	13,839,000	3,699,000	2,140,000	1,559,000
Djibouti	959,000	632,000	169,000	98,000	71,000
Eritrea	3,453,000	1,853,000	495,000	286,000	209,000
Ethiopia*	109,224,000	60,855,000	9,247,000	5,390,000	3,857,000
Gambia	2,280,000	1,212,000	323,000	187,000	136,000
Guinea	12,414,000	6,607,000	1,766,000	1,022,000	744,000
Guinea-Bissau	1,874,000	1,028,000	275,000	159,000	116,000
Haiti	11,123,000	6,875,000	1,837,000	1,063,000	774,000
Lesotho	2,108,000	1,315,000	351,000	203,000	148,000
Liberia	4,819,000	2,680,000	716,000	414,000	302,000
Madagascar*	26,262,000	14,798,000	3,287,000	1,738,000	1,549,000
Malawi*	18,143,000	9,698,000	3,130,000	1,670,000	1,460,000

Country	Total population: 2018	15–64-year-old population: 2018	Total business creators	Business creators: men	Business creators: women
Mali	19,078,000	9,529,000	2,546,000	1,473,000	1,073,000
Mauritania	4,403,000	2,500,000	669,000	387,000	282,000
Mozambique	29,496,000	15,467,000	4,133,000	2,391,000	1,742,000
Niger	22,443,000	10,643,000	2,844,000	1,645,000	1,199,000
Nigeria*	195,875,000	104,570,000	41,082,000	21,741,000	19,341,000
Papua New Guinea	8,606,000	5,227,000	1,397,000	808,000	589,000
Rwanda	12,302,000	7,023,000	1,877,000	1,086,000	791,000
Senegal*	15,854,000	8,539,000	3,358,000	1,754,000	1,604,000
Sierra Leone	7,650,000	4,282,000	1,144,000	662,000	482,000
South Sudan	10,976,000	6,013,000	1,607,000	930,000	677,000
Sudan	41,802,000	23,371,000	6,246,000	3,613,000	2,633,000
Syria*	16,945,000	10,858,000	915,000	749,000	166,000
Tanzania	56,313,000	30,015,000	8,022,000	4,641,000	3,381,000
Togo	7,889,000	4,402,000	1,177,000	681,000	496,000
Uganda*	42,729,000	21,847,000	7,010,000	3,755,000	3,255,000
Yemen	28,499,000	16,389,000	4,380,000	2,606,000	1,774,000
Total	923,215,000	498,200,000	139,716,000	78,285,000	61,431,000

Note: * Prevalence rates based on Global Entrepreneurship Monitor consolidated file (Reynolds, 2021). Estimates for other countries based on average values of countries with surveys. Population estimates based on United Nations (2019b).

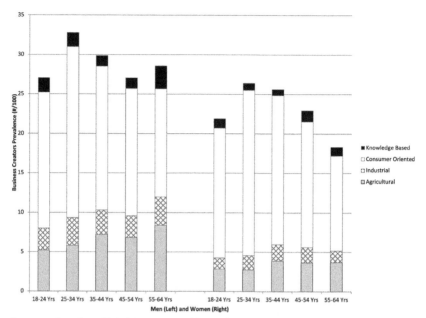

Source: Data from Global Entrepreneurship Monitor (Reynolds, 2021) averaged across all
years for each country where surveys were completed, then averaged across countries for nine
Agricultural economies.

Figure 4.1   Business creation participation by age, gender, and sector

While new businesses are being started in all sectors, more than half are in
consumer-oriented ventures such as market stalls, restaurants, lodging, transportation, and the like. While over half of established work is in agriculture,
only about one-fourth of business creators are involved in farming, forestry, or
fishing. Both men and women are creating new firms in industrial sectors (construction, manufacturing, utilities). Very few are pursuing business creation in
sectors that require technical or educational training, such as health, education,
social, business, or financial services.

A large proportion of adults in Agricultural economies have very modest
personal resources. This would include personal income and the skills and
knowledge provided by an education, often referred to as human capital. Based
on surveys of representative adults, reflected in Figure 4.2, about three-tenths
of the adults in agricultural economies have a daily income of about $3.30.[11]
Another three-tenths have a daily personal income of $6.60 and two-fifths
a daily income of $13.20, although some are much higher. There is little differ-
ence between adult men and women with regards to daily income.

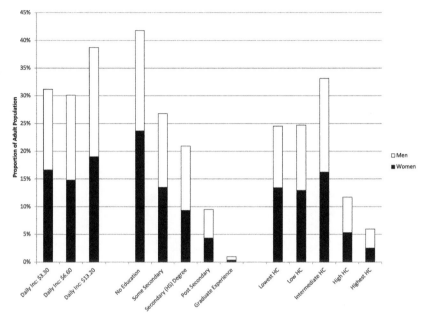

Source: See Figure 4.1, source.

Figure 4.2   Population human capital

Educational attainment, also presented in Figure 4.2, indicates a large proportion of adults, two-fifths, with no educational experience. Almost half have some primary or secondary experience, with one-fifth earning a secondary degree. About one-tenth have some post-secondary experience. Men and women with graduate training are scarce. Men are slightly more likely than women to have received some education.

These two measures can be used to create an index of personal human capital (details of which are in the appendix at the end of this chapter). As shown in the right section of Figure 4.2, one-quarter of adults have the lowest levels of personal resources—or human capital. These individuals have the lowest level of income and have not completed secondary (high) school. At the other extreme, those with post-secondary education and income in the upper third are the 6% at the highest level of human capital. About one-third have an intermediate level of human capital, reflecting intermediate levels of personal income and a secondary school degree, low education and high level of personal income, or low personal income and post-secondary education. One-eighth are in the high and one-fourth are in the low human capital categories.

The index facilitates exploring the relationship between human capital and participating in business creation. As shown in Figure 4.3, three-tenths or more of men with the three highest levels of human capital and one-fourth of women with the four highest levels of human capital are active in business creation. Among men and women with the lowest levels of human capital, one-fifth or more are active.

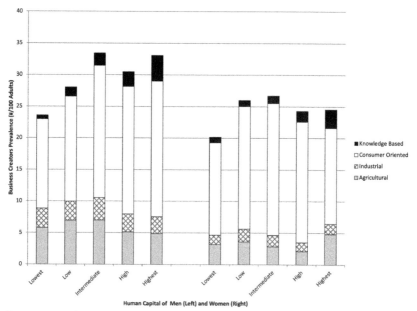

Source: See Figure 4.1, source.

Figure 4.3   *Business creation participation by human capital, gender, and sector*

There is some relationship between human capital and the sectors emphasize in business creation. Most men and women focus on consumer-oriented sectors, with a slight decrease among those with the highest levels of human capital. Those with more human capital, men and women, have a greater emphasis on knowledge-based sectors. Among men with greater human capital there is a decrease in emphasis on agricultural sectors. Among women, the emphasis on agricultural sectors is highest among those with the highest levels of human capital. Industrial sector business creation is similar among those with all levels of human capital.

There is some relationship between human capital and the sectors empha-sized in business creation. Most men and women focus on consumer-oriented sectors, with a slight decrease among those with the highest levels of human capital. Those with more human capital, men and women, have a greater emphasis on knowledge-based sectors. Among men with greater human capital there is a decrease in emphasis on agricultural and industrial sectors. Among women, the emphasis on agricultural sectors is highest among those with the lowest and the highest levels of human capital.

The labor force status of nascent entrepreneurs, those just entering business creation, is presented in Figure 4.4. There are few differences between men and women. One-third of those with full- or part-time jobs are involved in business creation. Only one-seventh of those unemployed and seeking work are involved. There is even less participation, at 1 in 20, among homemakers or students. Retired men are about as active as unemployed men, while retired women are much less active than any other category.

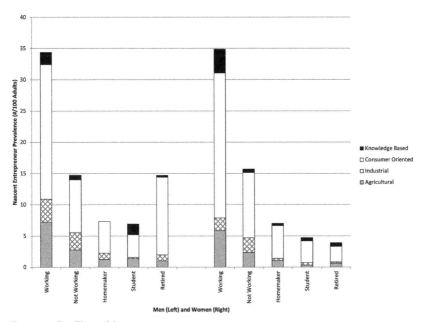

Source: See Figure 4.1, source.

Figure 4.4   *Nascent entrepreneur participation by labor force status, gender, and sector*

In Agricultural economies:

- Men and women of all ages are very active (20 to 30 per 100) in business creation in all sectors.
- While there is great diversity in human capital in Agricultural economies, all are very involved in business creation. Men and women with the lowest levels of human capital only slightly less active than those with more resources.
- Those working full or part time are much more involved than those with other roles in the labor force.

Business creation is a major activity among working adults.

WHO ARE THE BUSINESS CREATORS?

Those who pursue business creation form a dynamic community. It is useful—particularly for policy development—to know something about this group. The age and gender of those active in the four major sectors is presented in Figure 4.5: total percentages for each sector equal 100%. There is, however,

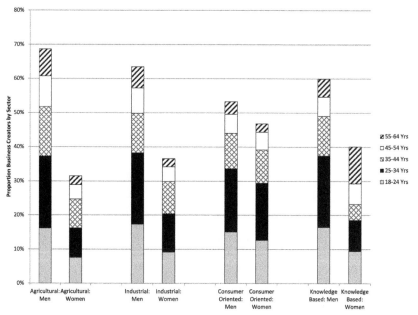

Source: See Figure 4.1, source.

Figure 4.5   *Age and gender proportions of business creators by sector*

considerable diversity in the amount of activity in the different sectors. About three-fourths of business creators' ventures are oriented toward consumers, one-seventh are in farming, forestry, or fishing, 1 in 11 in an industrial sector, and a small remainder in knowledge-based activities.

In all sectors, one-fourth of business creators are under 25 years of age. About a third are from 25 to 34 years old, and one-fifth are from 35 to 44 years old. Those 45 to 64 years old are three-tenths of business creators in knowledge-based sectors, slightly less than one-quarter in agriculture and industrial sectors, but one-sixth in consumer-oriented sectors.

All sectors have men and women of all ages involved. Consumer-oriented businesses, where half of the activity occurs, have almost as many women as men. Women are two-fifths of those active in knowledge-based sectors and about one-third in the industrial and agricultural sectors.

Business creators with different levels of human capital are found in all sectors, as shown in Figure 4.6. There is no significant difference in the distribution of human capital between men and women business creators. Most business creators in all sectors have low or intermediate levels of human capital.

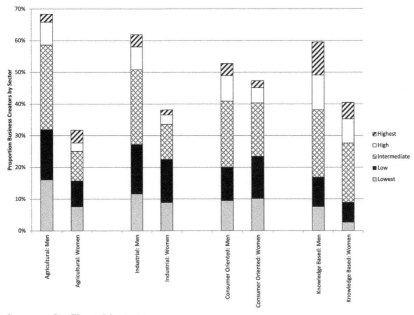

Source: See Figure 4.1, source.

Figure 4.6   *Human capital and gender proportions of business creators by sector*

They are 60% in agriculture, 64% in industrial, 62% in consumer-oriented, and 56% in knowledge-based sectors. The largest proportion of those with high or the highest levels of human capital are in knowledge-based and consumer-oriented sectors. They are one-sixth of business creators in agricultural and industrial sectors. All sectors have some business creators with low levels of human capital, including those where some knowledge may be required for success. Low human capital business creators are one-fourth of those in agriculture, one-fifth of those in industrial and consumer-oriented sectors, and one-tenth of those in knowledge-based sectors. The presence in knowledge-based sectors may reflect savvy, industrious individuals that compensate for a lack of formal training with self-education and more sophisticated work experience.

What are people doing when they first get involved in starting a business? The overwhelming majority, from 82% to 91%, of active business creators—men and women—are engaged in full- or part-time work as they pursue business creation, as shown in Figure 4.7. New ventures do not usually receive full-time attention until success is assured. There are some small differences

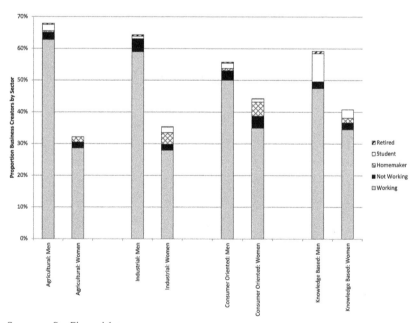

Source: See Figure 4.1, source.

Figure 4.7   *Labor force status and gender proportions of nascent entrepreneurs by sector*

related to labor force status at entry into a start-up. Women are more likely to be active nascent entrepreneurs while they continue as homemakers. Students are a slightly higher proportion of those pursuing knowledge-based new ventures. The dominant pattern, however, is one of individuals migrating from paid work to become independent business owner-managers.

Given that most nascent entrepreneurs are working as they enter the start-up process, why are they pursuing business creation? In Agricultural economies about one-fifth are pursuing opportunities to gain more autonomy and three-tenths seek greater income. A small proportion, 1 in 30, hope to maintain their existing level of income. These may be attracted to new business opportunities. Three-tenths find they have no better options for participating in the economy and one-fifth have a mix of motives.

The proportion with different motives shifts for those with different amounts of human capital presented in Figure 4.8. The proportions with different motivations are indicated for men and women with each level of human capital. The total for each category equals 100%. For both men and women motives shift with the amount of human capital. Those with more personal resources have a greater interest in opportunities that provide greater autonomy or income. At every level of human capital, a small proportion hope to maintain

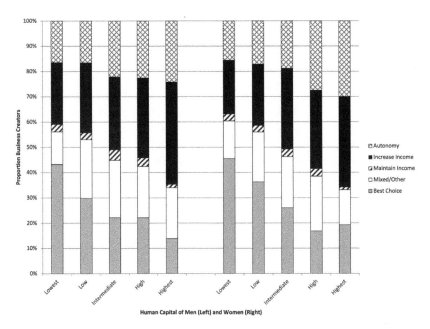

Figure 4.8   Business creator motivation by human capital and gender

their current level of income. Those with fewer resources are more likely to consider business creation their best choice for work.

The motives among all business creators with different amounts of human capital are provided in Figure 4.9. Again, men and women with different levels of human capital are identified, the overall total is 100%. Two-fifths of all business creators have intermediate levels of human capital. Those seeking autonomy or more income, however, are found among those with all levels of human capital. Those who consider business creation their best work option are concentrated among men and women with the lowest, low, or intermediate levels of human capital.

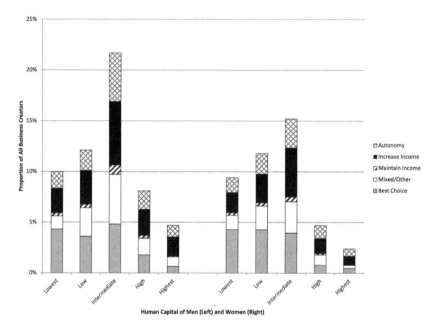

Figure 4.9   *Proportion of business creators by motivation, human capital, and gender*

For both men and women, the proportion pursuing business opportunities increases for those with more human capital, particularly for those at the high and highest levels. Among those with the lowest human capital, over two-fifths report it is their best choice, compared to one-fifth among those with the highest human capital. Among those with the highest levels of human capital, two-thirds report the attraction of a business opportunity, compared to two-fifths of those with the lowest human capital.

Among the community of business creators in agricultural economies:

- There are slightly more men than women.
- The majority are from 25 to 44 years old.
- The majority have low to intermediate levels of human capital.
- Four-fifths are working full or part time as they pursue business creation.
- Those with less human capital see business creation as their best choice for participating in the economy.
- An interest in work autonomy and greater income attract those with more human capital.
- Those with a variety of backgrounds and interests are involved in business creation in all sectors.

These are, then, the individuals making bottom-up contributions to Agricultural economies.

NEW VENTURES AND CONTRIBUTIONS

The 140 million business creators in 36 Agricultural economies are involved in creating 98 million early-stage ventures, as listed in Table 4.2. More than half of early-stage ventures are pre-profit, the remainder are new firms up to 42 months old. These estimates involve adjustments to account for the fact that about half of business creation is a team effort. While most start-up teams involve two people, teams of four, five, or six are not uncommon. The average start-up team sizes among Agricultural economies varies from 1.5 to 2.0. The largest country, Nigeria, has about 30 million new ventures, 20 million in the pre-profit stage and 11 million with initial profits. The smallest, Comoros, has 82,000 ventures, 45,000 in the pre-profit stage, and 37,000 with profits.

There is much diversity in the economic emphasis and contributions provided by these new ventures. The contributions can be considered in terms of job creation, expectations for growth, out-of-country exports, impact on the markets in which they will compete, and the presence of high-impact ventures. The proportions of new ventures making contributions is summarized in Figure 4.10. While contributions are provided by ventures in all sectors, three in four are consumer-oriented businesses.

All new ventures provide some jobs. About half are sole proprietorships, providing work for the owners. About one-third create from one to four jobs, 1 in 14 provide five to nine jobs, and 1 in 30 provide ten or more jobs. Many new ventures have expectations for growth, and 13% expect to create ten or more jobs in the next five years. While most expect modest growth, this includes a small proportion of the extremely optimistic that expect to have hundreds of employees in five years. While the majority are focused on local or national

Table 4.2   *Pre-profit ventures and new firms in Agricultural economies*

Country	15–64-year-old population	Total early-stage ventures	Pre-profit ventures	New firms
Afghanistan	20,194,000	3,482,000	1,919,000	1,563,000
Benin	6,236,000	1,076,000	593,000	483,000
Burkina Faso*	10,398,000	2,271,000	1,278,000	993,000
Burundi	5,839,000	1,007,000	555,000	452,000
Central African Republic	2,468,000	426,000	235,000	191,000
Chad	7,800,000	1,345,000	741,000	604,000
Comoros	478,000	82,000	45,000	37,000
Congo (Demo Republic)	42,720,000	7,367,000	4,060,000	3,307,000
Cote d'Ivoire	13,839,000	2,386,000	1,315,000	1,071,000
Djibouti	632,000	109,000	60,000	49,000
Eritrea	1,853,000	319,000	176,000	143,000
Ethiopia*	60,855,000	7,059,000	2,458,000	4,601,000
Gambia	1,212,000	209,000	115,000	94,000
Guinea	6,607,000	1,139,000	628,000	511,000
Guinea-Bissau	1,028,000	178,000	98,000	80,000
Haiti	6,875,000	1,185,000	653,000	532,000
Lesotho	1,315,000	227,000	125,000	102,000
Liberia	2,680,000	462,000	255,000	207,000
Madagascar*	14,798,000	2,649,000	1,404,000	1,245,000
Malawi*	9,698,000	2,806,000	1,206,000	1,600,000
Mali	9,529,000	1,644,000	906,000	738,000

Country	15-64-year-old population	Total early-stage ventures	Pre-profit ventures	New firms
Mauritania	2,500,000	432,000	238,000	194,000
Mozambique	15,467,000	2,667,000	1,470,000	1,197,000
Niger	10,643,000	1,835,000	1,011,000	824,000
Nigeria*	104,570,000	31,641,000	20,158,000	11,483,000
Papua New Guinea	5,227,000	902,000	497,000	405,000
Rwanda	7,023,000	1,211,000	667,000	544,000
Senegal*	8,539,000	1,940,000	1,152,000	788,000
Sierra Leone	4,282,000	738,000	407,000	331,000
South Sudan	6,013,000	1,036,000	571,000	465,000
Sudan	23,371,000	4,030,000	2,221,000	1,809,000
Syria*	10,858,000	459,000	175,000	284,000
Tanzania	30,015,000	5,176,000	2,853,000	2,323,000
Togo	4,402,000	759,000	418,000	341,000
Uganda*	21,847,000	5,004,000	1,647,000	3,357,000
Yemen	16,389,000	2,827,000	1,558,000	1,269,000
Total	498,200,000	98,085,000	53,868,000	44,217,000

Note: * Prevalence rates based on Global Entrepreneurship Monitor consolidated file (Reynolds, 2021). Estimates for other countries based on average values of countries with surveys. Population estimates based on United Nations (2019b).

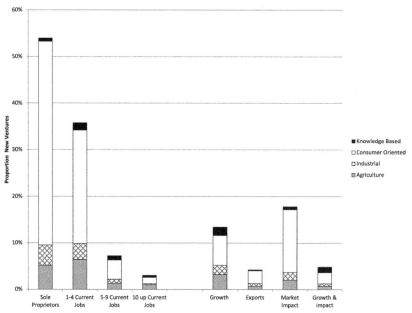

Note: The proportion of ventures with different characteristics was calculated for all cases
with useful data. The total number of ventures was then adjusted based on these estimates.
Following this, the estimates for Agricultural economies was computed following the procedures
outlined in Figure 4.1, source.

Figure 4.10   New venture contributions by sector

customers, a small proportion, 4%, expect half or more of their sales to go to
those living outside the country. Many new firms expect to provide new or
distinctive goods and services. About one-sixth (18%) of these new ventures (4
per 100 adults) anticipate small or major impacts on the markets in which they
will compete. While the individual impacts on exports or market adaptation
may be small, the aggregate impact can be substantial.

One in 20 expect growth and a major impact on the markets in which
they operate; they might be considered "entrepreneurial." While these high
potential ventures are present in all sectors, they are slightly more likely to be
involved in knowledge-based sectors.

New ventures reflecting the entire range of motivations are making economic contributions, as shown in Figure 4.11. While new ventures reflecting
the pursuit of autonomy or income are the source of most contributions, ventures initiated by those who consider it their best option are a significant source
of contributions. Those involved as their best choice or for mixed motives are

half of ventures providing five to nine jobs, one-third of those providing ten or more jobs, two-fifths of ventures expecting growth, three-tenths of those with substantial exports, two-fifths of those expecting to have an impact on their markets, and one-third of the high potential efforts expecting growth and an impact on their markets.

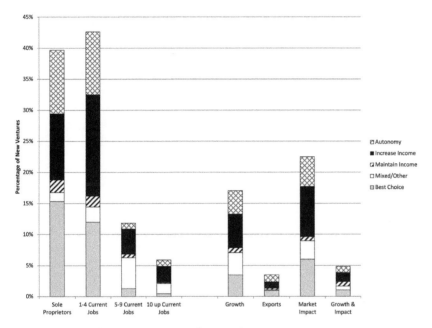

Figure 4.11   *New venture contributions by motivation*

Two features of business creation led to substantial contributions to national economies. First, the high prevalence rate of activity in all Agricultural economies. Second, the large proportion of new ventures expected to have a positive impact. Estimates of the national contributions of 98 million new ventures in these 36 Agricultural economies is provided in Table 4.3.

Most of the variation reflects differences in the population base. In Chad, with about 8 million in the workforce, 77,000 early-stage ventures are providing ten or more jobs, which is at least 770,000 new positions. In Nigeria, with 105 million in the labor force, 1.7 million early-stage ventures are providing ten or more jobs, at least 17 million new positions. Most of these new jobs will be in unregistered businesses and not reflected in "official" statistics. Even so, this is a major contribution to providing citizens with productive roles in the economy.

Table 4.3   *New venture contributions in Agricultural economies*

Country	Current jobs: 10 or more	Growth	Exports	Market impact	Growth and impact
Afghanistan	199,000	615,000	147,000	816,000	173,000
Benin	62,000	190,000	45,000	252,000	54,000
Burkina Faso*	69,000	274,000	43,000	200,000	32,000
Burundi	58,000	178,000	42,000	236,000	50,000
Cent African Rep	24,000	75,000	18,000	100,000	21,000
Chad	77,000	237,000	57,000	315,000	67,000
Comoros	5,000	15,000	3,000	19,000	4,000
Congo (Demo Rep)	421,000	1,301,000	310,000	1,727,000	367,000
Côte d'Ivoire	136,000	421,000	101,000	559,000	119,000
Djibouti	6,000	19,000	5,000	26,000	5,000
Eritrea	18,000	56,000	13,000	75,000	16,000
Ethiopia*	367,000	903,000	289,000	2,786,000	170,000
Gambia	12,000	37,000	9,000	49,000	10,000
Guinea	65,000	201,000	48,000	267,000	57,000
Guinea-Bissau	10,000	31,000	7,000	42,000	9,000
Haiti	68,000	209,000	50,000	278,000	59,000
Lesotho	13,000	40,000	10,000	53,000	11,000
Liberia	26,000	82,000	19,000	108,000	23,000
Madagascar*	21,000	43,000	20,000	654,000	22,000
Malawi*	10,000	26,000	211,000	900,000	19,000
Mali	94,000	290,000	69,000	385,000	82,000

Country	Current jobs: 10 or more	Growth	Exports	Market impact	Growth and impact
Mauritania	25,000	76,000	18,000	101,000	21,000
Mozambique	153,000	471,000	112,000	625,000	133,000
Niger*	105,000	324,000	77,000	430,000	91,000
Nigeria	1,655,000	7,592,000	1,815,000	6,316,000	2,051,000
Papua New Guinea	52,000	159,000	38,000	211,000	45,000
Rwanda	69,000	214,000	51,000	284,000	60,000
Senegal*	85,000	441,000	38,000	418,000	122,000
Sierra Leone	42,000	130,000	31,000	173,000	37,000
South Sudan	59,000	183,000	44,000	243,000	52,000
Sudan	231,000	712,000	170,000	945,000	201,000
Syria*	35,000	171,000	48,000	16,000	6,000
Tanzania	296,000	914,000	218,000	1,213,000	258,000
Togo	43,000	134,000	32,000	178,000	38,000
Uganda*	73,000	347,000	122,000	455,000	51,000
Yemen	610,000	965,000	9,000	1,320,000	668,000
Total	5,294,000	18,076,000	4,339,000	22,775,000	5,204,000

Note: * Prevalence rates based on Global Entrepreneurship Monitor consolidated file (Reynolds, 2021). Estimates for other countries based on average values of countries with surveys.

While perhaps they are overly optimistic, 18 million of these early-stage ventures expect to have more than ten employees in the next five years. A substantial minority have growth aspirations.

The impact of other contributions may be more difficult to measure. But 23 million early-stage ventures expect major or significant impacts on their markets, generally by providing new goods and services to a local community. More than 4 million expect half or more of their sales to be exports. The proportion of new exporting firms is generally higher in small countries which have significant trade with their neighbors. All countries have ventures expecting both growth and market impacts, a total of 5 million among Agricultural economies.

There is no question that early-stage new firms are making major contributions to their national economies. Because much of this activity is informal and unregistered, these contributions to the job pool, market innovation, or exports may not be widely recognized.

STRUCTURAL ADAPTATION

In Agricultural economies, business creation reflects a considerable shift from agriculture, forestry, and fishing toward consumer-oriented sectors such as trading, lodging, food services, and real estate and administrative services. Figure 4.12 presents the proportion of established jobs (white bars), new venture jobs (black bars), and shifts in the proportion of jobs (grey bars) for 14 sectors. Sectors with the greatest increases in the proportion of new jobs are on the left and those with the greatest reductions to the right.

In Agricultural economies 18% of the established jobs are in trade but 46% of new jobs are in this sector, an increase of 28%. The proportion of new jobs in lodging, food services, bars, real estate, and business services is 5% greater than among established jobs. This is offset by a shift away from the agricultural sector, from 42% of established jobs to 18% of new venture jobs, a decrease of 24%. There is also a shift from construction, from 5% to 1%, a decrease of 4%. The lack of new venture jobs in public administration probably reflects the lack of new venture creation in public sectors. For nine sectors the relative emphasis is unchanged, reflecting no major adjustments in the relative scope of these sectors.

For Agricultural economies, the sectors emphasized among new ventures are a clear indicator of the future economic structure, a reduced emphasis on farming, forestry, and fishing and a greater focus on consumer-oriented activity.

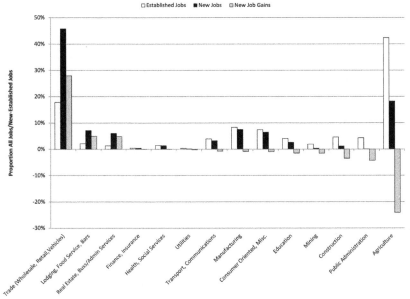

Note: Details in Tables B.1 and B.7. Established jobs, new venture jobs, and new job gains represent the averages across nine Agricultural economies.

Figure 4.12   Established jobs, new jobs, and new job gains by sector

MAJOR CHALLENGES, OR WHY QUIT?

In dynamic economies the constant introduction of new firms is matched with a constant outflow of business terminations. Complications associated with firm survival are reflected in the reasons for business terminations, presented in Table 4.4. The major reason for these shutdowns is a lack of profitability, given as the primary reason for quitting in 28% of the cases. Either the venture is unable to attract customers or cannot sell their output at an acceptable profit.

The second major reason is complications associated with family or personal issues, reported by 15%. Problems with gaining financial support or a planned shutdown of a business each account for about 10% of the cases. Many new ventures are implemented with the expectation of a limited period of profitability and one in ten complete a pre-planned exit. Complications related to government regulations or taxes account for about 1 in 100 of the terminations. This may reflect the high proportion of unregistered firms in agricultural economies, where most of the business activity is "off the books" and there is no interaction with government entities.

Table 4.4   *Primary reason for a business termination*

Not profitable	27.9%
Family, personal issues	15.3%
Lack of financial support	11.8%
Pre-planned exit	10.1%
Major incident	8.2%
Other career opportunities	3.4%
Retirement	1.4%
Government regulations, taxes	1.1%
Sold business	0.1%
Miscellaneous other	20.8%
Total	100.0%

Note: Based on representative samples of 324 discontinued businesses in 2 agricultural economies.

Two major issues receiving considerable attention in policy development—access to finance and the burdens of regulations and taxes—are given as major problems in about 13% of the cases. For every termination related to these two issues, there are seven reflecting other complications, particularly a lack of profits and family and personal issues. Given this, policy adjustments to reduce bureaucratic complications or improve financial support would have a modest impact on overall firm survival.

OVERVIEW

The most important features of business creation in Agricultural economies are:

- There is a lot of it, it appears to be the expected or default work career for all men and women. As more than one in four are involved there are 140 million in 36 Agricultural economies.
- There is a high level of activity among men and women of all ages.
- Those with all levels of human capital are active in business creation; with slightly less participation by those with little income and education.
- Those working are two to six times more active than those in other labor force situations.
- Among business creators most are from 25 to 44 years old and working.
- Motives are diverse, with the majority seeking autonomy or greater income and a substantial minority find it is their best option for work.
- High-potential business creators tend to have more human capital.

- Almost half of new ventures will provide jobs for others, and 5 to 10% expect growth, exports, or a market impact.
- One in 20, the high-potential ventures, expect to have both growth and market impact.
- There is a shift away from agriculture toward trade and other consumer-oriented sectors.
- A lack of profits, complications involving family and personal issues, and issues with financial support are the major factors leading to firm terminations.

In short, a large proportion of the adult population is initiating a tsunami of business creation that is adjusting the economic structure and providing both personal and societal benefits.

Perhaps the most striking feature of the business populations in Agricultural economies is the low proportion of registered firms; most economic activity occurs in unregistered, informal ventures. Business organizations, as legally recognized independent actors, account for a minority of jobs and outputs. This lack of established firms represents both an opportunity for business creators and a challenge for governments; they may not have developed the institutional infrastructure to monitor and supervise a highly formalized—registered—economy.

Business creators pursuing opportunities in Agricultural economies confront several challenges. These include modest or non-existent educational backgrounds, a lack of access to external financial support, complications in obtaining legal title to physical or intellectual assets, and dealing with the complications of formal registration. Those without current information about products, costs, and potential competition can also be at a disadvantage.

Most fundamental at the personal level is access to education. Two-fifths of the adult population have no basic education and half are not considered literate.[12] The inability to read, write, and do basic calculations is a major constraint on the capacity to create and manage a substantial business. In addition, a major challenge for those with growing businesses is locating skilled, educated employees. Many business activities, even simple market stalls, are more effective if the workers have a basic education. A better educated labor pool can be a major asset.

All businesses require some working capital, even if they are only modest outlays for tools, supplies, or inventory. The first source is always the personal savings of the start-up team. Beyond that, resources may be provided by family, neighbors, or friends. About 10% of adults in agricultural economies report providing financial support to business creators.[13] In seven in ten cases this is support to close family members (49%) or relatives (22%). One-fifth of recipients are friends or neighbors (22%). A small proportion goes to work colleagues (3%) or strangers with a good idea (3%).[14] Domestic financial institutions, which provide about $600 in credit per person or one-third of the annual GDP per person, are not a major source of loans for most of the population.[15]

A major source of support is moneylenders operating informal, unregistered financial operations. Interest rates and constraints are often substantial. There have been, however, recent changes in the availability of micro-credit to small-scale businesses. Access to micro-finance is expanding in Agricultural economies. The initial focus was support for the small-scale enterprises of women in rural villages. By 2018 about 13 per 1,000 adults in Agricultural economies, over half women and 40% in rural areas, had micro-loans averaging $900.[16] The institutionalization of national micro-loan programs avoids the high costs and onerous conditions associated with informal moneylenders. Promoting "financial inclusion" has become a major feature of many development efforts.[17] There is a massive, unmet demand for micro-loans in Agricultural economies. Given that they have become profitable for private-sector initiatives, expansion of micro-loan programs should be expected.

Many business owners do not consider the benefits of business registration justified by the costs and complications associated with business registration. In Agricultural economies, registration may require from five to ten procedures that take three weeks to complete and the cost (average of $1,210) is over half the average annual income.[18] For individual businesses, this is often associated with tax administration, whereby the businesses are expected to pay property, sales, or value-added taxes. Registered businesses may be expected to file annual statements describing their financial status and transactions and, in turn, submit financial payments. Nascent entrepreneurs may not consider the advantages for participating in national systems worth the effort. The advantages are not widely promoted.

The major asset in Agricultural economies is land, the source of production and the site for physical structures. The complications and benefits associated with recognition of land ownership have been a major issue for all cultures and societies. Individuals and households with legally recognized ownership of land are more likely to invest time and resources into productive endeavors. Business creators benefit when national administrations can provide legally recognized titles to assets. In Agricultural economies it is difficult to secure legal title to land, which may be the most important asset for many potential business creators. In many countries land administration does not provide full coverage and the records are not well maintained.[19] Property registration may require six procedures, take several months to complete, and cost 8% of the value of the property. The lack of clear title to such an asset can limit the potential for obtaining an asset-backed loan from an established financial institution.

Relatively speaking, Agricultural economies have not fully developed legal recognition of physical and intellectual property rights,[20] which would discourage investments in these assets and encourage informal mechanisms to discourage infringement.

Most new firms involve participation in national or regional markets. While many consumer-oriented or knowledge-based sectors serve local communities, they may involve inputs—inventory, parts, components, etc.—from national or international sources. Some new ventures, even in agriculture, expect to serve regional or national customers. In terms of both inputs and sales, there are advantages to having current information about prices, availability, and the competition. Those in rural areas may be at a substantial disadvantage if they do not have access to communications and electronic infrastructures. Only about one in five (18%) have internet access in Agricultural economies, cell phone distribution (at 70 per 100) is not yet universal, and governments are spending about $3 per year per person on communication support.[21] As with many other issues, a lack of education may be a serious disadvantage even if the communications infrastructure is present.

In Agricultural economies, those with limited resources and in disadvantaged situations are not able to rely on government assistance. Annual spending on social protection is about $8 per person, less than 1% of the annual GDP per capita. And nine-tenths of retirees have no access to a pension. This is associated with widespread acceptance of traditional authority and individual survival values, which emphasize self-reliance.[22]

This may be why there is substantial cultural support for business creation.[23] Three-fifths of adults strongly support entrepreneurial efforts, with four-fifths considering it a good career choice and a source of status. Perhaps reflecting both opportunities and social support, two-fifths of adults are ready for an entrepreneurial career, with three-fifths or more seeing good business opportunities, knowing an active entrepreneur, and confident of their ability to pursue business creation.

Those in Agricultural economies confront a lack of established jobs and little social protection from the government but considerable cultural support and personal confidence in their entrepreneurial skills. In such circumstances, developing some type of task specialization or a business venture may not just be the best option, but the only option.

With limited options and confronting a fluid, unstructured economy, it is no surprise that almost three in ten of those in Agricultural economies pursue business creation despite the challenges. In turn, they are a major source of contributions to economic growth and adaptation.

NOTES

1. Summarized from Koop et al. (2000, pp. 73–75). Fictitious name.
2. Bety (2011).
3. Details in Table B.2.
4. Details in Table B.1.
5. Details in Table B.1.
6. Details in Table B.1.
7. Details in Table B.3.
8. Details of sources in Table B.1.
9. Average across nine Agricultural economies is 27 per 100, but the range is from 15 per 100 to 39 per hundred; see Table B.6.
10. Details in Table B.3.
11. Development of estimates of household daily income discussed in Appendix A and Table B.5.
12. Table B.3.
13. Respondents report informal investments over the previous three years and details on the most recent investment (Reynolds, 2021).
14. Details in Table B.4.
15. Details in Tables B.3 and B.5.
16. Details in Table B.4.
17. EIU (2020).
18. Details in Table B.3.
19. Table B.4.
20. Details in Table B.4.
21. Details in Table B.4.
22. Details in Tables B.2 and B.3.
23. Details in Table B.4.
24. Based on consideration of several national household income distributions, the lowest third was assigned a median value equal to one-half of the intermediate third. The highest third was assigned a median value equal to twice the median value.

APPENDIX: HUMAN CAPITAL SCALE DEVELOPMENT

Relative standing on annual household income and educational attainment were combined to create a human capital scale. The distributions were computed for each annual GEM survey in each of nine Agricultural economies. Cases were weighted to represent the population of adults 18–64 years old in each country. For each country, the results were averaged across all years for which surveys were completed. The results for all countries were averaged to represent Agricultural economies. The distribution across five levels of human capital for the adult populations in Agricultural economies is presented in the second column in Table 4A.1. The presentation reflects data on an average of 4,222 adults in each of nine countries, a total of 38,013 respondents.

Most GEM surveys obtained estimates of pre-tax annual household income, which was recoded into low, intermediate, and high thirds (or tertile) for each country. It is assumed that the respondents' personal annual income is typical for households in the lowest, middle, or highest tertile in that country. Respondents in the middle third were assumed to have an annual income equal to the 2018 annual GDP per capita, adjusted for purchasing power parity (2011 dollars).[24] Annual personal incomes were converted to daily household incomes to provide a better indicator of the situation confronted by the typical citizen.

Each row in Table 4A.1 provides an overview of the proportion of cases with each level of income and educational attainment. The overall distribution for adults is presented in the bottom row of the table. Two-fifths are in the upper third of the national distribution with daily personal income of $13.20. Three-tenths are in the intermediate group, with daily personal incomes of $6.60, and three-tenths are in the lowest group with daily personal incomes of $3.60. In terms of education, over two-fifths have no educational experiences and three-tenths have completed secondary school or more. About 1% have graduate educational experiences.

The same procedures were followed to create descriptions of the human capital among business creators in nine Agricultural economies, an average of 1,156 per country for a total of 10,408. Distributions were computed for each survey year, averaged across years for each country, and averaged across all countries to represent Agricultural economies. The distribution of personal daily income and educational attainment for the five levels of human capital are provided in Table 4A.2. Business creators have a slightly higher level of human capital than the adult population.

At one extreme are 6% of active business creators with the greatest human capital. They have personal incomes in the highest category and have post-secondary educational experience; 10% of this group have graduate or

Table 4A.1   *Human capital in the adult population*

Human capital category	Proportion	Personal daily income				Educational attainment					
		$3.30	$6.60	$13.20	Total	None	1–11 years	High school degree	13–16 Years	17–20 years	Total
Highest	6%			100%	100%				88%	12%	100%
High	10%		23%	77%	100%			77%	21%	2%	100%
Intermediate	30%	5%	22%	72%	100%	42%	30%	22%	5%		100%
Low	27%	24%	76%		100%	47%	29%	24%			100%
Lowest	26%	100%			100%	61%	39%				100%
Total	100%										
Proportion		31%	30%	39%	100%	42%	26%	21%	10%	1%	100%

Table 4A.2   Human capital among business creators

Human capital category	Proportion	Personal daily income				Educational attainment					
		$3.30	$6.60	$13.20	Total	None	1–11 years	High school degree	13–16 years	17–20 years	Total
Highest	6%			100%	100%				90%	10%	100%
High	12%		34%	66%	100%			66%	32%	2%	100%
Intermediate	33%	5%	20%	75%	100%	50%	25%	20%	5%		100%
Low	27%	15%	85%		100%	58%	27%	15%			100%
Lowest	22%	100%			100%	68%	32%				100%
Total	100%										
Proportion		28%	33%	38%	99%	47%	23%	18%	11%	1%	100%

professional training. At the other extreme are 22% of business creators with the lowest human capital. All have personal incomes in the lower third and 68% have no educational experience. The three intermediate levels—high, intermediate, and low—represent different combinations of access to personal income and educational training.

5. Agricultural-Industrial economies: Industry and service

[One] woman ... had a beauty salon and a fleet of taxis. She had persuaded her brother, who had a taxi license for a run-down car and had just bought a new vehicle, to let her have the old car and the license. She hired a good mechanic and launched her business, buying more cars with her profits. She didn't miss a trick with her beauty business either; nearby was a large agribusiness plantation that employed many women workers for the harvest, which was then in progress. She dispatched two of her operators to open a makeshift beauty salon in the field, correctly guessing that these women would want to spend some of the money they were making to get fixed up before returning to their families.[1]

Ashok Khade, a descendant from the lowest Indian Hindu caste, the Chamhars, was one of six children born to agricultural day laborers living in a mud hut in 1955. Very bright, he won admission to a charity run high school and worked hard to graduate near the top of his class in 1973. An older brother was an apprentice welder at the ship building company Mazagon Dock and helped Ashok get a position as an apprentice draftsman. He did well and was sent to Germany in 1983 to work on a submarine project. The good life in Germany encouraged him to consider business creation. Upon return he organized a subcontracting firm emphasizing the welding skills of two brothers. Their first big order for work on offshore oil rigs came in 1993. The dramatic growth of the Indian economy and need for energy allowed them to expand their services to include refurbishing and building oil rigs and it now does work for the royal family of Abu Dhabi. By 2011 the firm has 4,500 employees and is valued at $100 million. Ashok Khade is proud to have gone from "village to palace."[2]

About 30% of the global population, 2.2 billion individuals, live in 35 Agricultural-Industrial economies like Bangladesh, Ghana, India, Namibia, and Vietnam. While two-fifths work in agriculture, fishing, or forestry, about one-fifth work in industrial sectors, three-tenths in consumer-oriented sectors, and one-seventh in activities that require post-secondary education.

THE NATIONAL CONTEXT

Agricultural-Industrial economies are dominated by young people, where three-tenths are under 16 years old and 6% are over 64 years of age. Most have some basic education, with three-fourths considered literate and one-third having completed secondary schooling. Adults with post-secondary education are still rare, at 1 in 17. Almost two-thirds of adults are in the labor force, three-fourths of men and half of women. Most jobs do not require a high level of skill and a third are working for less than \$3.60 a day. Two-thirds of retirees do not have any pension; they are presumably relying on family and relatives for support.[3]

Government spending is about \$1,800 per year for each citizen, about three-tenths of the annual GDP of \$6,200 per person. Annual spending on health care is about \$317 per person, for education about \$246 per person, and \$102 per person for all forms of social protection.[4]

Compared to Agricultural economies, living in Agricultural-Industrial economies is somewhat better. Life expectancy is 68 years, average adult education is 12 years, and annual income is about \$6,000 per year, three times that of those in Agricultural economies. More than two-thirds have confidence in the national government and the legal system and feel safe outside at night. Three-fourths are satisfied with their local community and their freedom of choice. About two-thirds are satisfied with their standard of living and the quality of the educational and health-care systems. Only two-fifths consider the local labor market "good."[5] Most citizens support traditional authority values and accept personal survival as an appropriate individual emphasis. Overall, the citizens of Agricultural-Industrial economies seem satisfied with and supportive of their governments and consider they are responsible for their own situation.

CAREER OPTIONS

Most adults work in Agricultural-Industrial economies. Slightly more than four-fifths of the jobs are in unregistered ventures—the informal sector. About three-fifths of the jobs involve one-person self-employment. One-fifth of jobs are in unregistered firms with several employees. Slightly less than one-fifth are jobs in registered enterprises and only one-eighth are in registered firms with ten or more employees. While some may be able to get a registered firm job, most will have little choice but to participate in the informal sector, often as a sole proprietor.[6]

Business creators will have a lot of company—and competition, as one in four adults are starting new ventures. Over half know someone active in business creation. Seven-tenths consider business creation a good career choice and a route to status and prestige. Most feel prepared to pursue business creation—over three-fifths see good business opportunities where they live and feel they have the skill and knowledge to create a new firm. Business creation is not only expected of those entering the workforce, but there is also considerable informal support.[7]

Economic development in Agricultural-Industrial economies provides considerable opportunity to develop businesses in expanding market sectors, sectors where there are few established registered enterprises.

Table 5.1   Business creators in Agricultural-Industrial economies

Country	Total population: 2018	15–64-year-old population: 2018	Total business creators	Business creators: men	Business creators: women
Angola*	30,810,000	15,705,000	4,640,000	2,392,000	2,248,000
Bangladesh*	161,377,000	108,341,000	13,835,000	11,475,000	2,360,000
Bhutan	754,000	515,000	125,000	74,000	51,000
Cabo Verde	544,000	362,000	88,000	52,000	36,000
Cambodia	16,250,000	10,437,000	2,532,000	1,501,000	1,031,000
Cameroon*	25,216,000	13,778,000	4,616,000	2,468,000	2,148,000
Congo (Republic of)	5,244,000	2,913,000	707,000	419,000	288,000
El Salvador*	6,421,000	4,147,000	700,000	364,000	336,000
Equatorial Guinea	1,309,000	791,000	192,000	114,000	78,000
Eswatini	1,136,000	658,000	160,000	95,000	65,000
Ghana*	29,767,000	17,662,000	6,139,000	2,824,000	3,315,000
Guatemala*	17,248,000	10,479,000	2,027,000	1,145,000	882,000
Guyana	779,000	509,000	123,000	73,000	50,000
Honduras	9,588,000	6,095,000	1,478,000	876,000	602,000
India	1,352,642,000	903,115,000	100,894,000	65,576,000	35,318,000
Iraq*	38,434,000	22,403,000	5,434,000	3,221,000	2,213,000
Kenya	51,393,000	29,745,000	7,215,000	4,276,000	2,939,000
Kiribati	116,000	70,000	17,000	10,000	7,000
Kyrgyzstan	6,304,000	3,981,000	965,000	572,000	393,000
Laos	7,062,000	4,471,000	1,085,000	643,000	442,000

Country	Total population: 2018	15-64-year-old population: 2018	Total business creators	Business creators: men	Business creators: women
Micronesia	113,000	72,000	17,000	10,000	7,000
Morocco*	36,029,000	23,700,000	2,216,000	1,464,000	752,000
Myanmar	53,708,000	36,438,000	8,839,000	5,239,000	3,600,000
Namibia*	2,448,000	1,456,000	390,000	196,000	194,000
Nepal	28,096,000	17,941,000	4,352,000	2,579,000	1,773,000
Nicaragua	6,466,000	4,174,000	1,012,000	600,000	412,000
Pakistan*	212,228,000	128,223,000	15,684,000	13,964,000	1,720,000
São Tomé and Príncipe	211,000	115,000	28,000	17,000	11,000
Solomon Islands	653,000	367,000	89,000	53,000	36,000
Tajikistan	9,101,000	5,478,000	1,329,000	788,000	541,000
Timor-Leste	1,268,000	734,000	179,000	106,000	73,000
Vanuatu*	293,000	168,000	92,000	52,000	40,000
Viet Nam*	95,546,000	66,454,000	10,222,000	5,143,000	5,079,000
Zambia*	17,352,000	9,190,000	3,577,000	1,830,000	1,747,000
Zimbabwe	14,439,000	7,892,000	1,915,000	1,135,000	780,000
Total	2,240,345,000	1,458,579,000	202,913,000	131,346,000	71,567,000

Note: * Prevalence rates based on Global Entrepreneurship Monitor consolidated file (Reynolds, 2021). Estimates for other countries based on average values of countries with surveys. Population estimates based on United Nations (2019b).

HOW MUCH ACTIVITY?

Among the 1.4 billion in the Agricultural-Industrial economy labor force about 203 million are in the early stages of business creation, as shown in Table 5.1. About two-thirds, 131 million, are men and one-third, 72 million, are women. The three largest sources of business creators are the countries on the Indian sub-continent. Together, Bangladesh, India, and Pakistan account for two-thirds of the business creators. Even in smaller countries, like Kiribati, Micronesia, and São Tomé and Príncipe, tens of thousands are involved. Many are in the early stages of the start-up process and their efforts may not be easy to detect.

WHO PURSUES BUSINESS CREATION?

In Agricultural-Industrial economies 24 per 100 adults are engaged in business creation. There is a considerable range in participation, from less than 15 per 100 in Bangladesh, India, Morocco, and Pakistan to over 35 per 100 in Ghana, Vanuatu, and Zambia.[8]

Gender and age have a major impact on participation in business creation, as shown in Figure 5.1. For both men and women participation is highest among

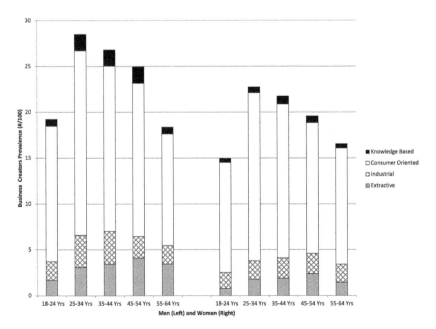

Figure 5.1   Business creator participation by age, gender, and sector

those 25 to 54 years old, and somewhat reduced among those 18 to 24 and over 55 years old. Participation among men, at 27 per 100, is about 30% higher than among women, at 21 per 100.[9] Women's participation is somewhat lower in all age categories, but there is almost gender equality among those of 55 to 64 years old.

Business creation is found in all economic sectors, with three-fourths in consumer-oriented sectors. About one-tenth are in industrial and agricultural sectors. One in 25 are in knowledge-based sectors. Women are slightly more likely to pursue consumer-oriented ventures and slightly less likely to emphasize agricultural sectors. The proportion engaged in industrial sectors is about the same for men and women.

Personal resources, household income, and educational attainment are assets when pursuing business creation. Human capital in the population of Agricultural-Industrial economies is described in Figure 5.2. Details are presented in the appendix to this chapter.

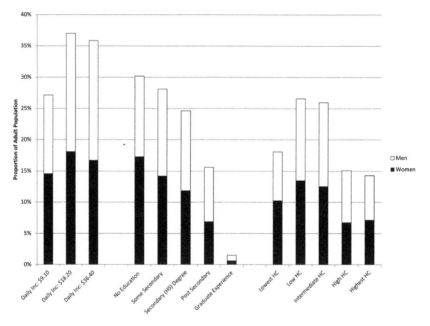

Figure 5.2   Population human capital

About one-fourth of adults have a personal daily income of $9.10; the remainder are equally divided between those with daily incomes of $18.20 and $36.40. Three-tenths have received no formal education and slightly more than half have been to secondary school or more. Almost one-fifth have education beyond secondary school. One in 50 have graduate experience. Slightly more men are represented among those with more education.

The distribution of human capital, an index based on income and education, in the adult population is shown to the right of Figure 5.2. About half the population has low or intermediate human capital, about one-fourth a high or highest level of human capital, and slightly less than one-fifth the lowest level. Men are a slightly larger proportion of those with more human capital.

Men with greater human capital are more likely to be involved in business creation, as shown in Figure 5.3. One-third of those with the highest human capital are active. For women, however, participation is similar among those with low, intermediate, high, or the highest levels of human capital. Men and women with little education and limited access to wealth are the least active.

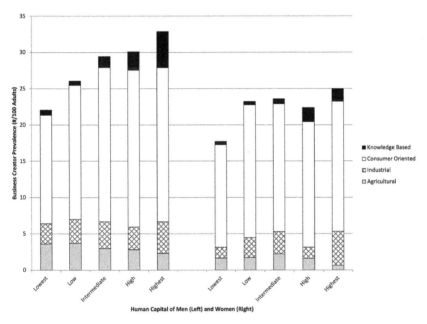

Figure 5.3   *Business creator participation by human capital, gender, and sector*

Across all levels of human capital, seven-tenths pursue new ventures in consumer-oriented sectors (this is slightly less for men with the highest level of human capital). Considering both men and women, the proportion pursuing agricultural new ventures declines with more human capital, from 13% to 5%. About one-eighth focus on the industrial sector, but this is not related to the amount of human capital. Those with more human capital, men and women, are more likely to pursue new ventures in knowledge-based sectors. This varies from 3% for those with the lowest human capital to 11% for those with the highest amount.

Men and women working full or part time are the most likely to pursue business creation, as shown in Figure 5.4. About 30 per 100 are working on a pre-profit start-up while they are working full or part time. Those not working or with responsibilities as homemakers are much less likely to pursue firm creation. Smaller proportions of students are active nascent entrepreneurs, while the retired and disabled are slightly more active than students.

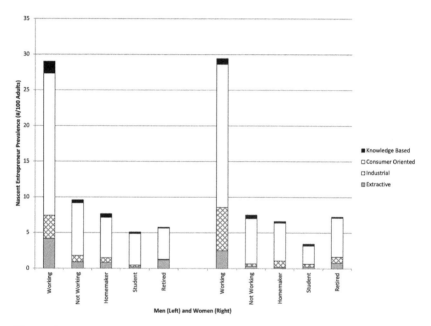

Figure 5.4　　*Nascent entrepreneur participation by labor force status, gender, and sector*

In Agricultural-Industrial Economies:

- Men and women of all ages are active in business creation in all sectors; there is less activity among the youngest or oldest working-age adults.
- Except for those with the lowest level of human capital, all men and women are very active in business creation, particularly men with the highest human capital.
- Those working full or part time are much more likely to enter the start-up process.

Business creation is very prevalent among working-age adults.

WHO ARE THE BUSINESS CREATORS?

The nature of the business creator community is of interest for both practical and policy considerations. The age and gender composition of those pursuing business creation in the four market sectors is provided in Figure 5.5. The total for each sector equals 100%.

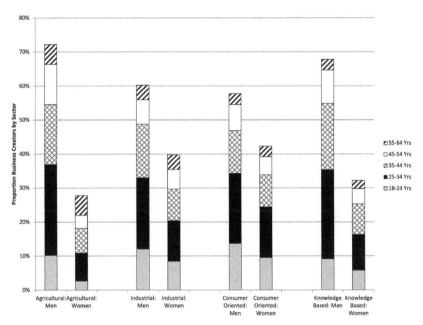

Figure 5.5   Age and gender proportion of business creators by sector

About two-thirds of all business creators are men, slightly more in agriculture and knowledge-based sectors. The industrial and consumer-oriented sectors have the largest proportions of women, about two-fifths. Over half of all business creators are between 25 and 44 years old. Men 45 and older are a larger proportion of those involved in agricultural business creation. There are slightly fewer young women, 18 to 24 years old, in all sectors. Young women in Agricultural-Industrial economies may be distracted by child-rearing responsibilities.

Business creators with a wide range of human capital are involved in all economic sectors, as shown in Figure 5.6. Again, the total for each sector equals 100%.

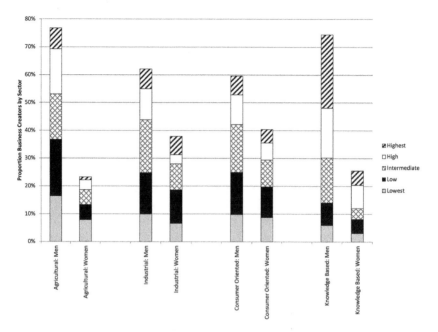

Figure 5.6   *Human capital and gender proportions of business creators*
                by sector

Among men, more than half have intermediate or high levels of human
capital. Among women, about half have the low or lowest levels of human
capital. Women with more human capital may be less attracted to business
creation. Half of those involved in agricultural-sector business creation have
the low or lowest levels of human capital. In contrast, three-fifths of those
involved in knowledge-based sectors have the high or highest levels of human
capital. The distribution of human capital is similar for business creators in
industrial and consumer-oriented sectors.

In every sector, four-fifths of nascent entrepreneurs are working full or
part time when they get involved in a pre-profit start-up venture, presented
in Figure 5.7. A smaller proportion, 8%, would be considered unemployed.
Together homemakers, students, and those retired or disabled are one-tenth of
the business creators.

Across all those involved in Agricultural-Industrial business creation, about
half see a business opportunity that will provide greater work autonomy, more
income, or allow them to maintain their current level of income. Three-tenths
consider business creation their best option and one-fifth have mixed motives.

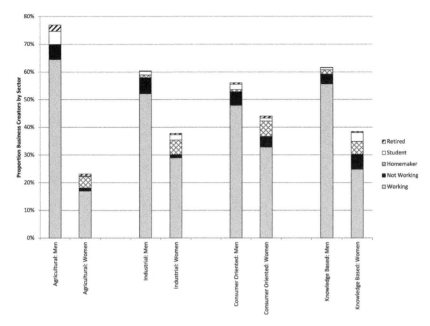

Figure 5.7   Labor force status and gender proportions of nascent
entrepreneurs by sector

Slightly more women emphasize business creation as their best choice, while slightly more men emphasize business opportunities.

There is a systematic shift in motives for both men and women related to their human capital. While two-fifths of those with the lowest level of human capital consider business creation their best choice for work, this is less than one-fifth among those with the highest level of human capital, as shown in Figure 5.8. About three-fifths of those with the highest level of human capital but less than half of those with the lowest level are pursuing business opportunities.

The proportions of all business creators with different motives and different levels of human capital are presented in Figure 5.9. The total for all ten categories equals 100%. Three-fifths are men and women with low or intermediate levels of human capital. Within this group, about half, or one-fourth of all business creators, are pursuing a business opportunity, one-quarter have mixed objectives and another quarter see this as their best choice. About one-fourth of business creators are men and women with the high or highest level of human resources. Most of this group are pursuing business opportunities.

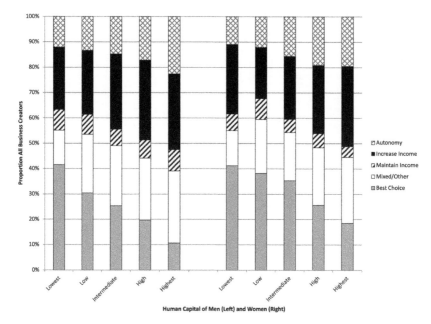

Figure 5.8   Business creator motivation by human capital and gender

Among the 203 million business creators in Agricultural-Industrial economies:

- Men are about two-thirds of the total.
- Half are young adults 25 to 44 years old.
- Business creators are active in all economic sectors.
- Four-fifths are working full or part time as they pursue business creation.
- One-sixth have the lowest level of human capital, three-fifths have low or intermediate levels of human capital, and one-quarter have high or the highest levels of human capital.
- Those with more human capital are attracted to business opportunities to gain greater work autonomy, more income, or maintain their current income.

These business creators are a major source of economic adaptation and growth.

NEW VENTURES AND CONTRIBUTIONS

The 203 million business creators in 35 Agricultural-Industrial economies are, once the size of start-up teams is taken into account, involved in 137 million

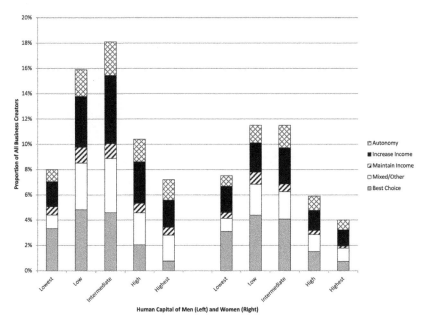

*Figure 5.9   Proportion of business creators by motivation, human
capital, and gender*

early-stage ventures. Table 5.2 provides the estimated counts for each country, which includes 84 million pre-profit nascent ventures and 53 million new firms.

As might be expected half of the total are in India, with 67 million, followed by Pakistan with 11 million, and Bangladesh with 10 million. Even a smaller country such as Kiribati, 33 islands south of Hawaii, has 11,000 new ventures, while Micronesia, a collection of Islands north of Indonesia, is the context for 12,000. There is substantial activity in all countries.

Early-stage ventures in all sectors are a source of contributions for Agricultural-Industrial economies. The proportion making contributions in the four major sectors is shown in Figure 5.10. Three-fourths are in consumer-oriented ventures.

Three-fifths of the ventures are providing jobs for others and 1 in 25 is providing ten or more jobs. About two-fifths are providing work for the firm owners and have no employees. Most of these informal jobs will not be included in official employment statistics. A small, but significant, proportion, one-sixth, have plans to grow and provide ten or more jobs in five years. One in 14 expect half of their sales to go outside their country. One in seven are

Table 5.2   Pre-profit ventures and new firms in Agricultural-Industrial economies

Country	15–64-year-old population	Total early-stage ventures	Pre-profit ventures	New firms
Angola*	15,705,000	2,987,000	1,941,000	1,046,000
Bangladesh*	108,341,000	10,079,000	4,886,000	5,193,000
Bhutan	515,000	81,000	45,000	36,000
Cabo Verde	362,000	58,000	32,000	26,000
Cambodia	10,437,000	1,654,000	915,000	739,000
Cameroon*	13,778,000	2,889,000	1,914,000	975,000
Congo (Republic of)	2,913,000	461,000	255,000	206,000
El Salvador*	4,147,000	459,000	243,000	216,000
Equatorial Guinea	791,000	125,000	69,000	56,000
Eswatini	658,000	105,000	58,000	47,000
Ghana*	17,662,000	4,945,000	1,915,000	3,030,000
Guatemala*	10,479,000	1,319,000	776,000	543,000
Guyana	509,000	81,000	45,000	36,000
Honduras	6,095,000	966,000	534,000	432,000
India*	903,115,000	66,827,000	45,341,000	21,486,000
Iraq	22,403,000	3,551,000	1,964,000	1,587,000
Kenya	29,745,000	4,714,000	2,608,000	2,106,000
Kiribati	70,000	11,000	6,000	5,000
Kyrgyzstan	3,981,000	631,000	349,000	282,000
Laos	4,471,000	709,000	392,000	317,000

Country	15–64-year-old population	Total early-stage ventures	Pre-profit ventures	New firms
Micronesia	72,000	11,000	6,000	5,000
Morocco*	23,700,000	1,370,000	531,000	839,000
Myanmar	36,438,000	5,775,000	3,195,000	2,580,000
Namibia*	1,456,000	250,000	153,000	97,000
Nepal	17,941,000	2,844,000	1,573,000	1,271,000
Nicaragua	4,174,000	662,000	366,000	296,000
Pakistan*	128,223,000	11,577,000	9,905,000	1,672,000
São Tomé and Príncipe	115,000	18,000	10,000	8,000
Solomon Islands	367,000	58,000	32,000	26,000
Tajikistan	5,478,000	868,000	480,000	388,000
Timor-Leste	734,000	116,000	64,000	52,000
Vanuatu*	168,000	57,000	30,000	27,000
Viet Nam*	66,454,000	6,557,000	1,137,000	5,420,000
Zambia*	9,190,000	2,208,000	1,323,000	885,000
Zimbabwe	7,892,000	1,251,000	692,000	559,000
Total	1,458,579,000	136,274,000	83,785,000	52,489,000

Note: * Prevalence rates based on Global Entrepreneurship Monitor consolidated file (Reynolds, 2021). Estimates for other countries based on the average values of countries with surveys. Population estimates based on United Nations (2019b).

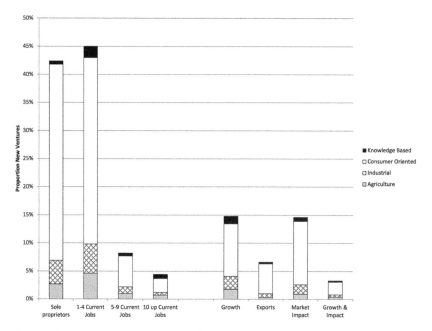

Figure 5.10   New venture contributions by sector

doing something different from their competitors and expect to have some impact on the markets in which they compete. In many cases these new ventures will be in villages or communities where they are the first to introduce a new product or service.

About 1 in 30 new ventures are emphasizing both growth and changes in the market, perhaps the most entrepreneurial group. While they are present in all sectors, over three-fifths are in the consumer-oriented sectors.

Business creators pursuing opportunities are associated with most new ventures creating jobs, expecting growth, contributing to exports, or expecting to affect their market sectors, as shown in Figure 5.11. Those pursuing business creation as their best choice, however, are associated with more than one-fifth of those providing ten or more jobs or expecting future growth and more than one-quarter of those emphasizing exports or a market impact. Those pursuing attractive business opportunities are three-fifths of the high potential ventures, expecting growth and market impacts. New ventures reflecting a range of motives are making significant economic contributions.

While the proportion of new ventures with impacts on jobs, exports, and market innovation may seem small, the large amount of business creation

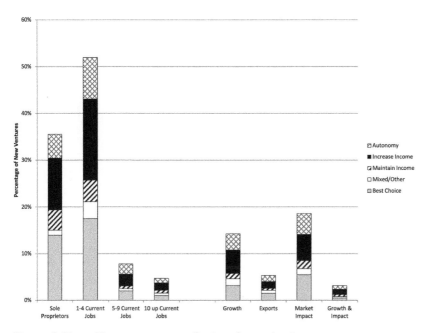

Figure 5.11   New venture contributions by motivations

activity means that the total contributions can be substantial. This is reflected in the counts for each country provided in Table 5.3.

Across the 35 countries 9 million early-stage ventures are providing ten or more jobs, a total of at least 90 million jobs. For India, with 900 million adults in their working years, this would be almost 6 million new firms providing 60 million jobs. For Vanuatu, with 168,000 working adults, this would be 700 new firms providing 7,000 jobs. The same levels of impact are related to market innovations. These early-stage ventures are also a source of exports with 6%, or about 8 million, providing goods or services to those living outside their country. A total of 30 million ventures across the 35 Agricultural-Industrial economies would be changing the markets in which they compete. About 5 million might be considered high potential, expecting both growth and a market impact.

STRUCTURAL ADAPTATION

Business creation represents a shift away from agricultural and industrial work toward more consumer-oriented activities, as reflected in Figure 5.12. The proportion of established jobs (white bars) is provided along with the

Table 5.3   *New venture contributions in Agricultural-Industrial economies*

Country	Current jobs: 10 or more	Growth	Exports	Market impact	Growth and impact
Angola*	373,000	828,000	533,000	834,000	205,000
Bangladesh*	516,000	864,000	681,000	228,000	33,000
Bhutan	4,000	12,000	5,000	15,000	3,000
Cabo Verde	3,000	8,000	4,000	11,000	2,000
Cambodia	80,000	235,000	111,000	307,000	53,000
Cameroon*	97,000	524,000	113,000	296,000	69,000
Congo (Republic of)	22,000	66,000	31,000	86,000	15,000
El Salvador*	7,000	71,000	12,000	21,000	8,000
Equatorial Guinea	6,000	18,000	8,000	23,000	4,000
Eswatini	5,000	15,000	7,000	19,000	3,000
Ghana*	89,000	585,000	141,000	305,000	43,000
Guatemala*	14,000	130,000	38,000	96,000	13,000
Guyana	4,000	11,000	5,000	15,000	3,000
Honduras	47,000	137,000	65,000	179,000	31,000
India*	5,569,000	12,551,000	3,417,000	19,938,000	3,423,000
Iraq	172,000	504,000	239,000	659,000	113,000
Kenya	228,000	669,000	317,000	875,000	151,000
Kiribati	500	1,600	700	2,100	400
Kyrgyzstan	31,000	90,000	42,000	117,000	20,000
Laos	34,000	101,000	48,000	132,000	23,000

Country	Current jobs: 10 or more	Growth	Exports	Market impact	Growth and impact
Micronesia	600	1,600	800	2,100	400
Morocco*	44,000	222,000	92,000	726,000	108,000
Myanmar	279,000	819,000	389,000	1,072,000	184,000
Namibia*	20,000	49,000	45,000	105,000	23,000
Nepal	137,000	403,000	191,000	528,000	91,000
Nicaragua	32,000	94,000	45,000	123,000	21,000
Pakistan*	845,000	1,657,000	909,000	1,429,000	107,000
São Tomé and Príncipe	900	2,600	1,200	3,400	600
Solomon Islands	3,000	8,000	4,000	11,000	2,000
Tajikistan	42,000	123,000	58,000	161,000	28,000
Timor-Leste	6,000	17,000	8,000	22,000	4,000
Vanuatu*	700	1,000	2,600	5,300	200
Vietnam*	530,000	1,119,000	160,000	698,000	150,000
Zambia*	50,000	134,000	114,000	518,000	47,000
Zimbabwe	60,000	177,000	84,000	232,000	40,000
Total	9,351,700	22,247,800	7,921,300	29,793,900	5,021,600

Note: * Prevalence rates based on Global Entrepreneurship Monitor consolidated file (Reynolds, 2021). Estimates for other countries based on average values of countries with surveys.

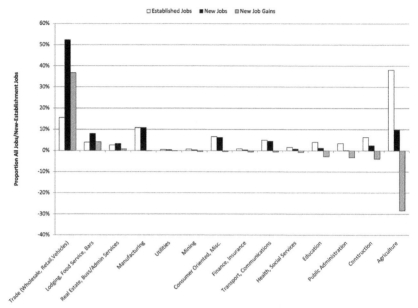

Note: Details in Tables B.1 and B.7. Established jobs, new venture jobs, and new job gains represent the average values across 13 Agricultural-Industrial economies.

Figure 5.12   Established jobs, new jobs, and new job gains by sector

proportion of new jobs (black bars) provided by new ventures. The difference, which reflects shifts from established to new firm jobs, is represented by grey bars. Sectors with the greatest job gains are presented to the left, those with the greatest job losses to the right. An expansion in jobs is greatest in trading activities (from 16% to 52%) followed by lodging, food service, and bars (from 4% to 8%). This is offset by a reduction in agricultural work (from 38% to 10%) as well as construction (from 6% to 2%). For seven sectors—real estate and business services, manufacturing, utilities, mining, consumer oriented, finance and insurance, and transportation and communications—there is little net change. New firm jobs in these sectors will reflect the normal churning among existing businesses. The lack of new jobs in public administration and education probably reflects the lack of private opportunities in sectors dominated by public organizations.

The future structure of these economies seems to reflect more firms in the consumer-oriented sectors of trade, lodging, food service, and bars and less emphasis on agriculture and construction.

MAJOR CHALLENGES, OR WHY QUIT?

Complications associated with firm creation are reflected in the primary reasons for business termination, presented in Table 5.4. One-third (34%) report the most common problem is a lack of profit. The owners are either losing money or working for nothing.

Table 5.4   Primary reason for a business termination

Not profitable	34.3%
Family, personal issues	13.6%
Lack of financial support	13.3%
Sold business	8.9%
Government regulations, taxes	6.8%
Other career opportunities	5.9%
Major incident	4.9%
Pre-planned exit	2.6%
Retirement	0.6%
Miscellaneous other	9.1%
Total	100.0%

Note: Based on representative samples of 1,099 discontinued businesses in five Agricultural-Industrial economies.

Two other issues account for three-tenths of the terminations—complications with family and personal issues (14%) and lack of financial support (14%). The other third of the cases are responding to a range of issues—sale of the business (9%), issues with government regulations and taxes (7%), other—presumably attractive—career opportunities (6%), some type of incident (5%), planned exit from the business (3%), as well as retirement (1%) and a variety of other complications (9%).

Most critical, however, is the ability to manage the firm to provide an acceptable level of profit, which is mentioned half again as much as financial issues and complications with governments and taxes.

OVERVIEW

Business creation in Agricultural-Industrial economies:

•   Is very popular, pursued by one-fourth of adults; over 200 million in 35 countries are involved with 136 million new ventures.

- Involves men and women of all ages; those 25 to 54 years old are the most active.
- Except for those with the lowest human capital, men and women with all levels are quite active. It is greatest for men with the most education and income.
- Involves over four-fifths of business creators being working men and women.
- Is expected by business creators to lead to greater autonomy or more income; a substantial minority have mixed motives or find it their best choice for work.
- Has those pursuing high-potential new ventures tending to have more human capital.
- Will provide jobs for others in more than half of new ventures; from 5% to 15% expect growth, exports, or a market impact. One in 25 expect both growth and a market impact.
- Has new firms emerging in all sectors, with a greater emphasis on consumer-oriented sectors and a shift away from agriculture and construction.
- Reflects a lack of profit in one-third of firm terminations; another third involve family or personal complications or a lack of financial support.

Adults in Agricultural-Industrial economies are very active in creating new firms that provide both personal and economic benefits.

Business creators in Agricultural-Industrial economies are not confronted with established, registered firms dominating local markets. There are, however, some challenges. Some of these include modest educational backgrounds, limited access to financial support, complications in obtaining legal title to physical or intellectual assets, and dealing with the complications of formal registration. Lack of current information about products, costs, and potential competition can also be a disadvantage.

A substantial minority have limited education, one-fifth of adults have no primary education and one-quarter are not literate. An expansion of basic education would do much to facilitate the potential for creating more than a single-person venture. In addition, a major challenge for those with growing businesses is locating skilled, educated employees. A better educated labor pool can be a major asset.

All businesses require some working capital, even if they are only modest outlays for tools, supplies, or inventory. As one-third of the adults have a daily income of less than $10, other sources are necessary to fund even a modest operation. Others in their social network may help. About 10% of adults in Agricultural-Industrial economies report providing financial support to business creators.[10] In three-fifths of the cases this is support to close family members or relatives and in one-third the recipients are friends or neighbors. A small proportion goes to work colleagues or strangers with a good idea.[11]

Domestic financial institutions provide about $3,000 in credit per person, about half of the annual GDP per person.[12] Formal bank loans may be available for a small proportion of business creators. A major source of support for small-scale efforts are moneylenders operating informal, unregistered financial operations. Interest rates and constraints are often substantial. Access to micro-finance is expanding in Agricultural-Industrial economies. By 2018 about 5 per 100 adults had a micro-finance loan; two-thirds were women and half were in rural areas. The average loan was $1,624.[13] Efforts to improve "financial inclusion" are a major feature of many developments, with some success in Agricultural-Industrial economies.[14] The unmet demand for micro-loans suggests that further expansion of these private-sector programs may be expected.

The costs and complications associated with business registration may not justify the benefits. In Agricultural-Industrial economies, registration may require nine or more procedures, take over a month to complete, and the cost (average of $2,417) is one-third of the average annual income.[15] For individual businesses, this is often associated with tax administration, whereby the businesses are expected to pay property, sales, or value-added taxes and comply with a range of government regulations related to employment, safety, pollution, and the like. Nascent entrepreneurs may not consider the advantages for participating in national systems worth the effort. The advantages are not widely promoted.

Perhaps as important, it is difficult to secure legal title to land, which may be the most important asset for many potential business creators. The formal land administration provides some geographic coverage but there may be concerns regarding the quality of record keeping.[16] Property registration may require six procedures, take several months to complete, and cost 6% of the value of the property. The lack of clear title to such an asset can limit the potential for obtaining an asset-backed loan.

Most new firms involve participation in national or regional markets. While many consumer-oriented or knowledge-based sectors serve local communities, they may involve inputs—inventory, parts, components, etc.—from national or international sources. Some new ventures, even in agriculture, expect to serve regional or national customers. In terms of both inputs and sales, there are advantages to having current information about prices and availability and the competition. Those in rural areas may be at a substantial disadvantage if they do not have access to communications and electronic infrastructures. While mobile phones are almost universal among adults, only a third have internet access in Agricultural-Industrial economies. Annual government support for communications is less than 1% of the spending, about $8 per person.[17] As with many other issues, a lack of education may be a serious disadvantage even if the communications infrastructure is present.

With limited resources, Agricultural-Industrial economies are not providing a social safety net for ordinary citizens; annual per capita spending on social protection is about $100 per person, or 2% of the annual GDP per capita.[18] The ordinary person must rely on their own and family resources for survival.

This may be associated with a traditional approach to authority and individual emphasis on survival, accompanied by strong cultural support for entrepreneurial careers. Seven in ten consider business creation a good career choice and a path to improved social status.

Fortunately, a large proportion of adults are ready to pursue business creation. Well over half of all adults have identified good business opportunities, know an active entrepreneur, and are confident in their capacity for business creation. There is, in addition, substantial cultural support for entrepreneurial careers.[19]

With limited work opportunities, little help from their governments, and considerable cultural support, one in four adults in Agricultural-Industrial economies are involved in business creation. This is a major source of contributions to national economic growth.

NOTES

1.		Blumberg (1995). Example from Swaziland, located in southern Africa between Mozambique and South Africa.
2.		Summarized from Polgreen (2011).
3.		See Table B.3 for details.
4.		See Table B.2 for details.
5.		See Table B.2 for details.
6.		See Table B.1 for details.
7.		See Table B.4 for details.
8.		This may reflect some lack of standardization regarding data collection procedures across these countries.
9.		See Table 2.F for details.
10.		Respondents report informal investments over the previous three years and details on the most recent investment (Reynolds, 2021).
11.		Details in Table B.5.
12.		Table B.5.
13.		Details in Table B.5.
14.		EIU (2020).
15.		Details in Table B.4.
16.		Table B.5.
17.		Details in Table B.5.
18.		Details in Table B.2.
19.		Details in Table B.4.
20.		Because of missing data, Vanuatu is not included.

APPENDIX: HUMAN CAPITAL SCALE DEVELOPMENT

The same procedures described in the appendix to Chapter 4 were utilized to create a human capital scale for those in Agricultural-Industrial economies, presented in Table 5A.1. The data represents an average of 6,539 adults in each of 13 countries, a total of 85,004 respondents.

The same procedures were followed to create descriptions of the human capital among 13,985 business creators in 12 Agricultural-Industrial economies (an average of 1,165 per country), presented in Table 5A.2.[20]

Business creators have a slightly higher level of human capital than the adult population.

Table 5A.1   Human capital in the adult population

Human capital category	Proportion	Personal daily income				Educational attainment					
		$9.10	$18.20	$36.40	Total	None	1–11 years	High school degree	13–16 Years	17–20 Years	Total
Highest	10%			100%	100%				90%	10%	100%
High	15%		33%	67%	100%			67%	30%	3%	100%
Intermediate	28%	13%	33%	54%	100%	25%	29%	33%	12%	1%	100%
Low	29%	24%	76%		100%	39%	36%	24%			100%
Lowest	18%	100%			100%	51%	49%				100%
Total	100%										
Proportion		27%	37%	36%	100%	30%	28%	25%	16%	2%	100%

Note: Data is based on representative samples of the adult population in 13 Agricultural-Industrial economies.

Table 5A.2   Human capital among business creators

Human capital category	Proportion	Personal daily income				Educational attainment					
		$9.10	$18.20	$36.40	Total	None	1–11 years	High school degree	13–16 Years	17–20 Years	Total
Highest	10%			100%	100%				90%	10%	100%
High	18%		30%	70%	100%			70%	27%	3%	100%
Intermediate	29%	10%	35%	55%	100%	25%	30%	35%	9%	1%	100%
Low	25%	24%	76%		100%	38%	38%	24%			100%
Lowest	18%	100%			100%	45%	55%				100%
Total	100%										
Proportion		27%	35%	39%	101%	25%	28%	28%	17%	2%	100%

Note: Based on 17,720 active business creators in 12 Agricultural-Industrial economies.

6.   Service-Industrial economies: Education and opportunity

In the summer of 1988, the Shining Path was disrupting farming in Peru and demanded payment to allow trucks carrying consumer goods, such as Coca-Cola and Pepsi, to rural areas. Forced to abandon agriculture the Aquino family, which included six brothers, mostly engineers, mortgaged their home and started a soft drink company focusing on poorer households. Initial distribution of Kola Real in recycled beer bottles was done informally in Ayacucho, a regional capital city. Strong acceptance led the family to found AJE in 1991 to serve all Peru. International expansion began in 1999 with sales in Venezuela, followed by Mexico, the rest of Central America, and in major Latin American countries. Sales began in Asia in 2006. The company now operates in 15 countries; in many the product is known as Big Cola.[1]

One … woman was the fifty-five-year-old household head with fourth-grade schooling and six dependent children. Although she was trained as a dressmaker, she finds she earns more running a backyard factory to make cement blocks—a highly non-traditional business for a female. In eighteen months with ADEMI [Association for the Development of Micro-Enterprises, Inc. in the Dominican Republic] she has had seven loans, increasing from DR$200 to DR$2,000. She has added two employees and, as is common among female MEs [micro-enterprises], most of her children also help when they are not in school. Her volume has increased from one to three truckloads of sand (to make blocks) delivered per week. "Sometimes I never even close; sometimes I'm up wetting the blocks at 6:00 A.M., but it doesn't bother me." She is proud of and pleased with her business's growth, and she now wants to buy more land to expand the business. Any small savings go for the children, "so that they can study," and for the house. And her modest home shows it: it contains a set of encyclopedias, a new refrigerator and the children's stereo.[2]

About 2.5 billion live in 54 Service-Industrial economies, 38% of the world population. Included are some of the largest countries in the world, such as Brazil, China, Indonesia, and Mexico. About one-third of work in Service-Industrial economies is in consumer-oriented sectors and one-quarter in knowledge-based sectors. Slightly more than one-fifth is in industrial sectors and about one-fifth in agricultural.[3]

THE NATIONAL CONTEXT

Two-thirds of the population in these countries are of working age, 15 to 64 years old, and about one-tenth are 65 or older; those under 15 years are one-quarter of the population. Three-fifths of adults are in the labor force, seven-tenths of the men and half of the women. About one-quarter of all jobs do not require much training or experience. Less than one-tenth provide wages of less than $3.60 per day. Three-fifths of retirees have some form of pension.[4]

Annual GDP per person is about $13,200, of which three-tenths is absorbed by government expenditures. Those in Service-Industrial economies have a life expectancy of 74 years and an average education of 14 years. Over nine-tenths are literate, and seven-tenths have completed secondary school. Annual health-care spending is about $841 per person and about $583 per year goes to education. About 5% of the annual GDP is reflected in government spending on social protection, an average of $466 per person.[5]

About two-fifths have confidence in the national government or the judicial system. Three-fifths feel safe outside at night. Three-fourths are satisfied with their local community and their freedom of choice. More than half are satisfied with the educational and health-care systems. One-third consider the local job market as good.[6]

CAREER OPTIONS

Much of business activity is formalized. Slightly more than half of firms are registered, and registered firms with ten or more employees are almost half of all businesses. In non-agricultural sectors slightly less than half of all jobs are unregistered firms. Five-sixths of all firms have employees, the remaining one-sixth reflect self-employment.[7]

There is support for entrepreneurial careers as three-quarters of all adults consider it a good career choice and a source of status. The majority have traditional or intermediate authority values, which emphasize self-reliance rather than expectations of government support. While twice as many emphasize personal values of survival rather than self-expression, two-fifths have an intermediate or mixed orientation. Among the adult population many are ready to pursue firm creation, as about half see good business opportunities or know an active business creator and three-fifths consider they have the skills and knowledge to start a new firm. Over half of the adults have finished high school and over nine-tenths are literate, so many have a basic education that would facilitate business creation.[8]

In such a context, many seeking an economic role have a choice between working for established organizations or pursuing business creation.

HOW MUCH ACTIVITY?

About one-sixth of working-age adults have chosen to pursue firm creation, although there is substantial variation, from less than one in ten in Bosnia and Herzegovina, Georgia, and Serbia to more than one-quarter in Botswana,

Entrepreneurship and economic development

Table 6.1   *Business creators in Service-Industrial economies*

Country	Total population: 2018	15–64-year-old population: 2018	Total business creators	Business creators: men	Business creators: women
Albania	2,883,000	1,977,000	334,000	198,000	136,000
Algeria*	42,228,000	26,810,000	3,125,000	2,022,000	1,103,000
Antigua and Barbuda	96,000	67,000	12,000	7,000	5,000
Armenia	2,952,000	2,011,000	339,000	201,000	138,000
Azerbaijan	9,950,000	7,008,000	1,184,000	701,000	483,000
Belize*	383,000	249,000	46,000	24,000	22,000
Bolivia*	11,353,000	7,009,000	2,350,000	1,256,000	1,094,000
Bosnia and Herzegovina*	3,324,000	2,286,000	173,000	117,000	56,000
Botswana*	2,254,000	1,390,000	407,000	219,000	188,000
Brazil*	209,469,000	146,090,000	23,550,000	12,539,000	11,011,000
China*	1,427,648,000	1,016,515,000	161,642,000	90,828,000	70,814,000
Colombia*	49,661,000	33,990,000	7,735,000	4,529,000	3,206,000
Costa Rica*	4,999,000	3,456,000	482,000	269,000	213,000
Dominica	72,000	48,000	8,000	5,000	3,000
Dominican Republic*	10,627,000	6,901,000	1,272,000	748,000	524,000
Ecuador*	17,084,000	11,073,000	3,092,000	1,618,000	1,474,000
Egypt*	98,424,000	60,010,000	6,742,000	5,105,000	1,637,000
Fiji	883,000	575,000	97,000	57,000	40,000

Country	Total population: 2018	15–64-year-old population: 2018	Total business creators	Business creators: men	Business creators: women
Gabon	2,119,000	1,259,000	213,000	126,000	87,000
Georgia*	4,003,000	2,615,000	251,000	154,000	97,000
Grenada	111,000	74,000	12,000	7,000	5,000
Indonesia*	267,671,000	180,923,000	35,334,000	17,251,000	18,083,000
Iran*	81,800,000	56,719,000	8,078,000	5,796,000	2,282,000
Jamaica*	2,935,000	1,980,000	419,000	228,000	191,000
Jordan*	9,965,000	6,169,000	765,000	541,000	224,000
Lebanon*	6,859,000	4,589,000	1,094,000	663,000	431,000
Libya*	6,679,000	4,494,000	625,000	422,000	203,000
Macedonia, North*	2,083,000	1,454,000	130,000	92,000	38,000
Maldives	516,000	393,000	66,000	39,000	27,000
Marshall Island	58,000	39,000	7,000	4,000	3,000
Mauritius	1,267,000	896,000	152,000	90,000	62,000
Mexico*	126,191,000	83,563,000	11,292,000	6,272,000	5,020,000
Moldova	4,052,000	2,945,000	497,000	294,000	203,000
Mongolia	3,170,000	2,077,000	351,000	208,000	143,000
Panama*	4,177,000	2,708,000	426,000	230,000	196,000
Paraguay	6,956,000	4,461,000	753,000	446,000	307,000
Peru*	31,989,000	21,152,000	6,124,000	3,285,000	2,839,000
Philippines*	106,651,000	68,166,000	13,041,000	6,010,000	7,031,000
Samoa	196,000	112,000	19,000	11,000	8,000
Serbia*	8,803,000	5,807,000	562,000	386,000	176,000

Entrepreneurship and economic development

Country	Total population: 2018	15–64-year-old population: 2018	Total business creators	Business creators: men	Business creators: women
South Africa*	57,793,000	37,913,000	2,891,000	1,694,000	1,197,000
Sri Lanka	21,229,000	13,869,000	2,342,000	1,387,000	955,000
St. Kitts and Nevis	56,000	37,000	7,000	4,000	3,000
St. Lucia	182,000	130,000	22,000	13,000	9,000
St. Vincent and Grenadines	110,000	75,000	12,000	7,000	5,000
Suriname*	576,000	380,000	18,000	12,000	6,000
Thailand*	69,428,000	49,303,000	11,113,000	5,604,000	5,509,000
Tonga*	103,000	61,000	11,000	5,000	6,000
Trinidad and Tobago*	1,390,000	957,000	173,000	99,000	74,000
Tunisia*	11,565,000	7,808,000	716,000	512,000	204,000
Turkmenistan	5,851,000	3,789,000	640,000	379,000	261,000
Ukraine	44,246,000	29,978,000	5,062,000	2,997,000	2,065,000
Uzbekistan	32,476,000	21,725,000	3,668,000	2,172,000	1,496,000
Venezuela*	28,887,000	18,796,000	4,158,000	2,252,000	1,906,000
Total	2,846,433,000	1,964,881,000	323,634,000	180,135,000	143,499,000

Note: * Prevalence rates based on Global Entrepreneurship Monitor consolidated file (Reynolds, 2021). Estimates for other countries based on average values of countries with surveys. Population estimates based on United Nations (2019b).

Ecuador, and Peru. Across these 54 Service-Industrial economies, listed in Table 6.1, 324 million are involved in business creation, two-fifths of the global total. Men are 56% of business creators, or 180 million, and women 44%, or about 144 million.

Some of the largest countries are Service-Industrial economies, like Brazil, China, and Egypt, as well as many smaller nations like Algeria, Costa Rica, and Tonga. China, with 162 million business creators among a billion adults in their working years, is the largest source of activity. Other large countries have millions of business creators, such as Indonesia (35 million), Brazil (24 million), the Philippines (13 million), and Mexico (11 million). But even some of the smaller countries have thousands of active business creators, such as Belize with 46,000 and Tonga with 11,000.

WHO PURSUES BUSINESS CREATION?

Men and women of all ages are active in business creation, as illustrated in Figure 6.1. Men, at 19 per 100, are slightly more active than women, at 14 per 100. Those 25 to 44 years old are the most active in business creation, followed by those 45 to 54 years old and young adults, 18 to 24 years old. Those 55 to 64 years old are the least active. Men and women of all ages are active in all

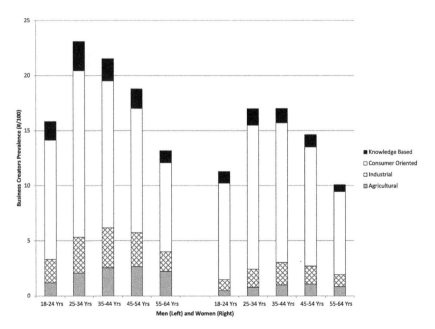

Figure 6.1   Business creation participation by age, gender, and sector

economic sectors, as shown in Figure 6.1. About seven-tenths are pursuing new firms in consumer-oriented sectors, one-eighth in industrial sectors, and one-tenth in agricultural or knowledge-based sectors.

Personal resources, income, and educational attainment vary among those in Service-Industrial economies, as shown in Figure 6.2.[9] About a third have a daily income of $20.75, another third a daily income of $41.50, and a final third a daily income of about $83.00. A majority, two-thirds, have completed secondary school. One-quarter have a post-secondary education and 1 in 20 are a graduate or have professional experience. A small proportion of adults, one-eighth, have no educational experience. Over nine-tenths would be considered literate.[10] There is gender equality in terms of personal resources.

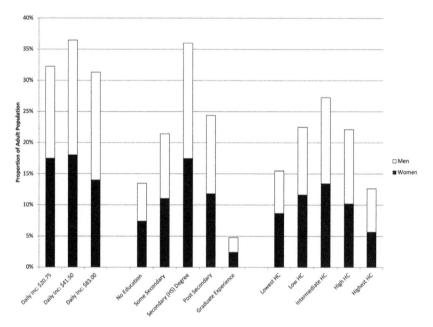

Figure 6.2   Population human capital

The distribution of human capital, based on personal income and educational attainment is presented as an index on the right of Figure 6.3. About a third are in the highest or high category, about one-quarter in the intermediate category, and two-fifths in the low or lowest categories.

Men and women with more human capital are the more active in business creation, as presented in Figure 6.3. Despite some disadvantages, those with the lowest levels of human capital are very much involved, albeit at two-thirds the level of the most active. Although consumer-oriented business creation is

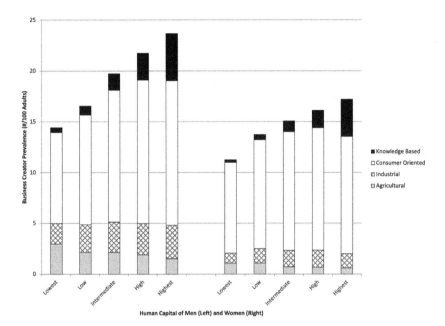

Figure 6.3   Business creation participation by human capital, gender, and sector

the most popular, men and women with more human capital are more involved in knowledge based sectors. The emphasis on agricultural and industrial sectors is similar for all levels of human capital.

One-fourth of men and women working full or part time are involved in business creation, as shown in Figure 6.4. They are implementing new firms in all sectors. They are three times more likely to be involved as those not working. Those not working seem to be more likely to pursue consumer-oriented businesses. One-tenth or less of those unemployed, homemakers, students, or retired are pursuing business creation.

In Service-Industrial economies:

- Men and women of all ages are active (14 to 19 per 100 adults) in business creation in all sectors.
- Seven-tenths of the activity is in consumer-oriented sectors.
- More human capital is associated with greater participation in business creation among both men and women, although more than one-tenth of the most disadvantaged are involved.
- Those working are four times more likely to be involved as adults with other roles in the labor force.

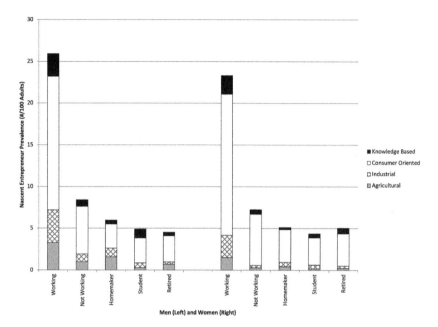

Figure 6.4   *Nascent entrepreneur participation by labor force status, gender, and sector*

WHO ARE THE BUSINESS CREATORS?

This churning mass of 324 million business creators has some distinctive features. Men are about two-thirds and women one-third of active business creators. There is some variation by gender for different sectors, as presented in Figure 6.5; each sector totals 100%. Men are three-fourths and women one-fourth of those pursuing agricultural new ventures. Men are three-fifths and women two-fifths of those pursuing industrial and knowledge-based new firms. Men are slightly more than half and women slightly less than half of those involved in new consumer-oriented ventures. Almost three-fifths of business creators are between 25 and 44 years old. Those 18 to 24 and 45 to 54 years old are about a third; less than a tenth are 55 to 64 years old. The age distributions are similar for men and women across all economic sectors.

All economic sectors have business creators with diverse levels of human capital. There are, however, some differences in the proportions. Two-thirds of those creating knowledge-based new firms have either high or the highest human capital, shown in Figure 6.6. In contrast, two-fifths of those involved in new agricultural firms have either the low or lowest human capital. The distri-

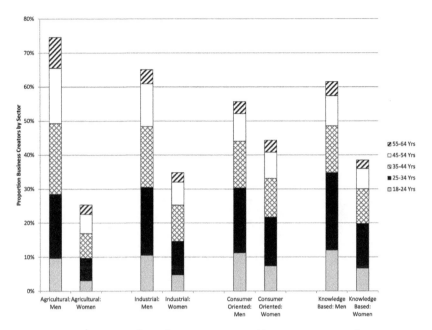

Figure 6.5   Age and gender proportions of business creators by sector

butions in industrial and consumer-oriented sectors are intermediate and very similar, with about three-tenths with the high or highest levels and one-third with the low or lowest levels.

Four-fifths of those nascent entrepreneurs entering the firm creation process do so while they have a full- or part-time job. As shown in Figure 6.7, about one in ten are not working while they pursue business creation, and the remaining tenth are homemakers, students, or retired. Women are slightly more likely to be homemakers, retired men are slightly more prevalent in agriculture. The proportion with different statuses in the labor market as they enter business creation is very similar across all economic sectors.

Not all business creators have the same objectives. In Service-Industrial economies about half seek a business opportunity that will provide more work autonomy, greater income, or maintain their current level of income. Slightly more than one-fourth consider business creation their best work opportunity and one-fifth have mixed motives. Slightly more women are pursuing their best work option, three-tenths compared to one-quarter for men.

The relationship of human capital and motivation among business creators is presented for men and women in Figure 6.8. Over three-fifths of those with the highest human capital are pursuing a business opportunity to gain

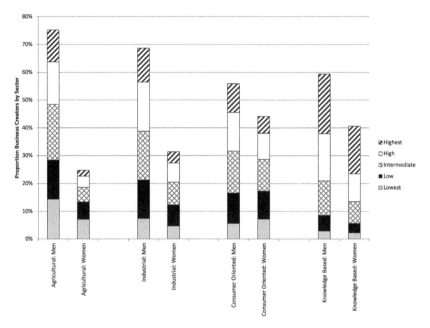

Figure 6.6   *Human capital and gender proportion of business creators by sector*

autonomy, more income, or maintain their income compared to two-fifths of those with the lowest level of human capital. This is offset by the half with the lowest human capital that are pursuing their best option, compared to less than one-fifth among those with the highest human capital. The proportion involved for mixed motives increases among those with more human capital. There are few significant differences between men and women.

Considering all business creators, two-thirds have intermediate, high, or the highest level of human capital, shown in Figure 6.9. Over half of these are pursuing a business opportunity, more than a third of all business creators. One-fifth have low levels of human capital and one-eighth the lowest level. While men are more involved than women, the proportion with different levels of human capital is similar. Business creators with diverse motivations are found among those with all levels of human capital.

AMONG THE 320 MILLION BUSINESS CREATORS IN SERVICE-INDUSTRIAL ECONOMIES:

• Men are two-thirds and women one-third.

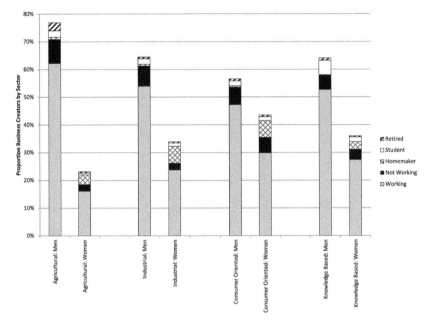

Figure 6.7   Labor force status and gender proportions of nascent entrepreneurs by sector

- Three-fifths are between 25 and 44 years old.
- While most of the activity is consumer-oriented, there is activity in all economic sectors.
- Four-fifths are working full or part time as they pursue business creation.
- Three-fifths have intermediate, high, or the highest level of human capital.
- Half are pursuing business opportunities that will provide autonomy, greater income, or income stability, slightly more than a quarter consider business creation their best choice, and about one-fifth have mixed motivations.

NEW VENTURES AND CONTRIBUTIONS

The 324 million business creators in Service-Industrial economies are working, alone or in teams, to implement 197 million new ventures. As shown in Table 6.2, 93 million are in the pre-profit start-up phase and 104 million are new firms. China has the largest share, with 94 million. Indonesia with 26 million and Brazil with 16 million are also major sources of new ventures.

Table 6.2   *Pre-profit ventures and new firms in Service-Industrial economies*

Country	15-64-year-old population	Total early-stage ventures	Pre-profit ventures	New firms
Albania	1,977,000	197,000	116,000	81,000
Algeria*	26,810,000	1,851,000	1,106,000	745,000
Antigua and Barbuda	67,000	7,000	4,000	3,000
Armenia	2,011,000	200,000	118,000	82,000
Azerbaijan	7,008,000	698,000	411,000	287,000
Belize*	249,000	20,000	14,000	6,000
Bolivia*	7,009,000	1,460,000	996,000	464,000
Bosnia and Herzegovina*	2,286,000	94,000	58,000	36,000
Botswana*	1,390,000	255,000	154,000	101,000
Brazil*	146,090,000	16,395,000	5,799,000	10,596,000
China*	1,016,515,000	94,285,000	40,440,000	53,845,000
Colombia*	33,990,000	3,792,000	2,116,000	1,676,000
Costa Rica*	3,456,000	291,000	219,000	72,000
Dominica	48,000	5,000	3,000	2,000
Dominican Republic*	6,901,000	827,000	432,000	395,000
Ecuador*	11,073,000	2,080,000	1,239,000	841,000
Egypt*	60,010,000	3,108,000	1,756,000	1,352,000
Fiji	575,000	58,000	34,000	24,000
Gabon	1,259,000	126,000	74,000	52,000
Georgia*	2,615,000	148,000	88,000	60,000
Grenada	74,000	7,000	4,000	3,000

Country	15–64-year-old population	Total early-stage ventures	Pre-profit ventures	New firms
Indonesia*	180,923,000	25,603,000	11,576,000	14,027,000
Iran*	56,719,000	4,325,000	2,556,000	1,769,000
Jamaica*	1,980,000	304,000	186,000	118,000
Jordan*	6,169,000	429,000	222,000	207,000
Lebanon*	4,589,000	762,000	294,000	468,000
Libya*	4,494,000	254,000	184,000	70,000
Macedonia, North*	1,454,000	80,000	50,000	30,000
Maldives	393,000	39,000	23,000	16,000
Marshall Island	39,000	4,000	2,000	2,000
Mauritius	896,000	90,000	53,000	37,000
Mexico*	83,563,000	6,798,000	5,043,000	1,755,000
Moldova	2,945,000	293,000	172,000	121,000
Mongolia	2,077,000	207,000	122,000	85,000
Panama*	2,708,000	288,000	182,000	106,000
Paraguay	4,461,000	444,000	261,000	183,000
Peru*	21,152,000	3,707,000	2,781,000	926,000
Philippines*	68,166,000	8,855,000	4,035,000	4,820,000
Samoa	112,000	12,000	7,000	5,000
Serbia*	5,807,000	361,000	235,000	126,000
South Africa*	37,913,000	1,646,000	1,015,000	631,000
Sri Lanka	13,869,000	1,380,000	812,000	568,000
St. Kitts and Nevis	37,000	4,000	2,000	2,000
St. Lucia	130,000	13,000	8,000	5,000

Country	15–64-year-old population	Total early-stage ventures	Pre-profit ventures	New firms
St. Vincent and Grenadines	75,000	7,000	4,000	3,000
Trinidad and Tobago*	957,000	114,000	66,000	48,000
Tunisia*	7,808,000	503,000	256,000	247,000
Turkmenistan	3,789,000	377,000	222,000	155,000
Ukraine	29,978,000	2,983,000	1,756,000	1,227,000
Uzbekistan	21,725,000	2,162,000	1,273,000	889,000
Venezuela*	18,796,000	2,197,000	1,553,000	644,000
Total	1,964,881,000	197,140,000	93,287,000	103,853,000

Note: * Prevalence rates based on Global Entrepreneurship Monitor consolidated file (Reynolds, 2021). Estimates for other countries based on average values of countries with surveys. Population estimates based on United Nations (2019b).

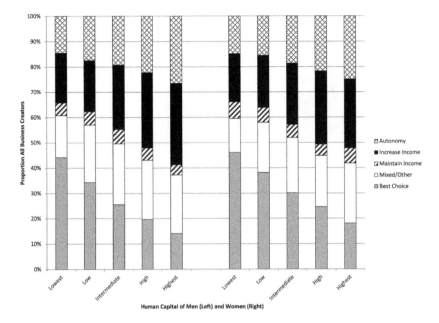

Figure 6.8   *Business creator motivation by human capital and gender*

New venture contributions among Service-Industrial economies are summarized in Figure 6.10. Two-thirds are a source of new jobs. More than half are providing one to four new jobs, one-tenth five to nine new jobs, and 1 in 20 ten or more jobs. About one-third are a source of employment for a sole proprietor.

Many of the new ventures will contribute to economic growth, exports, or adaptation. Almost one-fifth have growth aspirations, expecting to provide ten or more jobs in five years. One in 15 expect half or more of their customers to be outside the country. One-fifth consider their ventures a source of innovation in the markets, providing something new for their customers. About 1 in 25 is a high-potential new venture, expecting both growth and a market impact. About three-quarters of all new ventures are in the consumer-oriented or knowledge-based sectors.

Diverse motivations are associated with ventures making contributions to the Service-Industrial economies, as shown in Figure 6.11. The majority making contributions reflect a focus on business opportunities; the business creators are seeking greater autonomy, more income, or to maintain existing income stability. On the other hand, one-quarter of the ventures providing ten or more jobs, plans for growth, a focus on exports, or an impact on the markets

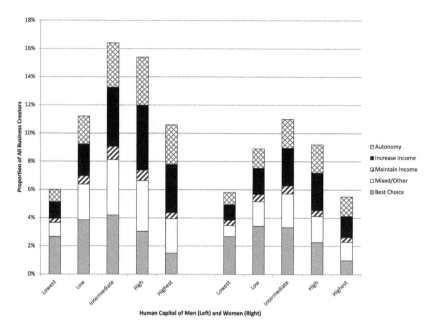

Figure 6.9   *Proportion of business creators by motivation, human*
                capital, and gender

reflect the best choice for the start-up team. Without these business creators,
there would be a substantial reduction in contributions.

Among those firms expecting to have growth and a market impact,
seven-tenths are pursuing business opportunities, most to gain work autonomy
or greater income. Those responding to labor market challenges by pursuing
firm creation as their best choice or with mixed motives are three-tenths of
high-potential new ventures.

The number of new firms making contributions to Service-Industrial economies is provided in Table 6.3. Most of the variation is related to the size of the
country. For example, China, with 94 million early-stage ventures, has about
16 million ventures providing ten or more jobs, 31 million expecting ten or
more jobs in five years, 2.5 million with substantial exports, 10 million providing a significant impact on the markets, and 4 million expecting both growth
and market impact. Smaller countries, as expected, will have fewer numbers
of ventures making contributions. Suriname (formerly Dutch Guinea on the
northern coast of South America) has about 12,000 early-stage new ventures
with 700 providing ten or more jobs, 500 expecting growth, 1,000 emphasizing
exports, 5,000 expecting a market impact, and 600 expecting both growth and

Table 6.3   New venture contributions in Service-Industrial economies

Country	Current jobs: 10 or more	Growth	Exports	Market impact	Growth and impact
Albania	12,000	42,000	17,000	41,000	9,000
Algeria*	156,000	475,000	107,000	400,000	121,000
Antigua and Barbuda	400	1,400	600	1,400	300
Armenia	13,000	43,000	17,000	42,000	9,000
Azerbaijan	44,000	148,000	59,000	147,000	30,000
Belize*	1,000	5,000	4,000	4,000	1,000
Bolivia*	31,000	212,000	62,000	167,000	39,000
Bosnia and Herzegovina*	14,000	24,000	13,000	23,000	5,000
Botswana*	8,000	79,000	13,000	25,000	11,000
Brazil*	316,000	1,714,000	396,000	586,000	96,000
China*	16,018,000	30,859,000	2,519,000	10,372,000	4,352,000
Colombia*	282,000	1,592,000	266,000	510,000	223,000
Costa Rica*	8,000	39,000	16,000	34,000	4,000
Dominica	300	1,000	400	1,000	200
Dominican Republic*	37,000	183,000	65,000	75,000	18,000
Ecuador*	37,000	186,000	80,000	148,000	26,000
Egypt*	404,000	897,000	265,000	912,000	295,000
Fiji	4,000	12,000	5,000	12,000	2,000
Gabon	8,000	27,000	11,000	26,000	5,000
Georgia*	2,000	36,000	18,000	5,000	2,000

Entrepreneurship and economic development

Country	Current jobs: 10 or more	Growth	Exports	Market impact	Growth and impact
Grenada*	500	1,600	600	1,600	200
Indonesia*	663,000	2,107,000	1,115,000	16,688,000	1,269,000
Iran*	354,000	1,158,000	182,000	274,000	86,000
Jamaica*	4,000	28,000	34,000	51,000	5,000
Jordan*	24,000	58,000	78,000	136,000	19,000
Lebanon*	25,000	85,000	91,000	362,000	33,000
Libya*	50,000	102,000	26,000	80,000	31,000
Macedonia, North*	13,000	27,000	14,000	24,000	9,000
Maldives	2,000	8,000	3,000	8,000	2,000
Marshall Island	200	800	300	800	200
Mauritius	6,000	19,000	8,000	19,000	4,000
Mexico*	190,000	945,000	302,000	870,000	173,000
Moldova	19,000	62,000	25,000	62,000	13,000
Mongolia	13,000	44,000	17,000	43,000	9,000
Panama*	6,000	19,000	31,000	48,000	2,000
Paraguay	28,000	94,000	37,000	93,000	19,000
Peru*	159,000	630,000	176,000	455,000	87,000
Philippines*	198,000	654,000	559,000	3,407,000	253,000
Samoa	700	2,400	900	2,300	500
Serbia*	32,000	96,000	31,000	46,000	20,000
South Africa*	119,000	398,000	299,000	494,000	105,000
Sri Lanka	87,000	294,000	117,000	290,000	60,000

Country	Current jobs: 10 or more	Growth	Exports	Market impact	Growth and impact
St. Kitts and Nevis	200	800	300	800	200
St. Lucia	800	2,800	1,100	2,700	600
St. Vincent and Grenadines	500	1,600	600	1,600	300
Suriname	700	500	1,100	5,100	600
Thailand*	390,000	1,000,000	220,000	1,241,000	166,000
Tonga*	200	2,000	900	2,400	300
Trinidad and Tobago*	8,000	27,000	4,000	5,000	1,000
Tunisia*	50,000	190,000	29,000	117,000	60,000
Turkmenistan	24,000	80,000	32,000	79,000	16,000
Ukraine	189,000	635,000	252,000	628,000	130,000
Uzbekistan	137,000	460,000	183,000	455,000	94,000
Venezuela*	89,000	495,000	98,000	346,000	64,000
Total	20,278,500	46,302,900	7,902,800	39,869,700	7,981,400

Note: * Prevalence rates based on Global Entrepreneurship Monitor consolidated file (Reynolds, 2021). Estimates for other countries based on average values of countries with surveys.

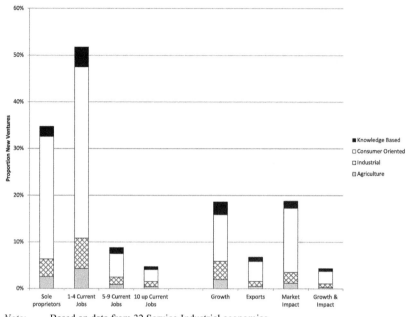

Note: Based on data from 32 Service-Industrial economies.

Figure 6.10   New venture contributions by sector

a market impact. Relative contributions are significant in all countries, regardless of the absolute size.

STRUCTURAL ADAPTATION

As with other stages of economic development, business creation reflects shifts into new economic sectors. There is some drift away from agriculture and construction and greater activity in consumer-oriented sectors. Figure 6.12 presents the established jobs (white bars), new venture jobs (black bars), and shifts in the proportion of jobs in each sector (grey bars). Major increases in the proportion of jobs are in trading activities (from 16% to 39%) an increase of 23%. There is also an increase in jobs related to lodging, food services, and bars (from 5% to 10%). There is a slight increase in real estate and business and administrative services jobs (from 5% to 7%). A reduced emphasis in jobs related to agriculture (from 18% to 10%) and construction (from 8% to 4%) offsets these gains. The lack of new jobs in education, health and social service, and public administration reflects the lack of new firms in sectors

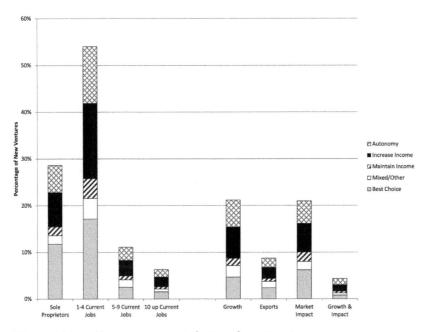

Figure 6.11   New venture contributions by motivation

dominated by public agencies. Hospitals and schools, once established, are a relatively stable source of employment and not sectors amenable to private initiatives. For six sectors—miscellaneous consumer, mining, transportation and communication, finance and insurance, utilities, and manufacturing—there is not much change in emphasis. New ventures in these sectors reflect the ongoing churning typical of established sectors.

Nonetheless, new ventures in Service-Industrial economies reflect a shift in the economic structure, reflecting indications of the future.

MAJOR CHALLENGES, OR WHY QUIT?

The problems that lead established firms to terminate reflect the challenges confronting business creation in Service-Industrial economies. The major complications are summarized in Table 6.4. The top problem is the inability to make money, reported by more than a third, followed by complications with developing financial support, reported by one-sixth.

Two issues related to the personal situation of the owners, family and personal issues and the development of other career opportunities, are reported in one-fourth of the cases. Systematic disengagements, including the sale of

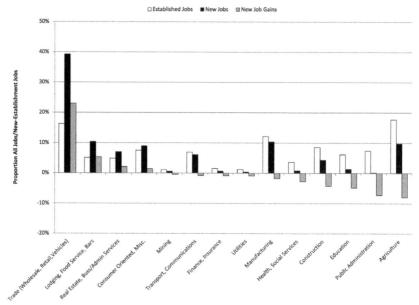

Figure 6.12   *Established jobs, new jobs, and new job gains by sector*

the business, retirement, and a pre-planned exit are the major factor for 1 in 11 cases. Other factors such as government regulations and taxes, a major incident, and miscellaneous complications account for one-seventh of the terminations.

The major focus of much public policy, financial support, regulations, and taxes account for one-fifth of the terminations. Clearly not as significant as the inability to make a profit.

OVERVIEW

Among the 2 billion working-age adults in 54 Service-Industrial economies:

- Business creation is a popular career choice pursued by one in six adults; over 324 million in 54 countries are involved with 197 million new ventures.
- While men are more active than women, women are more than one-third of active business creators; those 25 to 44 years old are the most active.

Table 6.4   *Primary reason for a business termination*

Not profitable	37.0%
Lack of financial support	17.3 %
Family, personal issues	16.0%
Other career opportunities	7.2%
Sold business	4.7%
Government regulations, taxes	4.7%
Major incident	2.7%
Pre-planned exit	2.5%
Retirement	1.5%
Miscellaneous other	6.5%
Total	100.0%

Note: Based on representative samples of 4,371 discontinued businesses in 19
Service-Industrial economies.

- Men and women with more human capital are more active, although the most disadvantaged are very much involved in business creation.
- Nine-tenths of business creators are involved while they are working full or part time.
- Half of business creators are less than 34 years old; half are 35 and older.
- Over half of business creators are expecting more autonomy or income, about a quarter see it as their best option, and others have mixed motives.
- About 4 in 1,000 adults are working on high-potential new firms, and four-fifths have intermediate, high, or the highest level of human capital.
- Two-thirds of new firms are expected to provide jobs for others, and from 5% to 20% will provide growth, exports, or a market impact.
- While new firms emerge in all sectors, there is a shift toward consumer-oriented markets; there is less activity in manufacturing, construction, and agriculture.
- Over a third of business terminations reflect a lack of profit; lack of financial support and family and personal issues account for another third.

Business creation is a major activity with significant contributions to Service-Industrial economies.

Business creators in Service-Industrial economies confront an economy where half of employment is in registered firms—businesses with an established presence in the economy. This may constrain opportunities for new firms. Other challenges may include issues with education, some constraints on financial support, and concerns about establishing legal title to assets or participating in the formal economy. Most seem to have access to current information about products, costs, and potential competition.

Over nine-tenths of adults are literate and had some primary school experience; over half have completed secondary school.[11] This not only improves the potential of those that pursue business creation but suggests there is a pool of qualified employees for new ventures. A major advantage for those that plan on a growth business.

All businesses require some working capital, even if they are only modest outlays for tools, supplies, or inventory. As one-third of the adults have a daily income of about $20, they may have limited funds to implement even small-scale enterprises. Financial support from social networks may be possible, as 6 in 100 adults have provided informal assistance for businesses.[12] In three-fifths of the cases this is support to close family members or relatives and in one-third the recipients are friends or neighbors. One in 10 provide support for work colleagues or strangers with a good idea.[13]

Domestic financial institutions provide about $10,000 in credit per person, slightly less than the annual GDP per person.[14] Formal bank loans may be available for a proportion of business creators. A major source of support for small-scale efforts are moneylenders operating informal, unregistered financial operations. Interest rates and constraints are often substantial. Micro-finance programs have developed Service-Industrial economies. By 2018 about 6% of adults had a micro-finance loan, three-fifths were to women and half were in rural areas. The average loan was $2,009.[15] Efforts to improve "financial inclusion" are a major feature, with more success in Service-Industrial economies.[16] There is probably an ongoing demand for micro-loans and private-sector initiatives may be emerging in response.

The costs and complications associated with business registration are an ongoing challenge in Service-Industrial economies. Registration may require eight or more procedures, take four weeks to complete, and the cost (average of $2,317) is one-fourth of the average annual income.[17] For individual businesses, this is often associated with tax administration, whereby the businesses are expected to pay property, sales, or value-added taxes and comply with a range of government regulations related to employment, safety, pollution, and the like. Nascent entrepreneurs may not consider the advantages for participating in national systems worth the effort. The advantages are not widely promoted.

It takes some effort to secure legal title to land, which may be the most important asset for many potential business creators. The formal land administration provides some geographic coverage but there may be concerns regarding the quality of record keeping.[18] Property registration may require seven procedures, take five weeks to complete, and cost 6% of the value of the property.[19] Without a legally recognized title, it is difficult to use an asset as collateral for a loan.

Most new firms involve participation in national or regional markets. While many consumer-oriented or knowledge-based sectors serve local communities, they may involve inputs—inventory, parts, components, etc.—from national or international sources. Some new ventures, even in agriculture, expect to serve regional or national customers. In terms of both inputs and sales, there are advantages to having current information about prices and availability and the competition. Mobile phones are universal among adults in Service-Industrial economies, but only three-fifths have internet access. Governments are, on average, spending $10 per year per person on communications infrastructure.[20] The minority of business creators without internet access may be at a disadvantage.

Those in Service-Industrial economies can expect to receive modest support if they confront complications, as annual government spending on social protection is about $466, or 4% of the annual GDP per capita. And two-fifths of retirees do not have access to a pension. Reservations about government assistance is reflected in the three-fourths that have a traditional or intermediate orientation toward authority. It is also associated with individual values which emphasize survival.[21]

Perhaps as a result, there is strong cultural support for entrepreneurial careers, with three-quarters of adults considering it a good career choice that leads to recognition and status. Many are well positioned to pursue business creation, with about half recognizing good business opportunities, knowing another entrepreneur, and confident in their business creation skills.[22]

Despite the challenges and reflecting the need for self-sufficiency and cultural support, from 10% to 30% of adults in Service-Industrial economies are involved in business creation. Their countries benefit from the substantial contributions from these new ventures.

NOTES

1. Nueno et al. (2011); Wikipedia (2021b).
2. Blumberg (1995).
3. Details in Table B.1.
4. Details in Table B.3.
5. Details in Table B.2.
6. Details in Table B.2.
7. Details in Table B.1.
8. Details in Table B.4.
9. Details in the appendix to this chapter.
10. Details in Table B.1.
11. Details in Table B.3.

12. Respondents report informal investments over the previous three years and details on the most recent investment (Reynolds, 2021).
13. Details in Table B.4.
14. Details in Table B.5.
15. Details in Table B.4.
16. EIU (2020).
17. Details in Table B.3.
18. Details in Table B.4.
19. Details in Table B.4.
20. Details in Table B.4.
21. Details in Tables B.2 and B.3.
22. Details in Table B.4.
23. Because of missing data, Tonga is not included.

APPENDIX: HUMAN CAPITAL SCALE DEVELOPMENT

The procedures described in the appendix to Chapter 4 were utilized to provide a description of the human capital among those living in Service-Industrial economies. The presentation in Table 6A.1 reflects average samples of 14,060 adults in each of 32 countries, a total of 449,926 respondents.

The same procedures were followed to create descriptions of the human capital among 72,997 business creators in 31 Service-Industrial economies (an average of 2,355 per country), provided in Table 6A.2.[23] As with other stages of development, business creators have a slightly higher level of human capital than the adult population.

Table 6A.1 Human capital in the adult population

Human capital category	Proportion	Personal daily income				Educational attainment					
		$20.75	$41.50	$83.00	Total	None	1–11 years	High school degree	13–16 years	17–20 years	Total
Highest	13%			100%	100%				80%	20%	100%
High	22%		48%	52%	100%			52%	40%	8%	100%
Intermediate	27%	24%	50%	26%	100%	9%	18%	50%	20%	3%	100%
Low	23%	45%	55%		100%	21%	34%	45%			100%
Lowest	15%	100%			100%	47%	53%				100%
Total	100%										
Proportion		32%	37%	31%	100%	13%	21%	36%	25%	5%	100%

Note: Based on representative samples of the adult population in 32 Service-Industrial economies.

Table 6A.2 Human capital among business creators

Human capital category	Proportion	Household income				Educational attainment					
		$12.75	$41.50	$83.00	Total	None	1–11 years	HSigh school degree	13–16 years	17–20 years	Total
Highest	16%			100%	100%				83%	17%	100%
High	22%		37%	63%	100%			63%	32%	5%	100%
Intermediate	26%	18%	50%	31%	99%	10%	21%	50%	16%	3%	100%
Low	22%	44%	56%		100%	19%	37%	44%			100%
Lowest	14%	100%			100%	39%	61%				100%
Total	100%										
Proportion		29%	33%	38%	100%	12%	23%	37%	24%	4%	100%

7. Progressive Service-Industrial economies: Values and knowledge based

Olga Slutsker, born in 1965, was not "academically inclined." With her parents' encouragement she emphasized sports and graduated from the St. Petersburg Academy of Physical Education with a focus on fencing. She became part of a national team, won a number of tournaments, and became a master of sports. In her early 20s she married and had two children. Traveling in Spain she visited a fitness club, enjoyed the experience, and wondered why they did not exist in Russia. At 27 Olga proceeded to create the first World Class fitness club in Moscow. She secured financing from relatives and an interest free loan from her successful businessman husband. He did not, however, invest equity and share ownership. The emphasis was on a quality gym experience and when the first club opened in 1993 it quickly attracted an influential clientele and favorable press coverage. Purchase of all rights to the name from a Swedish company in 1996 avoided complications for expansion. Completing a degree in management improved Olga's administrative skills and minimized the perception that her husband was the real source of business acumen. Her divorce in 2009 when the business was 17 years old led to a separation of her personal and business life. Her husband moved to Israel with the children, Olga retained ownership of the 49 World Class fitness clubs in four countries. The business is now widely regarded and the training venue for many Russian champions.[1]

Noriah, son of parents involved in business, completed secondary school and had several years of work experience. In his late 20s his application was accepted for the Factory Nursery Scheme (FNS), a program sponsored by the Development Bank of Malaysia. After a brief period of training, he began producing plastic bottles in the FNS incubator, contributing hard work, an agreeable disposition, and management expertise. A contract with the Ministry of Health was followed by private sector customers. The firm, located in the underdeveloped state of Kelantan on the east coast of the Malaysian peninsula, was profitable in the second year of operation, has good credit with the bank, and now exports to the adjacent states.[2]

Over half a billion live in 34 Progressive Service-Industrial economies, 8% of the world population. This group includes a wide range of countries, such as Argentina, Croatia, Italy, Qatar, and Russia. More than one-quarter of work is in industrial sectors, one-third in consumer-oriented sectors, and three-tenths in knowledge-based sectors. The agricultural sector accounts for about 1 in 20 of all jobs.

THE NATIONAL CONTEXT

Those in Progressive Service-Industrial economies have, relatively speaking, a pretty good life. While about two-thirds are in their working years, 15 to 64 years old, one-sixth are in their retirement years and one-fifth under 15 years of age. They live an average of 77 years. Literacy is virtually universal. Over four-fifths have completed high school and one-fifth have post-secondary education. Annual GDP per person is $34,000.[3]

While annual government expenditures are one-third of the GDP, at $13,000 per person, much is provided in personal benefits, such as $2,000 per person on health care, $1,500 per person on education, and $2,200 per person on a range of social protection programs. This may be why three-fifths are satisfied with the quality of the education and health-care systems. Four-fifths are satisfied in the community where they live, three-fourths are satisfied with their freedom of choice, and two-thirds feel safe outside at night. Two-fifths consider the local labor market as "good" and have confidence in the national government and the judicial system. Four-fifths of adults eligible for retirement have a pension.[4]

A distinctive feature of Progressive Service-Industrial economies, compared to those at earlier stages, is a major shift in national values. The half that emphasize secular-rational authority is twice that for Service-Industrial economies. Another third would find secular-rational values acceptable. This represents a widespread acceptance of collective, or government, solutions for social concerns and an assumption that governments should assist the disadvantaged. Three-tenths emphasize individual well-being values of self-expression, half again more than those in Service-Industrial economies. Those choosing to focus on distinctive personal life trajectories, rather than emphasizing economic survival, would receive sympathetic support.[5]

CAREER OPTIONS

Options for work are attractive. Two-thirds of non-agricultural jobs are in registered firms. Over four-fifths of firms are registered, and three-fifths of firms are registered with ten or more employees; two in five have fifty or more employees. Large, registered businesses are common, which is probably why four-fifths of eligible adults have pensions. This may also be why three-fifths of adults are in the labor force, seven-tenths of men and half of women. Three-fourths of jobs require some skill or training. Virtually no workers are paid less than $3.60 per day.[6]

There is some support for business creation. About two-thirds of adults consider this a good career choice, a route to status and respect, and are aware

Table 7.1   *Business creators in Progressive Service-Industrial economies*

Country	Total population: 2018	15–64-year-old population: 2018	Total business creators	Business creators: men	Business creators: women
Argentina*	44,361,150	28,444,936	4,063,575	2,471,229	1,592,347
Austria*	8,891,388	5,930,599	443,796	264,128	179,667
Bahamas	385,637	270,939	27,702	17,588	10,114
Bahrain	1,569,446	1,229,180	125,678	79,793	45,885
Barbados*	286,641	191,632	36,995	20,866	16,129
Belarus	9,452,617	6,455,089	660,001	419,034	240,966
Brunei Darussalam	428,963	309,284	31,623	20,077	11,545
Bulgaria*	7,051,608	4,540,010	201,357	117,649	83,708
Chile*	18,729,160	12,869,985	2,490,253	1,457,604	1,032,649
Croatia*	4,156,405	2,703,435	190,678	132,992	57,686
Czechia*	10,665,677	6,931,892	547,623	392,654	154,969
Estonia*	1,322,920	846,888	123,899	78,501	45,397
Hungary*	9,707,499	6,448,719	491,319	323,999	167,321
Italy*	60,627,291	38,752,480	1,937,022	1,247,102	689,920
Kazakhstan*	18,319,618	11,751,596	1,401,314	746,700	654,614
Kuwait	4,137,312	3,140,660	321,117	203,877	117,240
Lithuania*	2,801,264	1,832,378	204,302	139,936	64,366
Malaysia*	31,528,033	21,859,363	1,753,537	950,188	803,349
Malta	439,248	287,153	29,360	18,641	10,719
Montenegro*	627,809	419,474	63,238	41,161	22,077

Country	Total population: 2018	15–64-year-old population: 2018	Total business creators	Business creators: men	Business creators: women
Oman	4,829,473	3,639,525	372,123	236,261	135,862
Palau	17,907	12,306	1,258	799	459
Poland*	37,921,592	25,570,494	2,323,342	1,522,813	800,529
Portugal*	10,256,193	6,624,294	546,946	348,563	198,383
Qatar*	2,781,682	2,366,910	266,304	158,819	107,485
Romania*	19,506,114	12,898,758	1,053,724	698,689	355,034
Russia*	145,734,038	98,241,078	4,662,179	2,888,589	1,773,590
Saudi Arabia*	33,702,756	24,145,688	2,313,809	1,440,450	873,359
Seychelles	97,096	66,773	6,827	4,335	2,493
Slovakia*	5,453,014	3,758,469	443,597	287,099	156,497
Slovenia*	2,077,837	1,358,310	75,645	53,116	22,529
Turkey*	82,340,088	55,058,656	5,990,523	4,331,180	1,659,343
United Arab Emirates*	9,630,959	8,120,005	693,567	456,811	236,755
Uruguay*	3,449,285	2,227,462	322,934	209,589	113,345
Total	593,287,720	399,304,420	34,217,167	21,780,834	12,436,333

Note: * Prevalence rates based on Global Entrepreneurship Monitor consolidated file (Reynolds, 2021). Estimates for other countries based on average values of countries with surveys. Population estimates based on United Nations (2019b).

of media coverage of new business activity. Most adults, however, are not well positioned for entrepreneurship, as only two-fifths see good business opportunities or know an active entrepreneur. Half do not think they have the skill or knowledge to start a business. Two-fifths report that fear of failure would discourage business creation. On the other hand, two-thirds of adults would support pursuing self-fulfillment—doing their own thing. They would be sympathetic to efforts, such as business creation, that would reflect distinctive personal interests. If a start-up initiative is not successful, there is a range of social programs to provide a safety net.[7]

HOW MUCH ACTIVITY?

Business creation is pursued by about one in ten adults, with a range from 5 per 100 in Italy and Slovenia, to over 15 per 100 in Chile and Estonia.[8] About 34 million are involved in business creation in the Progressive Service-Industrial economies listed in Table 7.1. Across all countries, about 22 million men are two-thirds of the total, the other third are 12 million women. Larger countries have more people involved in business creation, such as 6 million in Turkey, 5 million in Russia, and 4 million in Argentina. But there is considerable activity

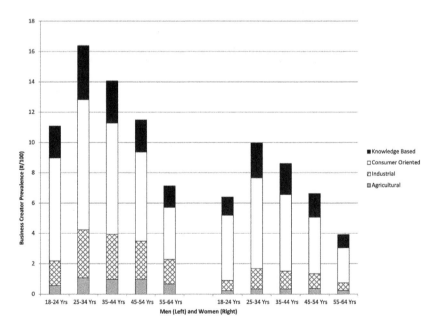

Figure 7.1   Business creation participation by age, gender, and sector

in smaller countries such as 7,000 in Seychelles and 30,000 in the Bahamas and Malta.

WHO PURSUES BUSINESS CREATION?

Participation in business creation varies with gender, age, personal human capital, and labor force activity. Men and women of all ages are involved in business creation, presented in Figure 7.1. Men, at 13 per 100, are about half again as active as women, at 8 per 100. Participation is highest among those 25 to 44 years old, slightly less among those 18 to 24 and 45 to 54 years old. Activity is the lowest among those 55 to 64 years old. The similarity of the patterns related to age among men and women suggests similarity in their responses to different life-course stages. Men and women of all ages are involved in all economic sectors. Slightly more than half are in the consumer-oriented sectors, one-fifth in knowledge-based sectors and industrial sectors, and 1 in 20 in agriculture.

Personal human capital, educational attainment and access to funds, varies across the adults in Progressive Service-Industrial economies, presented in Figure 7.2. Details are in the appendix to this chapter. For example, about a third of adults have a daily income of $201, another third a daily income

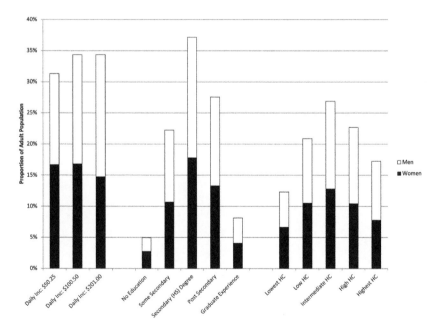

Figure 7.2   Population human capital

of $100, and slightly less than a third a daily income of $50. More than three-fifths have completed a secondary education and a quarter have gone beyond secondary school. One in 12 have a graduate experience and 1 in 20 have no education.

These two sources of personal capital are combined to create an index. The distribution among the adult population is shown to the right of Figure 7.2. Seven-tenths are in the three middle categories: low, intermediate, and high. About one-sixth are in the highest human capital category and one-eighth in the lowest.

There are some gender differences. A slightly greater proportion of men have higher income and more education than women (18% versus 16%). Slightly more women are in the lowest human capital category, 14% compared to 11% for men. On the other hand, the proportion with intermediate human capital is the same for both men and women.

Among men and women, those with more human capital are much more likely to be involved in business creation, as show in Figure 7.3. Compared to those with the lowest human capital, those with the highest level are three times more likely to be involved. Those with the lowest human capital are not well positioned for business creation and may have access to a social safety

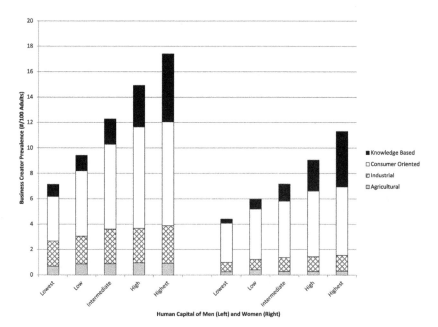

Figure 7.3   *Business creation participation by human capital, gender, and sector*

net. Personal human capital has some impact on choice of sector. While participation in agricultural or industrial sectors is similar across levels of human capital, those with higher levels of human capital are much more likely to pursue business creation in knowledge-based sectors and relatively less involved in consumer-oriented sectors.

The current role in the economy has a major impact on becoming involved in business creation. As shown in Figure 7.4, working men and women are four times as likely to enter business creation as nascent entrepreneurs as those not working, homemakers, students, or retired. And these new entrants are involved in all economic sectors.

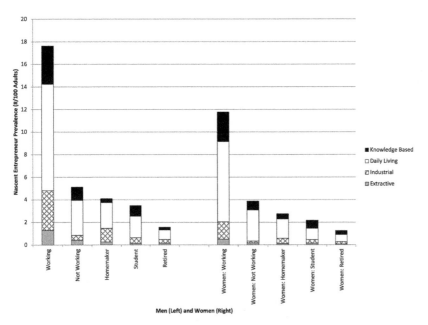

Figure 7.4   *Nascent entrepreneur participation by labor force status, gender, and sector*

In summary, the major patterns among business creators in these economies are:

• A moderate level of participation, at about 10 per 100 adults aged 15 to 64 years old.
• Men are about twice as active as women.
• The most active are mid-career adults, those 25 to 44 years old; least active are senior adults, 55 to 64 years old.

- For both men and women more human capital is associated with much higher levels of participation in business creation, and more involvement in knowledge-based sectors.
- Those with full- or part-time work as they enter business creation are four times as active as those not active in any work.

There is, then, considerable diversity among the 34 million business creators in the Progressive Service-Industrial economies.

WHO ARE THE BUSINESS CREATORS?

Participation in business creation involves joining a churning mass of entre-preneurs. Describing this active community is of some interest. What can be said about the 4 million in Argentina or the 500,000 in Hungary? Perhaps most significantly, men and women of all ages are involved in business creation in all sectors, as shown in Figure 7.5. The presentation focuses on four major economic sectors, the total for each equals 100%.

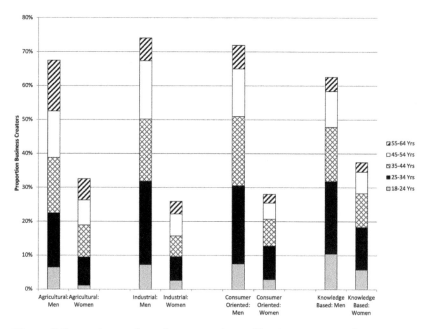

Figure 7.5   Age and gender proportions of business creators by sector

There are some differences related to gender and age. Men are seven-tenths of those in industrial and consumer-oriented sectors, women are three-tenths. Men are two-thirds of those in agriculture, women are one-third. Men are three-fifths of those in knowledge-based sectors, women are two-fifths. There are more younger people in knowledge-based and consumer service sectors. Those 18 to 34 years old are half of those involved in knowledge-based sectors and two-fifths of those in consumer services. In contrast, those 18 to 34 years old are one-third of those involved in agriculture, where two-fifths are 45 to 64 years old.

There is little overall difference among men and women business creators in terms of their human capital presented in Figure 7.6. Half have high or the highest levels of human capital, about one-quarter intermediate, and one-quarter low or the lowest level. One in 12 have the lowest human capital. There is, however, variation in human capital associated with the different sectors. Two-thirds of men and women creating new ventures in knowledge-based sectors have high or the highest levels of human capital, it is half of those in consumer-oriented sectors, and about two-fifths of business creators in the industrial and agricultural sectors.

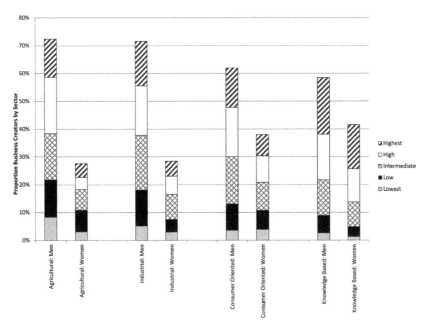

Figure 7.6   *Human capital and gender proportions of business creators by sector*

Almost nine-tenths of those entering business creation are doing so while they are working full or part time. The other one-tenth are unemployed looking for work, homemakers, students, or retired. As shown in Figure 7.7 there is little gender difference in this regard. A slightly larger proportion of women than men are homemakers while they pursue business creation. Business creators, working while they create new firms, are very busy people.

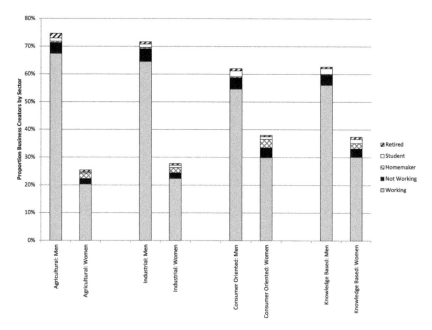

Figure 7.7   Labor force status and gender proportions of nascent entrepreneurs by sector

Motivation varies among business creators in Progressive Service-Industrial economies. Slightly more than half are pursuing a business opportunity, almost one-quarter to gain work autonomy, another quarter for greater income, and 1 in 20 to maintain their current level of income. Those who consider business creation as their best choice are one-fourth and those with mixed motives are a final one-fourth. Women are slightly more likely to consider business creation their best choice; men slightly more likely to pursue business opportunities.

For both men and women, however, motives vary among those with different amounts of human capital, presented in Figure 7.8. For example, among those with the highest level of human capital, three-fifths are pursuing a business opportunity and one-sixth consider business creation their best work option. Among those with the lowest level of human capital, two-fifths are pursuing a business opportunity and two-fifths consider it their best choice for participating in the economy. The same patterns are found among men and women.

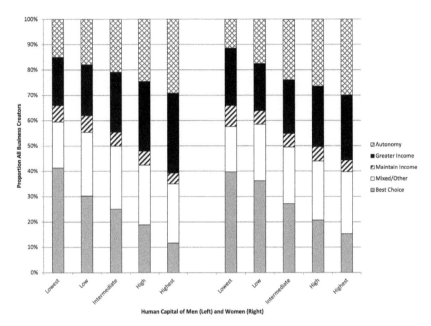

Figure 7.8   Business creator motivation by human capital and gender

Those with more human capital are the majority of those involved in business creation. As can be seen in Figure 7.9, almost four-fifths have inter-mediate, high, or the highest level of human capital. Those with the highest levels of human capital, which are those with post-secondary school education, are one-quarter of the total. Both men and women reflect a strong interest in greater work autonomy and more income. Those with the lowest amount of human capital, with low personal income and who have not completed sec-ondary school, are 1 in 15 of the business creators. The relationships between human capital and motivation are similar for men and women.

Among the 39 million business creators in Progressive Service-Industrial economies:

- About two-thirds are men.
- Over half are 25–44 years old.
- The vast majority are working full or part time when they enter business creation.

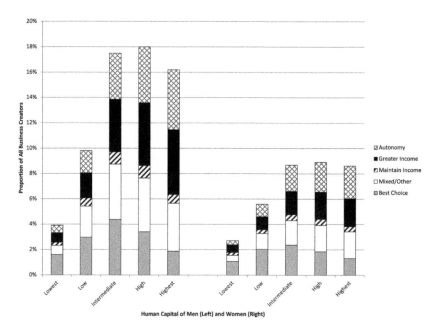

*Figure 7.9   Proportion of business creators by motivation, human
          capital, and gender*

- Three-fourths have intermediate, high, or the highest levels of human capital.
- Over half are pursuing a business opportunity for increased work autonomy or income.

Business creators represent some of the most active and well-prepared citizens in Progressive Service-Industrial economies.

NEW VENTURES AND CONTRIBUTIONS

The 34 million business creators in Progressive Service-Industrial economies are involved with 19 million new ventures, summarized in Table 7.2. About three-fifths, 11 million, are in the start-up, pre-profit stage and two-fifths, 8 million, have been profitable for up to 41 months. There is considerable variation in the scope of activity, large countries like Russia and Turkey have 3 million new ventures, while smaller countries like Austria, Belarus, Czechia, and Portugal have 300,000. Tiny Palau, with an adult labor force of 18,000, has almost a thousand new ventures.

Table 7.2   Pre-profit ventures and new firms in Progressive Service-Industrial economies

Country	15–64-year-old population	Total early-stage ventures	Pre-profit ventures	New firms
Argentina*	28,444,936	2,170,362	1,260,777	936,113
Austria*	5,930,599	255,050	172,916	79,826
Bahamas	270,939	15,150	9,811	5,282
Bahrain	1,229,180	68,733	44,510	23,961
Barbados*	191,632	24,139	15,950	7,794
Belarus	6,455,089	360,952	233,744	125,833
Brunei Darussalam	309,284	17,294	11,199	6,029
Bulgaria*	4,540,010	112,538	65,391	46,339
Chile*	12,869,985	1,359,460	853,298	509,648
Croatia*	2,703,435	110,646	81,920	28,906
Czechia*	6,931,892	308,023	225,126	79,136
Estonia*	846,888	65,094	45,523	19,642
Hungary*	6,448,719	283,474	186,001	96,447
Italy*	38,752,480	970,489	669,790	291,072
Kazakhstan*	11,751,596	904,850	599,393	308,392
Kuwait	3,140,660	175,618	113,726	61,223
Lithuania*	1,832,378	109,727	65,785	43,995
Malaysia*	21,859,363	1,177,518	612,254	565,895
Malta	287,153	16,057	10,398	5,598
Montenegro*	419,474	40,982	31,887	8,926
Oman	3,639,525	203,513	131,790	70,948

Country	15–64-year-old population	Total early-stage ventures	Pre-profit ventures	New firms
Palau	12,306	688	446	240
Poland*	25,570,494	1,590,275	1,023,515	561,191
Portugal*	6,624,294	301,135	191,984	109,691
Qatar*	2,366,910	106,161	75,813	30,953
Romania*	12,898,758	583,784	364,490	220,965
Russia*	98,241,078	2,763,009	1,498,549	1,292,445
Saudi Arabia*	24,145,688	1,100,341	610,365	482,421
Seychelles	66,773	3,734	2,418	1,302
Slovakia*	3,758,469	243,040	176,501	67,003
Slovenia*	1,358,310	40,442	24,104	17,009
Turkey*	55,058,656	3,081,630	1,844,746	1,211,523
United Arab Emirates*	8,120,005	299,542	159,984	136,284
Uruguay*	2,227,462	158,836	110,202	48,735
Total	399,304,420	19,022,286	11,524,305	7,500,767

Note: * Prevalence rates based on Global Entrepreneurship Monitor consolidated file (Reynolds, 2021). Estimates for other countries based on average values of countries with surveys. Population estimates based on United Nations (2019b).

Regardless of the actual scope of activity, new ventures in all sectors are making contributions to their national economies, as presented in Figure 7.10. While a quarter are sole-proprietorships, providing work for the owners, three-fourths have created employment and one-sixth have created ten or more jobs. One-third anticipate growth that will provide ten or more jobs over the next five years. One-eighth consider over half their sales are to those living outside their country, which would include income from tourists. Another one-eighth consider they have contributed to economic adaptation by having an impact on the markets in which they compete. One in 15 expect to have both high growth and an impact on the markets.

About three-fourths of all contributions will be in consumer-oriented or knowledge-based sectors.

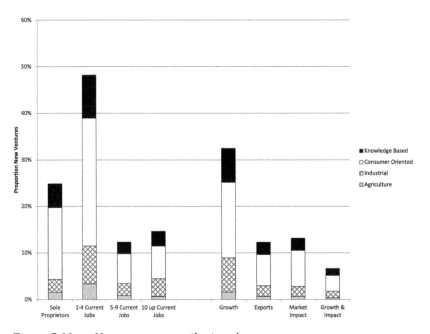

Figure 7.10   New venture contributions by sector

As shown in Figure 7.11, pursuit of business opportunities is associated with two-thirds of new ventures providing five or more jobs, expect growth, have a focus on exports, anticipate market impacts, or expect both growth and an impact. Those new ventures that were initiated as the best choice in a challenging labor market are one-fifth or more of all ventures making contributions. Progressive Service-Industrial economies are benefiting from new ventures reflecting a wide range of motivation.

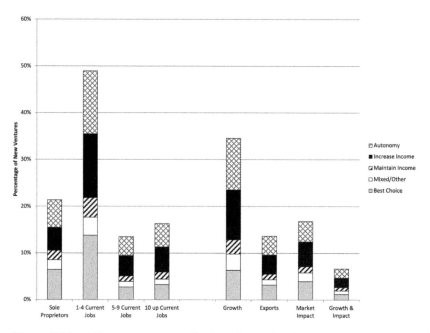

Figure 7.11   New venture contributions by motivation

The scope of activity in each Progressive Service-Industrial economy is presented in Table 7.3. Across all 34 countries with 19 million early-stage ventures, about 3 million are providing ten or more jobs, 7 million expect to grow to create ten or more jobs within five years, 2 million will be export oriented, 2.5 million expect to affect their markets, and 1 million expect to have both growth and a market impact.

While there is considerable variation among countries of different sizes, all economies are benefiting from the contributions of these new ventures. For example, new ventures are providing about 2 million new jobs in Argentina, at least 3 million in Russia, and 200,000 in Uruguay. New ventures expand employment in all countries.

STRUCTURAL ADAPTATION

The jobs produced by business creation reflect adjustments in the economic structure. Changes in the proportion of jobs in different sectors are presented as grey bars in Figure 7.12. The proportion of new jobs, shown in the black bars in Figure 7.12, exceed the proportion of existing jobs (shown in the white bars) for consumer-oriented activities.

Table 7.3   *New venture contributions in Progressive Service-Industrial economies*

Country	Current jobs: 10 or more	Growth: 10+ five-year jobs	Exports	Market impact	Growth and impact
Argentina*	175,000	538,000	77,000	221,000	78,000
Austria*	35,000	48,000	47,000	20,000	4,000
Bahamas*	2,000	5,000	2,000	3,000	1,000
Bahrain	11,000	23,000	10,000	11,000	5,000
Barbados*	1,000	3,000	2,000	2,000	400
Belarus	58,000	123,000	51,000	60,000	24,000
Brunei Darussalam	3,000	6,000	2,000	3,000	1,000
Bulgaria*	9,000	24,000	7,000	26,000	3,000
Chile*	155,000	483,000	107,000	265,000	106,000
Croatia*	20,000	45,000	28,000	25,000	10,000
Czechia*	58,000	118,000	43,000	70,000	30,000
Estonia*	6,000	20,000	9,000	9,000	3,000
Hungary*	29,000	77,000	35,000	26,000	10,000
Italy*	129,000	185,000	95,000	137,000	43,000
Kazakhstan*	154,000	436,000	99,000	132,000	76,000
Kuwait	28,000	60,000	25,000	29,000	12,000
Lithuania*	20,000	50,000	20,000	12,000	5,000
Malaysia*	51,000	115,000	66,000	188,000	16,000
Malta	3,000	5,000	2,000	3,000	1,000
Montenegro*	4,000	10,000	5,000	16,000	6,000

Country	Current jobs: 10 or more	Growth: 10+ five-year jobs	Exports	Market impact	Growth and impact
Oman	33,000	69,000	29,000	34,000	14,000
Palau	100	200	100	100	30
Poland*	156,000	541,000	136,000	82,000	32,000
Portugal*	35,000	75,000	46,000	33,000	7,000
Qatar*	51,000	62,000	22,000	40,000	24,000
Romania*	86,000	263,000	122,000	73,000	34,000
Russia*	336,000	1,131,000	96,000	270,000	106,000
Saudi Arabia*	364,000	476,000	256,000	339,000	142,000
Seychelles	600	1,000	500	600	200
Slovakia*	41,000	84,000	32,000	55,000	20,000
Slovenia*	6,000	14,000	8,000	5,000	2,000
Turkey*	711,000	1,556,000	344,000	203,000	101,000
United Arab Emirates*	127,000	196,000	109,000	81,000	56,000
Uruguay*	19,000	45,000	16,000	18,000	7,000
Total	2,916,700	6,887,200	1,948,600	2,491,700	979,630

Note: * Prevalence rates based on Global Entrepreneurship Monitor consolidated file (Reynolds, 2021). Estimates for other countries based on average values of countries with surveys.

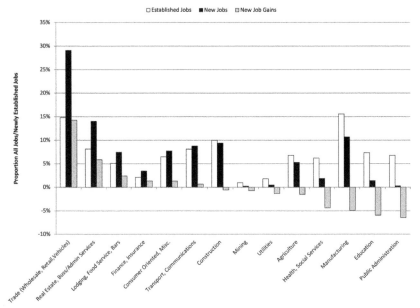

Figure 7.12   Established jobs, new jobs, and new job gains by sector

New jobs in trade (wholesale, retail) and lodging and food service are almost twice that of existing jobs in the same sectors (36% versus 20%). There is a larger proportion of new jobs in real estate and business services than among established jobs (14% versus 8%). There is an offsetting reduction in jobs in agriculture, manufacturing, and utilities; these sectors account for 24% of established jobs but 16% of new venture jobs. The low proportion of new jobs in education, public administration, and health and social services probably reflects the lack of business opportunities in sectors dominated by public organizations. For six sectors—finance and insurance, miscellaneous consumer services, transportation and communication (including media), construction, mining, and utilities—there is little difference in the proportion of existing and new jobs. New ventures in these sectors would reflect ongoing churning among established business sectors.

MAJOR CHALLENGES, OR WHY QUIT?

Problems encountered in managing businesses are reflected in the reasons for business terminations in Progressive Service-Industrial economies, summa-

Table 7.4   *Primary reason for a business termination*

Not profitable	29.7%
Family, personal issues	15.5%
Lack of financial support	12.1%
Other career opportunities	10.3%
Government regulations, taxes	7.5%
Sold business	6.5%
Retirement	4.0%
Pre-planned exit	3.2%
Major incident	2.4%
Miscellaneous other	8.8%
Total	100.0%

Note: Based on representative samples of 4,417 discontinued businesses in 20 Progressive Service-Industrial economies.

rized in Table 7.4. Almost half are associated with complications in managing the business. Most important is a lack of profit, followed by problems with financial support, and issues with government regulations and taxes. The lack of profit may reflect a shift in the market conditions, increased competition or reduced demand, and may reflect a shifting economic structure. Personal issues account for more than one-quarter of the terminations; most important are conflicts with family and personal responsibilities, cited in one-sixth of the cases. Other career opportunities, presumably more attractive, account for one-tenth and retirement for 1 in 25. Another one-tenth are related to the disposition of the venture, including a sale of the venture or a pre-planned exit. Miscellaneous other factors are responsible for the remaining one-tenth.

There is, then, no single problem that, if solved, would increase firm survival. Efforts to adjust public programs, simplifying regulations or reducing taxes, are unlikely to improve survival for most of the firms.

OVERVIEW

For the 400 million working-age adults in 34 Progressive Service-Industrial economies:

- Business creation is pursued by one-tenth, about 34 million individuals.
- Men are more active than women and are about two-thirds of active business creators.

- Men and women with the more human capital are the more active. Those with the lowest level of human capital are one-third as active as those with the most resources.
- Working men and women with intermediate, high, and the highest human capital are over half of all business creators; one-fifth are working men and women with low or the lowest human capital.
- Three-fourths of those pursuing high-potential start-ups are working men and women with intermediate, high, or the highest human capital.
- Over half of business creators, men and women, hope for greater work autonomy or higher incomes, one-quarter have mixed motives, and one-quarter consider it their best work option.
- Three-quarters of new ventures expect to provide jobs for others, three-tenths expect to grow, one-tenth expect exports or an impact on their markets, and 1 in 20 expect both growth and impact.
- New firms are created in all sectors, but there is an emphasis in trade, real estate and business services, and lodging and food services.
- Three-tenths of business terminations reflect a lack of profit, one-quarter a response to family and personal issues or other career opportunities, and one-sixth issues with financial support.

The millions of business creators making contributions to economic growth have both advantages and challenges.

Potential business creators in Progressive Service-Industrial economies confront an economy where four-fifths of employment is in registered firms—businesses with an established presence in the economy. Not only are there a multitude of formal job opportunities, established firms dominate most economic sectors. New firms will have significant competition in many markets. On the other hand, a number of features minimize challenges found in less developed economies related to education and policies related to property rights and business registration.

Both potential business creators and their employees have a basic education. Literacy is universal and three-fourths of adults have completed secondary school.[9] Some may have completed a module on business creation or entre-preneurship during their training. There should be few problems attracting employees with minimal qualifications.

Initial working capital may be available from the start-up team, as even the lower third has a daily income of $50 and those in the upper third $200 or more. Financial support from social networks may be possible, as 5 in 100 adults have provided informal assistance.[10] While more than half of informal support is for family members or relatives, one-third of the recipients are friends or neighbors, and 1 in 17 is a stranger with a good idea.[11]

Domestic financial institutions provide about $30,000 in credit per person, slightly less than the annual GDP per person.[12] Formal bank loans may be available for many business creators. While there are some micro-loan programs in Progressive Service-Industrial economies for women and those in rural areas, they are not a major source of support. About 2 per 100 have micro-loans, with an average balance of $3,571.[13]

Many Progressive Service-Industrial countries have attempted to minimize the costs associated with business registration. Registration may require seven procedures, take two weeks to complete, and the cost (average of $2,025) is about one-twentieth of the average annual income.[14] Given that most of the economic activity occurs in registered businesses, most business creators consider registration worthwhile.

Complications associated with property registration are also reduced. The formal land administration provides broad geographic coverage and there is confidence in the record keeping.[15] Property registration may require five procedures, take five weeks to complete, and cost 3% of the value of the property. Access to legally recognized ownership facilitates securing asset-backed loans.

Those in Progressive Service-Industrial economies have good access to market and economic information. Governments are spending $23 per year per person on communication infrastructure each year. There are 140 mobile phones for each 100 citizens and four-fifths have internet access.[16] The amount of information is probably not a problem, access to and interpreting the relevant material can be an issue.

Even with all these challenges, from 5 to 15 of each 100 adults are involved in business creation. This low level of activity probably reflects the extent of the established labor market, where a wide range of careers is available with existing businesses. In addition, there is an extensive social safety net, reflected in the annual per capita investment of $2,200 for social protection programs. This is consistent with the strong support for secular-rational authority values, which emphasize collective responsibility for all.[17]

There is, however, mixed support for entrepreneurial careers, as one-third of adults do not consider business creation a good career choice or a route to social status. Perhaps less than half are aware of good business opportunities, know an active entrepreneur, or have confidence in their ability to engage in business creation; only one in six adults have a high potential for business creation. Two-fifths report that fear of failure would discourage them from pursuing business creation. On the other hand, only one-third think individuals should focus on survival, the majority emphasize or accept self-expression as a primary individual value. And business creation is a major route for career self-expression.[18]

Even though Progressive Service-Industrial economies have created a context that facilitates business creation, only one in ten adults are involved in business creation—and nine in ten are not.

NOTES

1.   Seliverstova and Somkova (2018, pp. 38–40).
2.   Based on Noon (1989, pp. 92–93), fictitious name.
3.   Details in Tables B.2 and B.3.
4.   Details in Table B.2.
5.   Details in Table B.2.
6.   Details in Tables B.1 and B.3.
7.   Details in Tables B.2 and B.4.
8.   Details in Tables B.1 and B.7.
9.   Details in Table B.3.
10. Respondents report informal investments over the previous three years and details on the most recent investment (Reynolds, 2021).
11. Details in Table B.4.
12. Details in Table B.5.
13. Details in Table B.4.
14. Details in Table B.3.
15. Details in Table B.4.
16. Details in Table B.4.
17. Details in Table B.2.
18. Details in Tables B.2 and B.4.
19. Because of missing data, Montenegro is not included.

APPENDIX: HUMAN CAPITAL SCALE DEVELOPMENT

The procedures described in the appendix to Chapter 4 were utilized to provide a human capital scale for the adult populations in Progressive Service-Industrial economies. The description of the five levels of human capital in Table 7A.1 reflects average samples of 15,407 in each of 25 countries, a total of 385,168 respondents.

The same procedures were followed to create descriptions of the human capital among 44,897 business creators in 24 Progressive Service-Industrial economies (an average of 1,871 per country) presented in Table 7A.2.[19]

Table 7A.1   Human capital in the adult population

Human capital category	Proportion	Household daily income				Educational attainment					
		$50.25	$100.50	$201.00	Total	None	1–11 years	High school degree	13–16 years	17–20 years	Total
Highest	17%			100%	100%				70%	30%	100%
High	23%		49%	51%	100%			51%	37%	11%	99%
Intermediate	27%	29%	50%	21%	100%	3%	18%	50%	23%	5%	99%
Low	21%	56%	44%		100%	6%	37%	56%			99%
Lowest	12%	100%			100%	22%	78%				100%
Total	100%										
Proportion		31%	34%	34%	99%	5%	22%	37%	28%	8%	100%

Note: Data based on representative samples of the adult population in 25 Progressive Service-Industrial economies.

Table 7A.2   *Human capital among business creators*

Human Capital Category	Proportion	Household income				Educational attainment					
		$50.25	$100.50	$201.00	Total	None	1–11 years	High school degree	13–16 years	17–20 years	Total
Highest	27%			100%	100%				76%	24%	100%
High	26%		43%	57%	100%			57%	35%	8%	100%
Intermediate	24%	27%	49%	24%	99%	6%	18%	49%	22%	5%	100%
Low	16%	57%	43%		100%	10%	33%	57%			100%
Lowest	7%	100%			100%	31%	69%				100%
Total	100%										
Proportion		23%	29%	48%	101%	5%	15%	35%	35%	10%	100%

8.   Knowledge-Service economies: Expertise and fulfilment

Sanae's grandmother was an in-house sewing consignee in South Korea. As both her parents worked outside their home she spent her childhood with her grandmother, learning sewing. Once Sanae completed vocational school she worked as a dental nurse for ten years until she got married. She became a mother and started an internet blog discussing childcare, which attracted a following. Baby carrying slings are popular with Japanese mothers, but they are awkward and unattractive when no child is involved. She designed a storage bag for the slings that was well received by her blog audience. In her 30s she created a new business for the manufacturing and distribution of baby carrying sling storage bags. Sanae now has 12 full time employees and outsources work to 20 contract sewing partners.[1]

When his railway worker dad moved to A Coruña, Spain in 1950, fourteen-year-old Amancio Ortega Gaona worked for a local shirtmaker and as a tailor's assistant, learning to make clothes by hand. He became the manager of a clothing store catering to the elite in his early twenties. In 1963, when 27, he founded a bathrobe business, Confecciones Goa, which used less expensive materials, more efficient production, and lower prices to attract customers. When 39, in 1975, he opened the first Zara store, featuring low price copies of popular, high-end fashions; these items were popular and more stores were opened in Spain. In the 1980's, now in his 40s, Ortega changed the design, manufacturing, and distribution process to reduce lead times and quickly react to new trends, which he called "instant fashions." The parent company, established in 1985 as Inditex, supervises a more advanced version with teams of designers, extensive use of information technology, and acquiring systematic feedback from customers. Zara stores worldwide have a hundred thousand employees and annual sales approaching US$20 billion.[2]

About a billion people live in 26 Knowledge-Service economies, 13% of the global population. This includes most of Western Europe, Anglo spinoffs (Australia, Canada, New Zealand, and the United States) as well as advanced Asian economies (Hong Kong, Japan, South Korea, and Singapore).[3] Four-fifths of the work are in consumer-oriented or knowledge-based sectors, one-fifth in industrial sectors, and 1 in 33 jobs are in farming, fishing, or forestry.

THE NATIONAL CONTEXT

Most of those in Knowledge-Service economies are sharing a good life. They have the highest level of human development, with an average life expectancy of 82 years, adults with 17 years of education, and annual per capita income of $46,500.[4] But the range in annual personal income is considerable, from $26,000 for Greece and Latvia to $87,000 for Singapore and $97,000 for Luxembourg.[5]

Nine-tenths (87%) are satisfied in the community in which they live, four-fifths feel safe outside at night, three-fifths have confidence in the judicial system, and half confidence in the national government. Four-fifths are satisfied with their standard of living and their freedom of choice. Three-fifths are satisfied with the educational institutions and three-fourths with the health-care system. About half consider the local labor market as good.[6] Three-fifths of adults embrace secular-rational authority values which emphasize a shared responsibility for collective well-being, and one-quarter would find them acceptable. About one in eight embrace the traditional authority values emphasizing obedience, the family, and self-reliance. Three-fifths support individual values of self-expression and one-quarter would be sympathetic. Only one-eighth prefer that individuals focus on economic survival.[7]

While government spending absorbs two-fifths of the annual GDP per capita, much is spent on the people. Health care is supported by annual expenditures of $4,435 per person, education at $2,612 per person, and programs providing social protection absorb $5,121 per person.[8]

CAREER OPTIONS

There are a wide range of established firms that provide attractive jobs with benefits. Four-fifths of all jobs are in established, registered firms and two-fifths are firms with more than 50 employees.[9] Between public and private programs nine-tenths can expect to have a pension in retirement.[10] Many of these jobs, however, will require specialized education, often graduate training, and may involve substantial investments of time and money. There may be social and family pressure to capitalize on this educational investment by working for an established organization.

There is mixed support for business creation. On one hand there is a cultural emphasis on personal self-expression and business creation provides a route for developing a unique, personalized career. Political leaders continually encourage business creation. There is often considerable public recognition and attention given to successful entrepreneurs. Many educational programs have modules emphasizing entrepreneurship. Public programs may facilitate access to resources. Regulations may be adjusted to minimize complications associated with formal registration of new firms, which takes an average of 7.1 days to complete 4.3 procedures and costs US$1,219, about 3% of annual income.[11]

Table 8.1   *Business creators in Knowledge-Service economies*

Country	Total population: 2018	15–64-year-old population: 2018	Total business creators	Business creators: men	Business creators: women
Australia	24,898,000	16,222,000	1,948,000	1,195,000	753,000
Belgium	11,482,000	7,366,000	313,000	212,000	101,000
Canada	37,075,000	24,802,000	2,924,000	1,770,000	1,154,000
Cyprus	1,189,000	826,000	85,000	56,000	29,000
Denmark	5,752,000	3,666,000	193,000	131,000	62,000
Finland	5,523,000	3,431,000	212,000	137,000	75,000
France	64,991,000	40,300,000	1,997,000	1,357,000	640,000
Germany	83,124,000	53,962,000	2,707,000	1,744,000	963,000
Greece	10,522,000	6,763,000	507,000	333,000	174,000
Hong Kong	7,372,000	5,250,000	304,000	209,000	95,000
Iceland	337,000	220,000	27,000	18,000	9,000
Ireland	4,819,000	3,119,000	259,000	179,000	80,000
Israel	8,382,000	5,037,000	417,000	267,000	150,000
Japan	127,202,000	75,974,000	2,696,000	1,834,000	862,000
Korea (South)	51,172,000	37,155,000	3,690,000	2,592,000	1,098,000
Latvia	1,928,000	1,233,000	131,000	87,000	44,000
Luxembourg	604,000	423,000	38,000	24,000	14,000
Netherlands	17,060,000	11,037,000	837,000	534,000	303,000
New Zealand	4,743,000	3,069,000	464,000	280,000	184,000
Norway	5,338,000	3,491,000	266,000	189,000	77,000

Country	Total population: 2018	15–64-year-old population: 2018	Total business creators	Business creators: men	Business creators: women
Singapore	5,757,000	4,391,000	313,000	200,000	113,000
Spain	46,693,000	30,796,000	1,933,000	1,177,000	756,000
Sweden	9,972,000	6,215,000	356,000	230,000	126,000
Switzerland	8,526,000	5,667,000	406,000	241,000	165,000
United Kingdom	67,142,000	42,921,000	3,051,000	2,044,000	1,007,000
United States	327,096,000	214,193,000	25,251,000	15,223,000	10,028,000
Total	938,699,000	607,529,000	51,325,000	32,263,000	19,062,000

Note: Prevalence rates based on Global Entrepreneurship Monitor consolidated file (Reynolds, 2021). Population estimates based on United Nations (2019b).

On the other hand, potential nascent entrepreneurs may not have a personal relationship with others involved in business creation. Less than two-fifths personally know an entrepreneur. General cultural support for entrepreneurship may be mixed—almost half of adults do not consider business creation a good career choice. Only two-fifths think they have the skill and knowledge to start a business. Two-fifths are discouraged from being involved by fear of failure—which may lead to embarrassment for themselves and their family.[12] As more than half of nascent ventures do not reach profitability, this is not unrealistic.[13]

The choice may be between an acceptable, predictable life in an established career and the uncertainty that business creation will be successful, rewarding, and respected.

HOW MUCH ACTIVITY?

Among the 600 million working-age adults about 51 million, or 8 in every 100, are actively involved in business creation. There is some variation, from 4 per 100 in Belgium and Japan to more than 10 per 100 in Australia, New Zealand, and the United States. The amount of business creation in Knowledge-Service

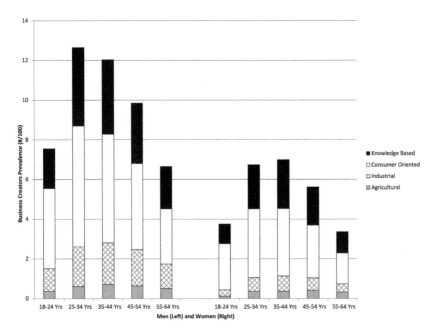

Figure 8.1   Business creation participation by age, gender, and sector

economies is presented in Table 8.1. The range is from 26,000 among the 220,000 working-age adults living in Iceland to 25 million among the 214 million in the United States. While about two-thirds are men, women are very much involved in all countries, with 10 million in the United States alone. Almost two-thirds of the activity involves very early-stage nascent enterprises.[14] Many, like teenage Ingvar selling door to door in rural Sweden, are not obvious. It was decades later when his efforts led to IKEA's international expansion and impact.

WHO PURSUES BUSINESS CREATION?

At every age, men are about twice as likely to pursue business creation as women, as shown in Figure 8.1. Participation, at 12 per 100, is highest among men 25 to 44 years of age and, at 7 per 100, among age-peer women. It is slightly lower among those 45 to 54 years old at 10 per 100 for men and 5 per 100 for women. Young adults, those 18 to 24 years old, and late career adults, 55 to 64 years old, are the least likely to pursue business creation.

Men and women of all ages pursue business creation in all sectors. About half are involved in consumer-oriented businesses and three-tenths in

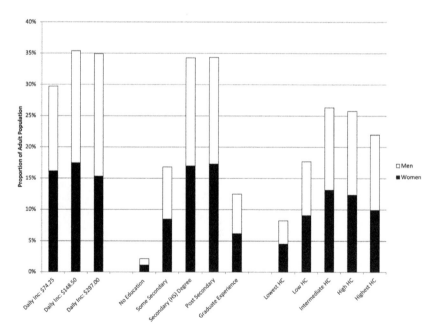

Figure 8.2   Population human capital

knowledge-based sectors. Men are slightly more likely to be involved in an industrial sector, women slightly more likely to pursue consumer-oriented or knowledge-based businesses. Young adults (under 25 years old) are less involved and senior adults (55 and older) slightly more involved in agricultural sectors.

Most adults in Knowledge-Service economies have significant human capital. They have funds and are well educated. As shown in Figure 8.2, even the three-tenths in the lowest category have a daily personal income of $74.25. Those in the highest income category have a daily personal income of $297.00. Over four-fifths have completed secondary school and almost half have post-secondary education. One in 8 have graduate or professional training and only 1 in 50 have no education. These assets are the basis for a five-category index of human capital, presented in Figure 8.2, the details of which are in the appendix to this chapter. With regards to human capital, there is gender equality in Knowledge-Service economies.

Participation for both men and women is greatest are among those with more human capital, as shown in Figure 8.3. Those with the highest levels are two and half times more active than those with the lowest levels of human capital. Those with the lowest human capital may not have the skills or

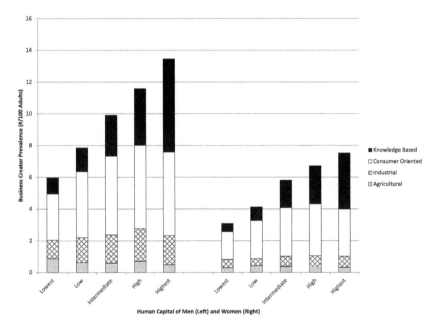

Figure 8.3   *Business creation participation by human capital, gender, and sector*

resources to proceed and are in countries with a wide range of established jobs and extensive social protection programs.

While the most popular sector for firm creation is consumer-oriented ventures, the emphasis on knowledge-based sectors increases among those with more human capital. More than two-fifths of men and women with the highest level of human capital are pursuing knowledge-based business creation. This reflects the match between educational attainment and the skills required for the knowledge-based sectors. This emphasis is offset by a reduced emphasis on business creation in agricultural sectors.

Those working have the highest level of participation as nascent entrepreneurs entering business creation, as shown in Figure 8.4. It is 14 per 100 for men and 8 per 100 for women. This is about three times the level of those not working. There is much less participation among those who are homemakers, students, or retired. Those from all labor force situations are involved in all market sectors.

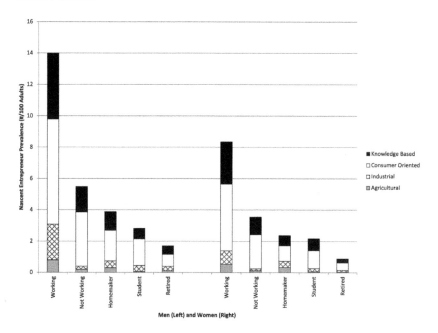

Figure 8.4   *Nascent entrepreneur participation by labor force status, gender, and sector*

In Knowledge-Service economies:

- Participation in business creation is modest, at 10 per 100 men and 6 per 100 women.
- Those most active are early-career adults, 25 to 44 years old, followed by mid-career adults, 45 to 54 years old.
- Men and women with the more human capital are more active in business creation, with a substantial emphasis on knowledge-based sectors.
- Those with full- or part-time work are three to four times as active in business creation as those with other roles in the labor force.

While business creators come from all segments of the adult population, younger people with human capital and jobs are the most likely to be involved.

WHO ARE THE BUSINESS CREATORS?

Men are about two-thirds of all active business creators, as shown in Figure 8.5. They are slightly more, at three-fourths, of the business creators in the industrial sector. In all sectors those 25 to 44 years old are over half of all active business creators. Those 45 to 54 years old are about one-fifth. Those 55 and older are one-fifth of those in the agricultural sector. There are slightly

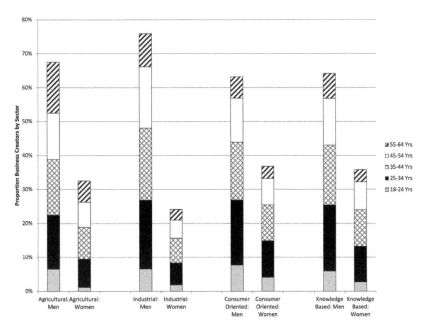

Figure 8.5   Age and gender proportions of business creators by sector

more young adults, 18 to 24 years old, involved in consumer-oriented sectors. There is much more activity in some sectors. About half of all business creation is in consumer-oriented sectors, one-third in knowledge-based sectors, one-seventh in industrial sectors, and 1 in 20 in agricultural sectors.[15]

There is much variation among business creators in the human capital they bring to the challenge. About two-fifths are from the highest third of their country's personal incomes, while one-fourth are from the lowest third. Over half have post-secondary education and almost one-fifth have university, graduate, or professional degrees. Only 1 in 100 have no educational experience. Four-fifths of business creators are in the three highest levels of human capital and only 1 in 20 in the lowest level. Clearly, most business creators bring above-average human capital to their initiatives.

The distribution of personal resources among business creators in different sectors is summarized in Figure 8.6. While there are differences in the amount of participation by men and women, no major gender differences are associated with human capital. There is little difference between the distributions for industrial and consumer-oriented sectors. But more of those in the agricultural sector have modest personal resources. A high proportion of those active in the

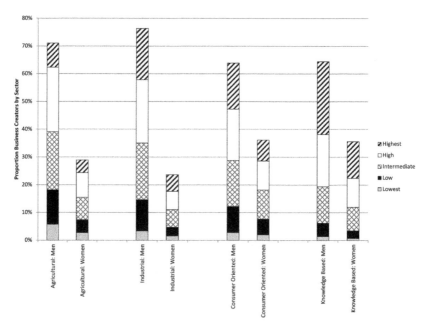

Figure 8.6   Human capital and gender proportions of business creators by sector

knowledge-based sectors have higher levels of personal resources; two in five come from high-income households and have advanced education.

Over four-fifths of nascent entrepreneurs working on pre-profit ventures in all sectors do so while working full or part time, presented in Figure 8.7. They are active in all sectors and there is little difference related to gender. Slightly more than 1 in 20 are not employed, and the remainder are homemakers, students, or retired. Slightly more women report they are homemakers as they pursue business creation, but they are still a small minority of active nascent entrepreneurs.

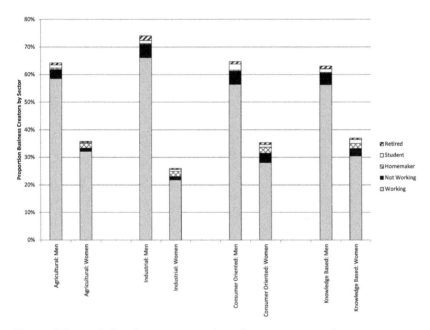

Figure 8.7   *Labor force status and gender proportions of nascent entrepreneurs by sector*

About three-fifths of the 51 million business creators in Knowledge-Service economies are attracted to a business opportunity. One-third because it may provide greater work autonomy and one-fifth expect an increase in their income. A small proportion hope for a more stable source of income. Slightly less than a fifth consider it their best choice for work and one-fifth have mixed motives. The range of motivations is similar for men and women.

There is a relationship between the amount of human capital and the motivation for pursuing business creation, presented in Figure 8.8. Among those with the highest human capital seven-tenths are pursuing a business opportunity and the dominant objective is to increase work autonomy. Among those with the lowest human capital about half are pursuing a business opportunity and more than a third consider this their best choice for work. The patterns are similar for men and women.

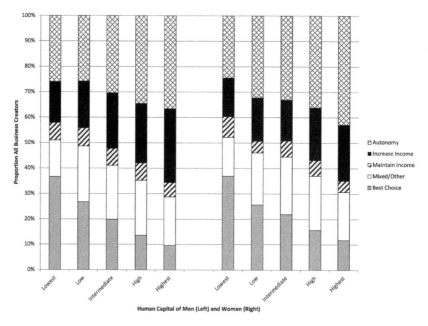

*Figure 8.8	Business creator motivation by human capital and gender*

Over four-fifths of all those involved in business creation have intermediate, high, or the highest levels of human capital, presented in Figure 8.9. Those with the highest level of human capital, with post-secondary education, are three-tenths of the total. Women are one-third of these business creators. Those with the lowest level of human capital, who have not completed secondary school, are 1 in 25 of all business creators. In Knowledge-Service economies, those with above-average personal resources, education, and income are the majority of business creators.

Among the community of business creators in Knowledge-Service economies:

- About two thirds are men, one-third are women.
- More than half are 25 to 44 years old.
- They are active in all sectors, but with an emphasis on consumer-oriented businesses.

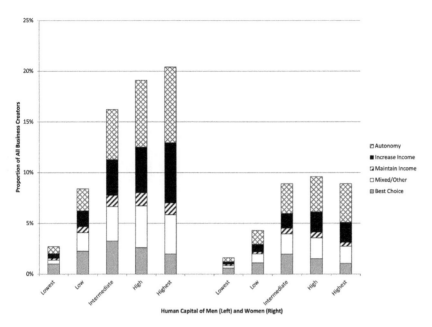

*Figure 8.9   Proportion of business creators by motivation, human
                   capital, and gender*

• Four-fifths are working full or part time as they enter business creation.
• Four-fifths have intermediate, high, or the highest level of human capital;
  a very small proportion have the lowest level.
• Those with more human capital are pursuing business opportunities to
  increase work autonomy, grow their income, or create more stable income.

Business creators are young and well prepared to make economic contributions with new firms.

NEW VENTURES AND CONTRIBUTIONS

The 51 million business creators in 26 Knowledge-Service economies are
involved with 29 million early-stage ventures.[16] As shown in Table 8.2, about
two-thirds or 18 million would be considered pre-profit nascent initiatives and
one-third or 11 million are new firms. The range is substantial, from 11,000 in
Iceland to 14 million in the United States.

   The average prevalence of the new ventures is about 5 per 100 adults. The proportion making economic contributions is presented for 26 Knowledge-Service
economies in Figure 8.10. Seven-tenths are creating jobs. Almost half are

Table 8.2   *Pre-profit ventures and new firms in Knowledge-Service economies*

Country	15–64-year-old population	Total early-stage ventures	Pre-profit ventures	New firms
Australia	16,222,000	1,112,000	621,000	491,000
Belgium	7,366,000	167,000	114,000	53,000
Canada	24,802,000	1,587,000	1,114,000	473,000
Cyprus	826,000	44,000	30,000	14,000
Denmark	3,666,000	103,000	53,000	50,000
Finland	3,431,000	108,000	62,000	46,000
France	40,300,000	1,079,000	806,000	273,000
Germany	53,962,000	1,572,000	969,000	603,000
Greece	6,763,000	306,000	190,000	116,000
Hong Kong	5,250,000	120,000	66,000	54,000
Iceland	220,000	11,000	7,000	4,000
Ireland	3,119,000	149,000	91,000	58,000
Israel	5,037,000	229,000	147,000	82,000
Japan	75,974,000	1,379,000	795,000	584,000
Korea (South)	37,155,000	2,504,000	1,141,000	1,363,000
Latvia	1,233,000	69,000	41,000	28,000
Luxembourg	423,000	20,000	16,000	4,000
Netherlands	11,037,000	506,000	274,000	232,000
New Zealand	3,069,000	262,000	150,000	112,000
Norway	3,491,000	126,000	67,000	59,000

Country	15–64-year-old population	Total early-stage ventures	Pre-profit ventures	New firms
Singapore	4,391,000	139,000	80,000	59,000
Spain	30,796,000	1,055,000	564,000	491,000
Sweden	6,215,000	185,000	116,000	69,000
Switzerland	5,667,000	225,000	124,000	101,000
United Kingdom	42,921,000	1,733,000	991,000	742,000
United States	214,193,000	14,017,000	9,544,000	4,473,000
Total	607,529,000	28,807,000	18,173,000	10,634,000

Note: Prevalence rates based on Global Entrepreneurship Monitor consolidated file (Reynolds, 2021). Population estimates based on United Nations (2019b).

providing one to four jobs, 1 in 9 five to nine jobs, and 1 in 8 ten or more jobs. Three-tenths are sole proprietorships, providing work only for the owners.

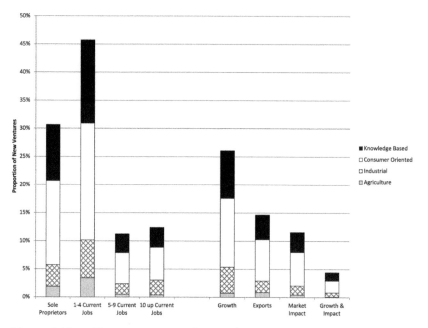

Figure 8.10   New venture contributions by sector

As can be seen in Figure 8.10, one-fourth expect growth that will require ten or more employees in the next five years. About 1 in 7 are delivering goods or services to those that live outside their country, a contribution to exports. One in 8 consider that they have made a major or significant impact on their markets providing new or innovative goods or services. One in 25 expect both growth and an impact on their markets. These contributions occur in all economic sectors, although about half are in consumer-oriented and three-tenths in knowledge-based sectors.

Over three-fourths of the ventures making contributions reflect the pursuit of business opportunities, shown in Figure 8.11. Initiatives are pursued to achieve greater autonomy, more income, or maintain current income. About 1 in 7 reflect efforts to pursue the best choices that were available to the nascent entrepreneurs. The proportion pursuing their best choices is somewhat higher, at one-fifth, for sole proprietorships or new ventures providing one to four new jobs. All motivations are associated with new ventures across a wide range of contributions.

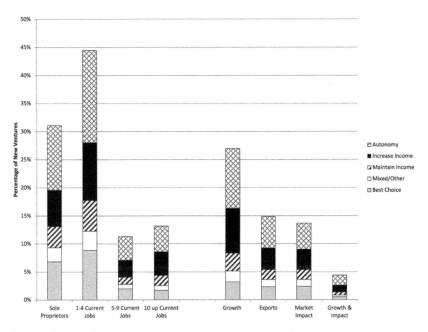

Figure 8.11   New venture contributions by motivation

The number of ventures making the different contributions for the 26 Knowledge-Service economies is presented in Table 8.3. For example, 100,000 early-stage ventures are providing ten or more jobs in France, which would be over a million jobs. Across the 26 countries, with 600 million in the labor force, the job contribution of new firms would probably be more than 30 million, a significant contribution. As many are associated with pre-profit nascent ventures, the jobs may be informal and unregistered and will not show up in administrative statistics until the venture is registered or reaches profitability and pays taxes. While many of these jobs will be short term, the ongoing flow of new ventures provides a constant source of new jobs. Many of these ventures will be significant job creators, as 1 in 4 expect to—or hope to—create at least ten jobs in the next five years.

While the majority are expecting to compete with established products or services, some anticipate having an impact on the markets. More than one-tenth, over 3 million, are providing innovations that will change the markets in which they compete. A significant minority, again one-tenth, anticipate that half or more of their sales will be exports. This proportion is generally larger in countries with small markets, where firm growth is dependent on exports. Over a million will be high-potential ventures, those expecting

Table 8.3   *New venture contributions in Knowledge-Service economies*

Country	Current jobs: 10 or more	Growth	Exports	Market impact	Growth and impact
Australia	101,000	300,000	110,000	150,000	52,000
Belgium	17,000	34,000	34,000	32,000	7,000
Canada	243,000	462,000	272,000	186,000	68,000
Cyprus	7,000	9,000	7,000	14,000	3,000
Denmark	13,000	29,000	20,000	11,000	4,000
Finland	6,000	16,000	10,000	11,000	2,000
France	99,000	238,000	154,000	189,000	63,000
Germany	210,000	372,000	175,000	138,000	52,000
Greece	23,000	35,000	38,000	67,000	10,000
Hong Kong	42,000	56,000	29,000	10,000	5,000
Iceland	2,000	4,000	2,000	2,000	1,000
Ireland	17,000	46,000	25,000	14,000	7,000
Israel	52,000	81,000	44,000	34,000	16,000
Japan	214,000	469,000	103,000	141,000	61,000
Korea (South)	184,000	625,000	224,000	208,000	92,000
Latvia	14,000	35,000	14,000	4,000	3,000
Luxembourg	3,000	5,000	5,000	4,000	1,000
Netherlands	47,000	86,000	50,000	41,000	10,000
New Zealand	25,000	62,000	40,000	38,000	12,000
Norway	14,000	26,000	14,000	17,000	5,000
Singapore	29,000	58,000	39,000	25,000	10,000

Country	Current jobs: 10 or more	Growth	Exports	Market impact	Growth and impact
Spain	63,000	129,000	91,000	90,000	13,000
Sweden	13,000	35,000	23,000	18,000	6,000
Switzerland	24,000	49,000	34,000	23,000	8,000
United Kingdom	159,000	450,000	215,000	559,000	154,000
United States	1,936,000	4,515,000	1,215,000	1,288,000	550,000
Total	3,557,000	8,226,000	2,987,000	3,314,000	1,215,000

Note: Prevalence rates based on Global Entrepreneurship Monitor consolidated file (Reynolds, 2021).

both growth and a market impact. While all countries have high-potential new ventures, almost half are in the largest country, the United States.

All Knowledge-Service economies benefit from new firm contributions to jobs, innovations, and exports.

STRUCTURAL ADAPTATION

In advanced economies, which has been the focus of much scholarly interest, there is little evidence of major shifts in the economic structure. The changes in the proportion of jobs in each sector is represented by the grey bars in Figure 8.12. It reflects the differences between new jobs (black bars) and established jobs (white bars).

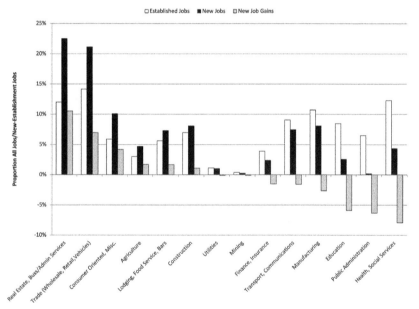

Note: Details in Tables B.1 and B.7. Current jobs, new jobs, and new job gains represent averages across 26 Knowledge-Service economies.

Figure 8.12   Established jobs, new jobs, and new job gains by sector

The largest expansion is among new jobs in real estate and business ser-vices, from 12% to 23%, a shift of 11%. This is similar to the shifts in two consumer-oriented sectors, trade and miscellaneous consumer oriented, from 20% to 31%, another shift of 11%. The major decreases in job shares, from

29% to 7%, are in three sectors dominated by public institutions: education, public administration, and health and social services. There are modest reductions in share of jobs in finance and insurance, transportation and communications, and manufacturing. There are small or negligible shifts associated with the churning in five sectors including agriculture; lodging, food service, and bars; construction; utilities; and mining.

Most new firm creation in Knowledge-Service economies is within established market sectors. Business creators are active in the sectors with low barriers to entry and where they have experience, commercial networks, and are confident about pursuing a business opportunity. This is consistent with more detailed assessments in the United States, which indicates that the distribution of new firms across 20 sectors is almost identical to that of established firms.[17]

MAJOR CHALLENGES, OR WHY QUIT?

Challenges associated with business creation and management are reflected in the reasons given for business terminations, presented in Table 8.4. Three complications account for over half of all terminations: inability to achieve profitability, family or personal issues that complicated business management, and other, presumably more attractive, career opportunities.

Table 8.4   Primary reason for a business termination

Not profitable	28.4%
Family, personal issues	16.1%
Other career opportunities	11.5%
Lack of financial support	8.3%
Government regulations, taxes	7.3%
Sold business	6.4%
Retirement	5.1%
Pre-planned exit	5.0%
Major incident	3.0%
Miscellaneous other	8.7%
Total	100.0%

Note: Based on representative samples of 3,357 discontinued businesses in 20 Knowledge-Service economies.

Two factors that receive most of the attention of policy makers are mentioned by 1 in 6, lack of financial support and issues with government regulations and taxes. A variety of other factors are mentioned in about one-fourth of the terminations, such as sale of the business, retirement, a pre-planned exit, or a major incident.

The major problem for business survival, then, is making enough money to justify continuing the business followed by personal challenges with family issues and alternative career opportunities. Improved financial support and fewer government complications can contribute to new firm survival but this is not relevant to the major challenges.

OVERVIEW

Among the 600 million in 26 Knowledge-Service economies:

- One in 12, or 51 million, are involved in business creation.
- Men are more active than women and are about two-thirds of active business creators.
- Early-career adults, 25 to 44 years old, are the most active in firm creation.
- Men and women with the highest levels of human capital are the most active; their participation is two and half times greater than those with the least human capital.
- Over three-fifths of business creators are involved to increase work autonomy or income, less than one-fifth consider it their best choice for work, and one-fifth have mixed motives.
- Working men and women are over four-fifths of business creators.
- One in 400 adults are pursuing a high-potential new venture; over three-fourths are men and women with intermediate, high, or the highest human capital.
- Seven-tenths of new firms expect to provide jobs for others, one-quarter anticipate growth, one-tenth exports, one-tenth a market impact, and one in twenty growth and a market impact.
- There is more activity in consumer-oriented sectors, but most firm creation reflects churning in established sectors.
- One-quarter of business terminations reflect a lack of profit and another quarter family or personal issues or other career opportunities. One in six are responding to a lack of financial support or issues with government regulations and taxes.

Business creation is occurring in a distinctive context provided by Knowledge-Service economies.

Knowledge-Service economies have the most extensive economic infrastructure and advanced business populations. Four-fifths of jobs are in registered firms, which dominate all market segments. While creating new market sectors is a major opportunity for business creation, they are rare events—although they attract considerable media attention. Most major institutions make an effort to facilitate new firm creation with few barriers and considerable support.

All adults are well educated. Literacy is universal, nine-tenths of the adults have completed secondary school, and two-fifths have post-secondary education. Both potential business creators and their employees have a basic education.[18] Modules on business creation or entrepreneurship are widely available in post-secondary programs. There should be few problems attracting employees with minimal qualifications, although shortages in specialized skills may exist.

Most adults have some personal resources to cover the initial costs of business creation; those in the lowest tertile have a daily income of $75 and those in the upper tertile $300 or more. There is some limited financial support from social networks, 1 in 25 adults are informal business angels.[19] Almost half of informal support is provided to family members or relatives, two-fifths to work colleagues, friends, or neighbors, and one-sixth to strangers with a good idea and others.[20] Seeking support from the local business community can be a viable, if time-consuming, option.

Domestic financial institutions are a major source of assistance, providing almost $80,000 in credit per person, almost twice the annual GDP per person.[21] Formal bank loans may be available for many business creators. Micro-loan programs, such as those providing modest support to women in rural areas of less developed economies, do not have a major presence.

Efforts to encourage business creation in Knowledge-Service economies has led to the simplification of registration procedures. It may take four procedures completed in one week and cost $1,000 to formally register a business; this is about 3% of the annual GDP per capita.[22] This may be why such a large proportion of firms are "on the books."

Complications associated with property registration are also minimized. The ownership of all land is legally registered and reflected in detailed record keeping.[23] Property registration may require five procedures, take three weeks to complete, and cost 5% of the value of the property. Land can be a major source of collateral for asset-backed loans.

Access to market and economic information is not a problem in Knowledge-Service economies. Nine-tenths have internet access and there are 126 mobile phones for each 100 citizens. Governments spend an average of $17 per person on communication infrastructure each year.[24] Information overload, not access, may be the major problem.

An extensive set of social protection programs, supported by $5,121 per year for each person, helps to support those not fully engaged with the economy. This reflects the strong support for secular rational authority values, which emphasize collective responsibility for the well-being of all. Those that choose not to take advantage of the jobs in established work organizations can expect some support while they sort out their career plans.

Few adults are enthusiastic about entrepreneurial careers; only three-tenths would provide strong support. More than a third do not consider it a good career choice, a source of status, or reflecting good media coverage. Only about 1 in 8 adults would be well prepared for business creation: those that see opportunities, know other entrepreneurs, and are confident in their own capacity to start a business. And two-fifths are discouraged by a fear of failure.

While Knowledge-Service economies have done the most to encourage business creation, they have the least amount of participation among a well-educated adult population. Even with all this support, only 5 to 12 per 100 adults are involved in business creation, an average of 8 per 100.

NOTES

1.   Kato and Miyake (2015).
2.   Based on Hansen (2012) and Wikipedia (2021a, 2021c).
3.   Taiwan is omitted because it is not included in the data supporting the United Nations 2019 Human Development Report (2019b).
4.   Details in Table B.2.
5.   World Economic Outlook (October 2019) adjusted for purchasing power parity.
6.   Details in Table B.1.
7.   Details in Table B.3.
8.   Details in Table B.1.
9.   Details in Table B.1.
10. Details in Table B.2.
11. Details in Table B.3.
12. Details in Table B.3.
13. Reynolds (2018, p. 130, figure 11.2).
14. National details in Table 8.3.
15. Details in Table B.6.
16. This reflects adjustments to account for average start-up team size.
17. Reynolds and Curtin (2009a, p. 195, table 7.8).
18. Details in Table B.3.
19. Respondents report informal investments over the previous three years and details on the most recent investment (Reynolds, 2021).
20. Details in Table B.4.
21. Details in Table B.5.
22. Details in Table B.3.
23. Details in Table B.4.
24. Details in Table B.4.

APPENDIX: PERSONAL HUMAN CAPITAL

The procedures described in Appendix A were utilized to create the human capital scale for Knowledge-Service adults. The results, based on average national samples of 29,032 in 26 countries, a total of 754,845 respondents, are presented in Table 8A.1.

The same procedures were followed to create descriptions of the human capital among 65,051 business creators in 26 Knowledge-Service economies (an average of 2,501 per country) provided in Table 8A.2. They have a slightly higher level of human capital than the adult population.

Table 8A.1   Human capital in the adult population

Human capital category	Proportion	Personal daily income				Educational attainment					
		$74.25	$148.50	$297.00	Total	None	1–11 years	High school degree	13–16 years	17–20 years	Total
Highest	22%			100%	100%				68%	32%	100%
High	26%		63%	37%	100%			37%	47%	16%	99%
Intermediate	26%	38%	48%	14%	100%	1%	13%	48%	29%	9%	99%
Low	18%	64%	36%		100%	4%	32%	64%			99%
Lowest	8%	100%			100%	16%	84%				100%
Total	100%										
Proportion		30%	35%	35%	100%	2%	16%	34%	35%	13%	100%

Note: Data based on representative samples of the adult population in 26 Knowledge-Service economies.

Table 8A.2   Human capital among business creators

Human capital category	Proportion	Personal daily income					Educational attainment					
		$74.25	$148.50	$297.00	Total	None	1–11 years	High school degree	13–16 years	17–20 years	Total	
Highest	27%			100%	100%				66%	34%	100%	
High	27%		60%	40%	100%			40%	42%	17%	99%	
Intermediate	26%	42%	39%	18%	99%	1%	18%	39%	27%	14%	99%	
Low	14%	59%	41%		100%	2%	39%	59%			100%	
Lowest	6%	100%			100%	7%	93%				100%	
Total	100%											
Proportion		25%	32%	43%	101%	1%	15%	30%	35%	18%	100%	

9. Transitions: Continuity and adaptation

Business creation is an important career option and makes a major contribution to economies at all stages of development. There are, however, similarities and differences in business creation between Subsistence economies emphasizing immediate survival and the most advanced countries emphasizing knowledge and service sectors. Comparison of activity across the stages of development reflects an evolution including shifts in those entering business creation, the character and motivation of the entrepreneur sector, complications that lead to business terminations, and the contributions and impact of the new ventures.

There is much anecdotal information about Subsistence economies—the economic life of indigenous people—which can provide informed estimates regarding many features of their work specialization and business creation. More precise comparisons, however, are possible for five stages of development, from Agriculture to Knowledge-Service economies.

PARTICIPATION IN BUSINESS CREATION

The dramatic decline in participation in business creation is the most striking feature associated with economic development. At the earliest stage of development, represented by the Subsistence economies of indigenous people, small-scale business activities are universal. All men and women are active with small businesses and many have several activities under way at the same time; serial and multi-tasking entrepreneurs are quite common.

National economies, where more precise information is available, show a consistent decline in participation with economic development. Participation is three times higher, 27 per 100, in Agricultural economies than in Knowledge-Service economies, at 8 per 100. The range and average values are presented in Figure 9.1. While there is considerable diversity in participation at each stage of development, from 15 to 39 per 100 in Agricultural economies and 5 to 12 per 100 in Knowledge-Service economies, the average values represent a consistent decline in participation.[1]

This decline is present for both men and women and all age groups, shown in Figure 9.2. At all stages of development participation it is greatest among those 25 to 44 years old and less among young adults, 18 to 24 years old, and senior adults, 55 to 64 years old. The only exception is a slight uptick among senior men in Agricultural economies. This would suggest that the impact of

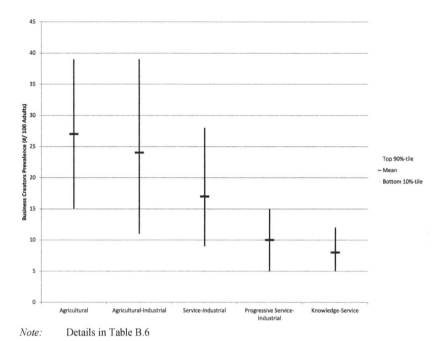

Note: Details in Table B.6

Figure 9.1   *Business creation participation by economic development*

personal life-course trajectories, whereby younger adults decide to pursue firm creation, is similar at all stages of economic development. Those old enough to have some work experience and young enough to have energy and optimism are the most active business creators.

Women are less likely to pursue business creation in more advanced economies. In Agricultural economies 24 per 100 women from 25 to 44 years old are involved in business creation, slightly less than the 30 per 100 for age-peer men. Compared to men, both the absolute and relative level of activity decline at later stages of economic development. In the most advanced Knowledge-Service economies 6 per 100 women 25 to 44 years old are involved in business creation, compared to 10 per 100 age-peer men. The reduction in participation by women may reflect greater expansion of job opportunities, mid-life child-rearing responsibilities, and a more conservative approach to work careers.

The reduced participation by the youngest adults, 18 to 24 years old, in more advanced societies may reflect participation in post-secondary education. Reduced participation by older adults, 55 to 64 years old, in advanced societies

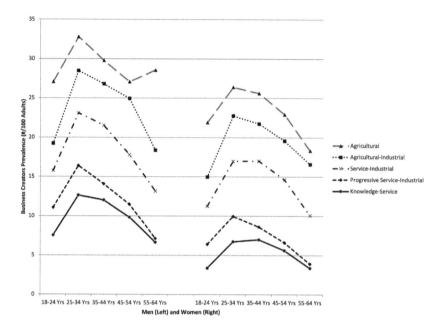

Figure 9.2   *Business creation participation by age, gender, and economic development*

may reflect greater access to retirement benefits. While 13% have access to pensions in Agricultural economies, it is 80% in Progressive Service-Industrial and 92% in Knowledge-Service economies.[2]

Participation associated with different levels of human capital, as shown in Figure 9.3, are broadly similar. For both men and women those with more human capital are more likely to be involved. There are, however, some differences. In Agricultural and Agricultural-Industrial economies there is less differences between those with the lowest and highest levels of human capital and, particularly among women, the participation is similar among those with low, intermediate, high, and the highest levels of human capital. This is contrast with the striking increased participation associated with more human capital in Service-Industrial, Progressive Service-Industrial, and Knowledge-Service economies.

In all stages of economic development those working full or part time are, by far, the most active in business creation, as shown in Figure 9.4. Working men and women are three to ten times more likely to enter business creation than those not working, homemakers, students, or retired. The patterns are almost the same regardless of the stage of economic development. The one exception

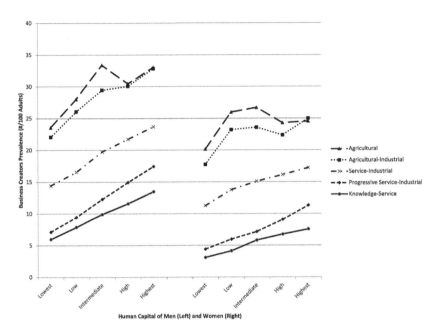

Figure 9.3   *Business creation participation by human capital, gender,*
and economic development

is a high level of activity among retired men in Agricultural economies. This
increased level of participation is also present among men 55 to 64 years old
in Agricultural economies. This may reflect the lack of support for retirees, as
87% of those in Agriculture economies have no pension.[3]

This suggests that across all stages of economic development, the effects
of labor force participation on entering business creation are much the same.
Those working see good opportunities, are confident in their business skills,
and their social milieu encourages entrepreneurial careers.

The similarity of patterns across the five levels of economic development is
striking, virtually all lines are parallel, varying only by the level of participation.[4] The most important aspects of participation in business creation in more
advanced stages of economies are:

- A decline in the tendency to become involved.
- A reduction in the relative participation by women.
- Highest level of activity among those 25–44 years old at all stages of
  development.
- Reduction in the absolute and relative participation by young adults, 18 to
  24 years old.

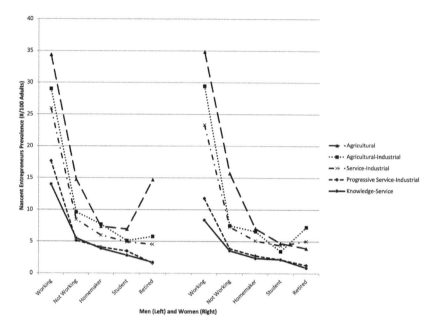

Figure 9.4   *Nascent entrepreneur participation by labor force status,*
                 gender, and economic development

• The highest levels of business creation among those with the highest levels
  of human capital at all stages of economic development.
• Major reduction in absolute and relative participation by those with the
  lowest levels of human capital.
• Most business creators get involved while they have full- or part-time
  work.

Clearly, economic development is associated with shifts in participation in
business creation.

There are striking similarities among of these three indicators of participation. The relation to age and gender in Figure 9.2, human capital and gender
in Figure 9.3, and working activity in Figure 9.4 indicate similar patterns for
all stages of economic development. The lines representing participation are
parallel across all stages of development. This would suggest that factors
affecting participation in business creation—like marriage or parenting—are
basic social processes. The only major difference is in the level of activity.

WHO ARE THE BUSINESS CREATORS?

In Subsistence economies, where virtually all adults have some business activity, there is little difference between business creators and the general population. Everybody, or almost everybody, is involved. But in national economies, particularly those at more advanced stages, business creators are a distinctive subset. They are not a representative cross-section of the general population.

The age and gender distribution among active business creators is broadly similar at all stages of economic development, presented in Figure 9.5. In this presentation the total for each stage of economic development equals 100%. Women are, however, a smaller proportion of business creators in more advanced economies. They are over two-fifths of business creators in Agricultural economies but one-third in Knowledge-Service economies.

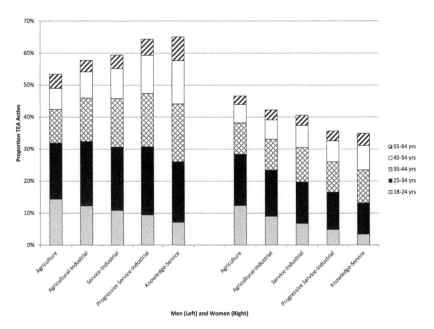

Figure 9.5   *Business creator proportions by age, gender, and economic development*

There is much similarity associated with age. In all economies early-career adults, men and women from 25 to 44 years old, are half of all business creators. A larger proportion of young adults are active in economies at earlier stages of development. This reflects countries with a larger proportion of young adults and a higher tendency to pursue business creation, shown in Figure 9.2. Those 18 to 24 years old are one-fourth of business creators in Agricultural economies. This proportion declines until it is one in ten in Knowledge-Service economies, countries where a large proportion of young adults are in post-secondary education. The proportion of older adults, those 45 to 64 years old, among business creators is greater in more advanced economies. This reflects, in part, the larger proportion of older adults in the population. They are about one-fifth of those active in business creation in Agricultural economies but one-third in Knowledge-Service economies. A slightly larger proportion of senior business creators are men in Knowledge-Service economies.

The proportion of business creators with different levels of human capital varies across stages of economic development. The proportion of business creators, men and women, with high and the highest levels of human capital is greater in Progressive Service-Industrial and Knowledge-Service economies, as shown in Figure 9.6.

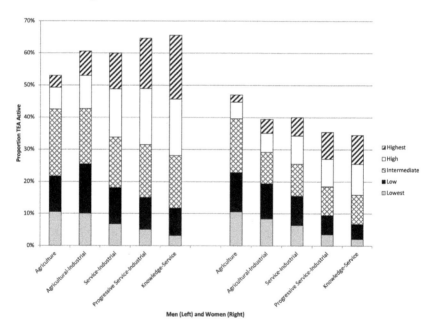

Figure 9.6   *Business creator proportions by human capital, gender, and economic development*

These differences are considerable. Less than one-fifth of business creators in Agricultural economies have high or the highest levels of human capital; this increases to over one half of those in Progressive Service-Industrial or

Knowledge-Service economies. Business creators with the low or lowest levels of human capital are over two-fifths of those in Agricultural economies to less than one-fifth in Knowledge-Service economies. The patterns are similar for both men and women. This reflects both the distribution of human capital in the adult population as well as differences in the pursuit of business creation by those with different levels of human capital.

In economies at all stages of development, four-fifths are working full or part time as they enter business creation as nascent entrepreneurs, reflected in Figure 9.7. This is slightly higher in Progressive Service-Industrial and Knowledge-Service economies. Those not working, who would be considered unemployed, are the next largest, though a small proportion of the total. The patterns, which are similar for men and women, are almost identical across stages of economic development. The only gender difference is a slightly higher proportion of women homemakers involved in business creation.

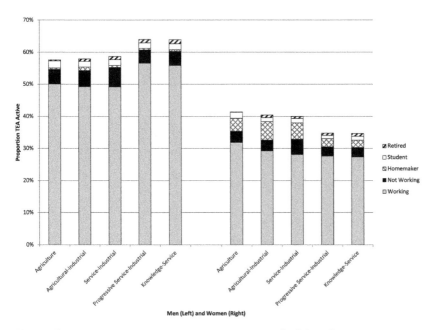

Figure 9.7   *Nascent entrepreneur proportions by labor force status,*
                 gender, and economic development

There are some subtle shifts in business creator motivations in economies at different stages of development, shown in Figure 9.8. About half of those in Agricultural, Agricultural-Industrial, and Service-Industrial economies are pursuing business opportunities to increase autonomy, income, or income stability. Three-tenths consider business creation their best choice for participating in the economy. In Knowledge-Service economies, three-fifths are pursuing a business opportunity and one-sixth consider business creation their best choice. Not a dramatic shift but one reflecting the greater human capital among business creators in more developed economies. The patterns for men and women, are similar. The proportion considering business creation their best work option declines in more advanced economies, reflecting the greater presence of jobs in established, registered businesses.

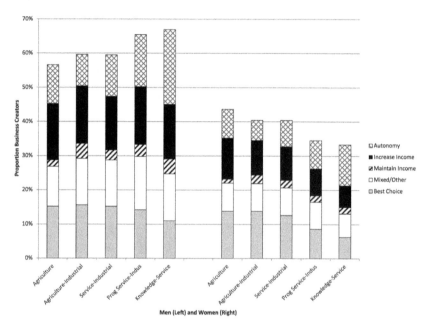

Figure 9.8   *Business creator motivation by gender and economic development*

There are some differences among those pursuing business creation, the entrepreneurial sector, by stage of economic development.

•   The proportion that are men increase from 57% in Agricultural economies to 66% in Knowledge-Service economies.
•   At all stages of economic development early-career men and women, 25 to 44 years old, are half of all business creators.
•   Those with intermediate levels of human capital are the majority of business creators at all stages of economic development. In Progressive Service-Industrial and Knowledge-Service economies those with the

highest level of human capital are one-quarter of the total; those with the lowest levels of human capital are 1 in 20.
• At all stages of economic development, over four-fifths are involved in work as they pursue business creation.
• The proportion pursuing business creation for an opportunity for more work autonomy, greater income, or to maintain their current income increases with economic development, from three-fifths to three-fourths. The proportion that considers business creation their best choice declines from one-third to one-sixth.

BUSINESS CHALLENGES

One of the distinctive features of subsistence business creation is the consistent reports of new ventures that are not able to continue because the customers would not pay for goods or services. Relatives, neighbors, and friends often feel that prior social exchanges with the businessperson make them a creditor, so the goods or services are considered compensation for a previous contribution. While the reason for a lack of profit may be distinctive in indigenous societies, the outcome is the same. The business cannot be sustained.

The dominant reason for a business termination in national economies at all stages of economic development is the inability to make a profit, or at least an acceptable profit. As shown in Figure 9.9, lack of profit is mentioned by one-quarter to one-third of those quitting a business. Other business-related issues are complications with attracting financial support and the challenge of dealing with government taxes and regulations. Across all stages of economic development, business-related issues are associated with about one-half of all business terminations.

Personal and family issues—dealing with complications in personal life or the attraction of other career opportunities—account for one-fifth to one-quarter of the terminations. The proportion leaving for other career options is higher in more advanced economies, from 3% to 12% of the terminations. This reflects both the increasing prevalence of established jobs and the higher level of human capital among business creators in more advanced economies. Disengagement reflecting a business sale, retirement, or a pre-planned exit are slightly higher among those in more advanced economies. A wide range of miscellaneous complications or a major incident leading to a termination are more prevalent in Agricultural economies, but one-tenth among those in other stages of economic development.

Overall, there is a striking similarity in the challenges confronted across all stages of economic development. Lack of profit and family and personal issues are universal problems. Locating financial support and dealing with

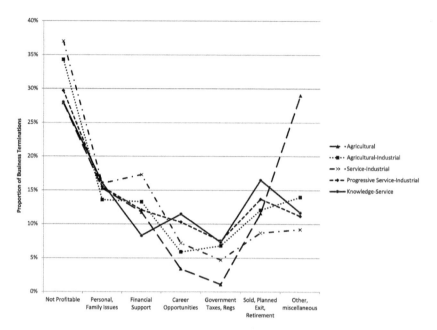

Figure 9.9   *Business termination issues by economic development*

government requirements are mentioned as a primary issue by one-fifth of those terminating a business.

NEW VENTURE IMPACT: ECONOMIC GROWTH

New ventures contribute to their economies through job creation, potential growth, export activity, and as a source of market adaptation. There are some variations at different stages of development. As shown in Figure 9.10, more than one-tenth of new ventures in Progressive Service-Industrial and Knowledge-Service economies are providing ten or more jobs, compared to less than 1 in 20 in earlier-stage economies. More than two-fifths of new ventures in Agricultural and Agricultural-Industrial economies are sole proprietorships, providing work for one person. At all stages of economic development half of new ventures provide one to four jobs and one-tenth from five to nine jobs. While many new ventures are small, there are millions of them, so the total impact is substantial.

One in 4 new ventures in Progressive Service-Industrial and Knowledge-Service economies anticipate growth (ten or more jobs in five years) compared to 1 in 6 in earlier-stage economies. A slightly larger pro-

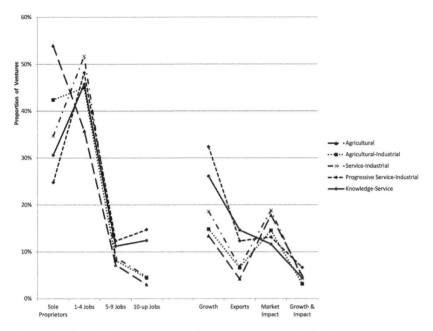

Figure 9.10   New venture contributions by economic development

portion of new ventures in the two advanced economies are export oriented, expecting more than half of their sales to go outside the country. At all levels of economic development, about the same proportion, one-sixth, expect to have some or more impact on the markets where they will compete.

In summary, more new ventures in advanced economies:

- Expect to provide more jobs.
- Expect to grow.
- Expect to export.

More new ventures in less advanced economies:

- Will be one-person, sole proprietorships.
- Expect to have a market impact.

The proportions expecting both growth and a market impact is about 1 in 20 in all stages of development.[5] The prevalence of high-potential business creators is 1 in 109 adults in Agricultural economies, four times higher than the 1 in 420 in Knowledge-Service economies.

NEW VENTURE IMPACT: STRUCTURAL ADAPTATION

Economic adaptation can occur at several levels. Changes in the proportion of existing jobs across economic sectors compared to new-venture jobs reflect adjustments in the economic structure. A greater proportion of jobs among new firms compared to existing jobs reflects an increased emphasis in a sector. Adaptation within market sectors, as when there is churning or turnover among firms in construction or trading or consumer services, is common in all economic systems. Job creation in market sectors without major shifts in the overall proportion of jobs would reflect churning within the sector, a micro-adjustment as new ventures displace established firms. It may reflect a traditional restaurant terminating operations and replaced with a new operation with a contemporary menu. New jobs are created, but there is no net change in the overall emphasis within the restaurant sector.

The shifts in job structure for the five stages of economic development are presented in Figure 9.11. For each stage of economic development and for 14 economic sectors the percentage of existing jobs is subtracted from the percentage of new-firm jobs. A sector associated with a negative change is one where the proportion of new-firm jobs is less than the proportion of existing jobs.

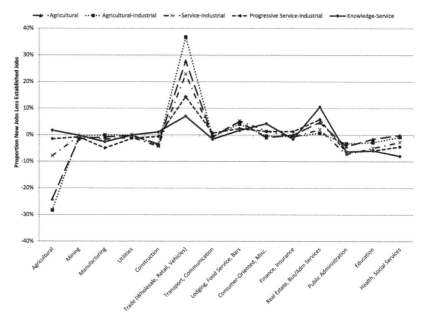

Figure 9.11   Shifts in economic structure by economic development

A sector associated with a positive change is one where the proportion of new venture jobs is greater than the proportion of established jobs. For example, the percentage of existing agricultural jobs in Agricultural-Industrial economies (38%) is less than the percentage of new-firm jobs (10%), a decrease of 28%. New firms are shifting jobs away from the agricultural (farming, forestry, fishing, hunting) sector. For Agricultural-Industrial economies, the decline in agricultural jobs is offset by a larger proportion of new jobs in trade (whole-sale, retail, motor vehicles). The proportion of new jobs, 52%, is 36% greater than the proportion, 16%, among existing jobs. Trade is, however, a sector with much firm—and job—churning, so this difference reflects both a shift in the economic structure and churning within the sector.

There are many sectors where the proportion of established and new-firm jobs is similar, suggesting that the proportion of economic activity is similar among established and new firms. This would include mining, util-ities, transportation and communication, and finance and insurance. Three sectors, dominated by large, established, mostly government organizations, are distinctive. The proportion of existing jobs in public administration, education, and health and social services increases from 10% in Agricultural and Agricultural-Industrial economies to 20% to 22% in Service-Industrial and Progressive Service-Industrial economies to 28% in Knowledge-Service economies. There is, then, less firm creation in sectors dominated by large public organizations.

Comparing the shifts associated across stages of economic growth, the major adjustments are from the agriculture to the trading sector for Agricultural and Agricultural-Industrial economies and, to a lesser extent, for Service-Industrial economies. There is a smaller sectoral shift among Progressive Service-Industrial and Knowledge-Service economies, where there are more new jobs in the real estate, business-administrative services sector, offset by a small proportion of new jobs in public administration, edu-cation, and health and social services.

This comparison makes clear that the jobs created by new ventures reflect both shifts in the economic structure and the ongoing "creative destruction" in existing sectors. Adaptations vary for economies at different stages of development.

NEW VENTURE IMPACT: OVERVIEW

The impact of new ventures varies by the stage of economic development, as summarized in Table 9.1. With development, there is a substantial decrease in the proportion of new ventures in Agriculture economies, from 17% to 5%. This is offset by a five-fold increase in the proportion in Knowledge-Based sectors, from 6% to 32%. There is a small increase in the proportion in

Table 9.1   New venture contributions by economic development: overview

	Agricultural	Agricultural-Industrial	Service-Industrial	Progressive Service-Industrial	Knowledge-Service
New-venture sectors					
Agricultural	17%	9%	10%	6%	5%
Industrial	9%	12%	15%	18%	15%
Consumer oriented	68%	73%	66%	55%	48%
Knowledge based	6%	5%	10%	22%	32%
Venture contributions					
Job creation	46%	58%	65%	75%	69%
Growth	13%	15%	19%	32%	26%
Exports	4%	7%	7%	12%	15%
Market impact	18%	15%	19%	13%	12%
High potential	5%	3%	4%	7%	4%
Shifts in sector emphasis					
Increase emphasis	Consumer oriented	Consumer oriented	Consumer oriented	Consumer oriented	Consumer oriented
Neutral	Industrial, knowledge based	Industrial, knowledge based	Agricultural, industrial	Agricultural, industrial	Agricultural, industrial
Decrease	Agriculture	Agriculture	Knowledge based	Knowledge based	Knowledge based

industrial sectors, from 9% to 15%. New consumer-oriented ventures are the majority in all stages but decline from seven-tenths to one-half of new ventures across the stages of economic development.

The proportion of new ventures that will provide jobs is greater for more advanced economies, from half to two-thirds. Self-employment is a larger share of new ventures in less developed economies. A larger proportion emphasize growth and exports in more advanced economies. Market impact is expected by a larger proportion of new ventures in less developed economies. In all stages of development a small proportion of new ventures expect to have high potential in both growth and impact.

The proportion of activity in consumer-oriented sectors is much greater than among existing firms in all stages of economic development. Consumer-oriented new firms may reflect both a shift toward consumer-oriented markets and greater business churning in these sectors. There is a clear shift away from agricultural work in less developed economies. In more advanced economies, there is less new-firm creation in knowledge-based sectors, many dominated by public organizations in health, education, and social services. At all stages of development, there is job churning in industrial sectors without much change in relative emphasis.

OVERVIEW

There are major similarities in business creation across all stages of economic development.

- There is start-up activity in all sectors.
- Men more active, but women are almost at parity in the early stages of development.
- Those intermediate in human capital are the most active.
- Men and women with greater human capital are more involved in business creation.
- Business creators enter the start-up process while they are working.
- Most business creators are pursuing attractive opportunities; a substantial minority consider it their best option for participating in the economy.
- Turnover (new jobs replacing existing jobs) without expansion occurs in many sectors.

There are, however, some major differences associated with the stage of economic development:

- There are much higher levels of business creation in early-stage economies.
- The lowest levels of overall and high-potential activity are in the most advanced stages.

- Women are a larger proportion of the activity in early-stage economies.
- There is more activity among those with less human capital in early-stage economies.
- There is more activity among those with more human capital in later-stage economies.
- A higher proportion pursue opportunities in later-stage economies.
- New ventures are associated with greater changes in the economic structures in early-stage economies.

NOTES

1. Some of the variation may reflect the lack of harmonization of data collection procedures in the national surveys. Small adjustments in the interview schedule have a major impact when attempting to identify infrequent events.
2. Details in Appendix Table B.3.
3. Details in Table B.3.
4. This provides confidence that the survey administration was harmonized across years and national populations.
5. The low prevalence of high potential new ventures would be associated with greater measurement error, precluding strong confidence in small differences across stages of development.

10. Overview and implications

My mom cried—she literally cried—and said: "What are you doing? You left your $150K corporate job for a (food) truck?" Dave, and his partner Tom, left promising business careers in 2010 to sell Mexican barbecue from a food truck in New York City. By 2015 they had three Mexicue restaurants, two hundred employees, and annual sales over $6 million.[1]

Across the globe 750 million individuals are implementing 550 million new ventures. But there is substantial variation in activity across countries at different stages of economic development. The decline in business creation with economic development represents a dramatic adjustment in labor force activity. While new firms are a major source of contributions to all economies, the nature and scope of contributions changes with economic development.

CONTRIBUTIONS

In earlier stages of economic development business creation improves the efficiency and effectiveness of basic economic activity, promoting individual, household, and tribal survival. Much business creation reflects the ongoing churning in traditional sectors, with more activity in sectors that represent adjustments in the economic structure—largely shifts out of farming and fishing and into trading.

In all economies new firms are a significant source of new jobs, exports, and market innovation. Perhaps their greatest ongoing contribution is the facilitation of churning in established market sectors—construction, transportation, manufacturing, retail, lodging, entertainment, restaurants, business services, and the like. These adjustments are reflected in the phrase "creative destruction." Here new firms are a continuous source of new procedures, new products, and improved productivity. Consumers, however, often benefit from adjustments by existing firms as they adjust to the new competition.

A small proportion of new firms in all economies expect to provide both innovation and growth. An even smaller proportion provide transformations that radically alter existing sectors, as in retail, or create entirely new sectors, such as automobiles, computers, or internet communication. These rare radical transformations seem to appear in larger (such as China, India, or the United States) or more advanced economies, where there is a substantial investment in education and research and development. More than a third of adults in the most advanced economies have advanced education, compared to 1 in 30 in Agricultural economies. Per capita spending on research and development from all sources is $1,108 in Knowledge-Service economies, 170 times greater than the $6 per person in Agricultural economies.[2]

Bottom-up business creation represents democratic initiatives that affect market structures—anybody can, and does, participate. This may pose, however, complications for national governments. It is often difficult to determine, in advance, the nature or scope of the effect of new firms. These new businesses can have a major impact on the economic structure. And the economic structure affects the political and institutional structures, which—in turn—affect citizen well-being and satisfaction. Top-down control of the economy may be challenged by attempts to control grass-roots business creation. Efforts to tightly control or prohibit grass-roots business creation generally lead to economic stagnation or decline, as in Cuba, North Korea, or the former Soviet Union.

A complementary problem occurs in more open economic systems. All governments have major problems tracking the emergence and impact of business creation. While many countries collect substantial data on business organizations and productive activities, none—not even the most advanced—have systematic programs to track bottom-up business creation. Relying on new registrations in existing administrative data sets may be a low-cost strategy to identify firm creation, but it does not provide information on the full scope of activity or efforts that precede the registration event. There can be a considerable lag between the emergence of new economic sectors and its appearance in administrative data sets. In such cases adjusting policy to reflect changes in the economic structure may be slow. It is ironic that economies with the most extensive statistical systems also have the least amount of business creation and have not developed systematic efforts to identify the emergence of nascent ventures.

This information lag would be shortened if modules tracking incipient business creation are incorporated in ongoing labor market surveys, which are based on interviews with representative samples of working-age adults.[3] This would facilitate estimates of the scope of human and financial resources devoted to business creation before and after they are included in administrative data sets. It would also allow determination of the proportion that reach profitability and become self-sustaining.

CONTEXT AND PARTICIPATION

Contextual features that affect career choices shift with economic development. These include changes in the availability of jobs in established organizations, the expansion of social protection programs, adjustments in national values and cultural support for business creation, as well as the proportion of adults that are confident they can succeed in business creation.

In early stages, represented by Subsistence and Agricultural economies, a large amount of small-scale business creation provides much of the population a path for short- and medium-term economic survival. The result is a mass of specialized ventures, each competing in markets which may be highly competitive. The net result is an improvement in effectiveness and productivity, compared to a collection of self-sufficient households, but a system that is less than optimal. As a major work option in early-stage economies, there is strong cultural support for business creation, many adults are confident of their capacity for business creation, orientations toward authority emphasize traditional values including self-reliance, and individual well-being emphasizes a focus on survival.

For the most desperate in the poorest economies, business creation is a better option than criminal pursuits, terrorism, dangerous migration, or the ultimate escape—suicide.

As communities coalesce to encompass more individuals and create nations, physical infrastructure improves, and a broader range of political institutions are developed. With a larger customer base, some new firms will grow and serve a wider range of customers. These growth firms may also develop a formalized structure, including stable, predictable employment with reliable benefits. These are attractive options when compared to small-scale self-employment. The improved productivity will lead to greater national wealth. Some of this increase will be, and apparently is, used to enhance a range of benefits for the citizens, improved health care, expanded education, and more social protection.[4]

The efficiency and reliability of large-scale organizations, and the need for such organizations for a range of societal functions, leads them to command a larger share of the economy. As part of this process, a larger share of jobs is provided by established firms—jobs that provide predictable rewards and benefits. This occurs at the same time that there are expansions of social protection, to provide support for the disadvantaged, including those without work.[5]

The presence of reliable jobs and expansion of social protection are associated with a decline in interest in business creation. There is also reduced cultural support for entrepreneurial careers, a reduction in the proportion of adults confident in their business creation skills, as well as more support for secular-rational authority values and self-expressive individual values. The net result is a decline in business creation activity at the later stages of economic development.

Even with less activity, business creation continues to provide major contributions in advanced economies. The majority is associated with churning in traditional market sectors, as a successful restaurant replaces another that has

214 Entrepreneurship and economic development

214 *Entrepreneurship and economic development*

214 	Entrepreneurship and economic development

214 Entrepreneurship and economic development

gone out of favor and a plumber trained in the latest techniques and procedures replaces an experienced legacy tradesman that retires. A small proportion provide new and transformative goods and services, creating entirely new market segments—as with social media—or transforming traditional sectors— as online shopping competes with in-person retail.

The decline of business creation in advanced economies reflects new firm contributions in the earlier stages of development.

POLICY OPTIONS

The most effective policy options will be different for different stages of economic development. In the earlier stages, where national economies are emerging, there is no need to encourage business creation—it is widely accepted as appropriate and many are involved. The most effective policies would emphasize improving the capacity of individuals to create and sustain new firms. This could include:

- Expanding education so all adults complete secondary school.
- Facilitating access to established financial institutions.
- Improving legal recognition of physical and intellectual property rights.
- Providing benefits for legally established businesses and minimizing the cost for registration.

There is great variation among developing countries with regards to these different features. As national resources vary the optimal mix of emphasis will differ for each emerging economy. Even a cursory internet search identifies public and private programs to sponsor business creation in the poorest of Agricultural economies. Most, however, emulate the programs promoted in the most developed countries with a focus on faddish growth businesses. Aside from the expansion of micro-finance institutions, there is little evidence of assistance for the mass of individuals, many with modest human capital, that are seeking to implement small-scale self-employment.

Advanced economies confront a quite different set of issues. There is widespread agreement that business creation provides substantial collective benefits. There is substantial public and private research and development, extensive support from the established financial institutions, a well-educated adult population, and strong legal recognition of physical and intellectual property rights. The presence of a wide range of satisfying careers in established organizations, an extensive social safety net, and ambivalent support from family and friends lead many to avoid entrepreneurial careers. Most adults choose not to be involved as nine-tenths are not active in business creation.

As substantial formal, institutional support for business creation is already in place, the policy challenge is to encourage more participation. Several strategies may be effective:

• Emphasize, in public forums, the public benefits from firm creation and recognize the contributions of responsible entrepreneurship.
• Include modules on business creation in all secondary and post-secondary education programs, so graduates are prepared to pursue an opportunity that may emerge during their work career.
• Develop national programs that provide health and retirement support regardless of employment status, to minimize the risk of benefit loss if leaving established employment or if a nascent venture is not successful.
• Develop separate agencies and programs for new businesses, separating them from efforts to serve the interests of small businesses. While most new businesses start small, most small businesses are not new. Many have been in place for decades, some family enterprises for generations. Established small businesses seldom welcome competition from new firms.
• Minimize the scope and impact of non-competition agreements, as most new firms reflect the efforts of individuals leaving established jobs to create new ventures in a sector they know well.
• Constrain occupational licensing and certification to only those arenas where public well-being is a major issue.

Again, different advanced economies have different situations and will need to identify a different set of priorities for policy adjustments.

CODA

Business creation is a fundamental feature of all societies, involving more adults than human creation. The major challenges are reducing the social costs—represented by investments in stillborn start-ups—and facilitating developments that promote responsible economic growth.

NOTES

1. Morrissey (2015).
2. Details in Table B.2.
3. The screening modules developed in the PSED (Curtin and Reynolds, 2018; Reynolds and Curtin, 2010) and GEM (Reynolds et al., 2005; Reynolds, 2021) programs have been extensively field tested, are in the public domain, and should facilitate modification of ongoing labor market interviews.
4. Details in Table B.2.
5. Details in Tables B.1 and B.2.

Appendix A Global Entrepreneurship Monitor program

In the late 1990s, national comparisons based on the Global Competitiveness Index and the World Competitiveness Rankings were considered a useful way to identify important contextual factors affecting national economic growth. This led to the development of a cross-national comparison of business creation activity, the Global Entrepreneurship Monitor (GEM) project. The primary focus was developing information about the role of business creation in national economic growth.[1] Critical to this objective was a capacity for standardized estimates of the amount of business creation in participating countries.

A research protocol was developed to identify those active in business creation in representative samples of the adult population in each country. Surveys of households are used to locate representative samples of adults. Case weights are developed such that the sample represents the national adult population. Standardized interview schedules made it possible to identify nascent entrepreneurs, or those actively involved in creating new firms that had not reached profitability; owner-managers of new firms with less than 3.5 years of profits; and owner-managers of firms that had been profitable for more than 3.5 years.[2] Those involved in start-ups or managing new firms were combined to create a measure of participation in the initial stages of the firm life course, the Total Entrepreneurial Activity[3] or TEA index.[4] This has varied from less than 3 per 100 adults of 18–64 years of age in Japan and Belgium to over 25 per 100 in Nigeria, Peru, and Uganda.[5]

From 2000 to 2017 harmonized national surveys were completed in 20 to 70 countries per year: a total of 869 surveys involving over 2.8 million respondents. As of 2017 data is available for 107 countries. These countries and the number of annual surveys is provided in Table A.1. Countries included in the GEM assessments are presented by the level of economic development in Table A.2 along with three different national identification codes. The right-hand column provides the average TEA index value. Because of complications associated with omissions in many cross-national data sets, three GEM countries (Kosovo, Puerto Rico, and Taiwan) are not assigned to any stage of development.

Table A.1   National participation in GEM annual surveys: 2000–2017

Country		Country		Country	
Algeria	4*	Guatemala	4*	Philippines	8
Angola	5	Hong Kong (SAR)	5	Poland	8
Argentina	19	Hungary	19	Portugal	15
Australia	13	Iceland	13	Puerto Rico	9
Austria	5	India	5	Qatar	12
Bangladesh	1	Indonesia	1	Romania	6
Barbados	5	Iran	5	Russia	10
Belgium	16	Ireland	16	Saudi Arabia	17
Belize	2	Israel	2	Senegal	13
Bolivia	3	Italy	3	Serbia	17
Bosnia and Herzegovina	8	Jamaica	8	Singapore	10
Botswana	4	Japan	4	Slovak Republic	16
Brazil	18	Jordan	18	Slovenia	3
Bulgaria	3	Kazakhstan	3	South Arica	5
Burkina Faso	3	Korea (South)	3	Spain	12
Cameroon	3	Kosovo	3	Suriname	1
Canada	12	Latvia	12	Sweden	12
Chile	15	Lebanon	15	Switzerland	1
China	14	Libya	14	Syria	1
Colombia	12	Lithuania	12	Taiwan	4
Costa Rica	3	Luxembourg	3	Thailand	5
Croatia	16	Macedonia (FYR)	16	Tonga	6

Entrepreneurship and economic development

Country	*
Cyprus	2
Czech Republic	3
Denmark	14
Dominican Republic	3
Ecuador	10
Egypt	6
El Salvador	3
Estonia	1
Ethiopia	1
Finland	17
France	17
Georgia	2
Germany	17
Ghana	3
Greece	15
Madagascar	1
Malawi	2
Malaysia	10
Mexico	13
Montenegro	1
Morocco	4
Namibia	2
Netherlands	17
New Zealand	5
Nigeria	3
Norway	16
Pakistan	3
Palestine (West Bank/Gaza)	3
Panama	3
Peru	15
Trinidad and Tobago	5
Tunisia	4
Turkey	8
Uganda	7
United Arab Emirates	6
United Kingdom	18
United States	18
Uruguay	12
Vanuatu	1
Venezuela	5
Vietnam	3
Yemen	1
Zambia	3

Note: * Total count of annual national surveys of the adult population.

There is substantial detail on the research protocol as well as access to the survey data files, including a harmonized adult population survey data set for the 1998 pretest to 2017.[6] More current data is available on the project website (www.gemconsortium.org), although there is a three-year lag before public dissemination.

Financial support for the initiation of the GEM project was provided by a major sponsor, the Kauffman Foundation, and funds raised by individual national teams. Once established, the project became self-supported through national team contributions. As each team covered the costs of their national data collection, minimizing data collection costs was important, particularly for developing countries. Hence, the minimum survey samples criteria were set at 2,000 cases, although some country teams implement much larger samples. There is, as a result, some variations among countries in the precision of the prevalence estimates. There is considerable year-to-year stability in participation in business creation.[7] Unless there are extraordinary circumstances, year-to-year changes greater than 10% probably reflect variations in the data collection procedures. As a result, the most accurate representations of national activity are provided by averaging annual estimates across the years in which the data was collected.

The GEM project, which has been in place for two decades, is the only cross-national, harmonized comparison of participation in business creation and owner-management in existence. Coverage of over 100 countries at all stages of economic development facilitates a wide range of assessments. Cross-national comparisons based on government-managed administrative data sets, most reflecting tax collection procedures, are not able to overcome national differences in requirements for inclusion and, critical for cross-national comparisons of firm creation, variation in procedures that incorporate new ventures in the national registries. New firms in different countries are included in administrative data sets at different stages in the firm creation process.

For many issues regarding participation in business creation, particularly for developing countries, there is no other harmonized source of data. The amount of research completed with the GEM data sets has grown considerably and there are several reviews of the amount and nature of analyses.[8]

The countries involved in the assessment are presented in Table A.2, sorted by stage of economic development. Three different schemes for coding the national identities are provided, that used in the World Economic Outlook, the three-character alpha character codes maintained by the International Organization of Standardization (ISO), and the international country phone codes used in the GEM project. (To avoid confusion with the United States, Canada was assigned an international phone code of 101.) The last column

Table A.2   GEM countries by economic development

Country	World Economic Outlook code	International Organization of Standardization code	International phone code (Global Entrepreneurship Monitor countries)	Average Total Entrepreneurial Activity index (#/100)
Knowledge-Service				
Australia	193	AUS	61	12.0
Belgium	124	BEL	32	4.2
Canada (assigned phone code)	156	CAN	101	11.8
Cyprus	423	CYP	357	10.2
Denmark	128	DNK	45	5.3
Finland	172	FIN	358	6.2
France	132	FRA	33	5.0
Germany	134	DEU	49	5.0
Greece	174	GRC	30	7.5
Hong Kong	532	HKG	852	5.8
Iceland	176	ISL	354	11.9
Ireland	178	IRL	353	8.3
Israel	436	ISR	972	8.3
Japan	158	JPN	81	3.5
Korea (South)	542	KOR	82	9.9
Latvia	941	LVA	371	10.7
Luxembourg	137	LUX	352	9.1
Netherlands	138	NLD	31	7.6

Country	World Economic Outlook code	International Organization of Standardization code	International phone code (Global Entrepreneurship Monitor countries)	Average Total Entrepreneurial Activity index (#/100)
New Zealand	196	NZL	64	15.1
Norway	142	NOR	47	7.6
Singapore	576	SGP	65	7.1
Spain	184	ESP	34	6.3
Sweden	144	SWE	46	5.7
Switzerland	146	CHE	41	7.2
United Kingdom	112	GBR	44	7.1
United States	111	USA	1	11.8
Progressive Service-Industrial				
Argentina	213	ARG	54	14.3
Austria	122	AUT	43	7.5
Bahamas	313	BHS		
Bahrain	419	BHR		
Barbados	316	BRB	246	19.3
Belarus	913	BLR		
Brunei Darussalam	516	BRN		
Bulgaria	918	BGR	359	4.4
Chile	228	CHL	56	19.3
Croatia	960	HRV	385	7.1
Czechia	935	CZE	420	7.9
Estonia	939	EST	372	14.6

Country	World Economic Outlook code	International Organization of Standardization code	International phone code (Global Entrepreneurship Monitor countries)	Average Total Entrepreneurial Activity index (#/100)
Hungary	944	HUN	36	7.6
Italy	136	ITA	39	5.0
Kazakhstan	916	KAZ	701	11.9
Kuwait	443	KWT		
Lithuania	946	LTU	370	11.1
Malaysia	548	MYS	60	8.0
Malta	181	MLT		
Montenegro	943	MNE	382	15.1
Oman	449	OMN		
Palau	565	PLW		
Poland	964	POL	48	9.1
Portugal	182	PRT	351	8.3
Qatar	453	QAT	974	11.3
Romania	968	ROU	40	8.2
Russia	922	RUS	7	4.7
Saudi Arabia	456	SAU	966	9.6
Seychelles	718	SYC		
Slovakia	936	SVK	421	11.8
Slovenia	961	SVN	386	5.6
Turkey	186	TUR	90	10.9
United Arab Emirates	466	ARE	971	8.5

Country	World Economic Outlook code	International Organization of Standardization code	International phone code (Global Entrepreneurship Monitor countries)	Average Total Entrepreneurial Activity index (#/100)
Uruguay	298	URY	598	14.5
Service-Industrial				
Albania	914	ALB		
Algeria	612	DZA	213	11.7
Antigua and Barbuda	311	ATG		
Armenia	911	ARM		
Azerbaijan	912	AZE		
Belize	339	BLZ	501	18.4
Bolivia	218	BOL	591	33.5
Bosnia and Herzegovina	963	BIH	387	7.6
Botswana	616	BWA	267	29.3
Brazil	223	BRA	55	16.1
China	924	CHN	86	15.9
Colombia	233	COL	57	22.8
Costa Rica	238	CRI	506	14.0
Dominica	321	DMA		
Dominican Republic	243	DOM	1809	18.4
Ecuador	248	ECU	593	27.9
Egypt	469	EGY	20	11.2
Fiji	819	FJI		
Gabon	646	GAB		

Entrepreneurship and economic development

Country	World Economic Outlook code	International Organization of Standardization code	International phone code (Global Entrepreneurship Monitor countries)	Average Total Entrepreneurial Activity index (#/100)
Georgia	915	GEO	995	9.6
Grenada	328	GRD		
Indonesia	536	IDN	62	19.5
Iran	429	IRN	98	14.2
Jamaica	343	JAM	876	21.1
Jordan	439	JOR	962	12.4
Lebanon	446	LBN	961	23.8
Libya	672	LBY	218	13.9
Macedonia, North	962	MKD	389	9.0
Maldives	556	MDV		
Marshall Island	867	MHL		
Mauritius	684	MUS		
Mexico	273	MEX	52	13.5
Moldova	921	MDA		
Mongolia	948	MNG		
Panama	283	PAN	507	15.8
Paraguay	288	PRY		
Peru	293	PER	51	28.9
Philippines	566	PHL	63	19.1
Samoa	862	WSM		
Serbia	942	SRB	381	9.7

Country	World Economic Outlook code	International Organization of Standardization code	International phone code (Global Entrepreneurship Monitor countries)	Average Total Entrepreneurial Activity index (#/100)
South Africa	199	ZAF	27	7.6
Sri Lanka	524	LKA		
St. Kitts and Nevis	361	KNA		
St. Lucia	362	LCA		
St. Vincent and Grenadines	364	VCT		
Suriname	366	SUR	597	4.8
Thailand	578	THA	66	22.5
Tonga	866	TON	676	18.6
Trinidad and Tobago	369	TTO	868	18.1
Tunisia	744	TUN	216	9.2
Turkmenistan	925	TKM		
Ukraine	926	UKR		
Uzbekistan	927	UZB		
Venezuela	299	VEN	582	22.1
Agricultural-Industrial				
Angola	614	AGO	244	29.5
Bangladesh	513	BGD	880	12.8
Bhutan	514	BTN		
Cabo Verde	624	CPV		
Cambodia	522	KHM		
Cameroon	622	CMR	237	33.5

Entrepreneurship and economic development

Country	World Economic Outlook code	International Organization of Standardization code	International phone code (Global Entrepreneurship Monitor countries)	Average Total Entrepreneurial Activity index (#/100)
Congo (Republic of)	634	COG		
El Salvador	253	SLV	503	16.9
Equatorial Guinea	642	GNQ		
Eswatini	734	SWZ		
Ghana	652	GHA	233	34.8
Guatemala	258	GTM	502	19.3
Guyana	336	GUY		
Honduras	268	HND		
India	534	IND	91	11.2
Iraq	433	IRQ		
Kenya	664	KEN		
Kiribati	826	KIR		
Kyrgyzstan	917	KGZ		
Laos	544	LAO		
Micronesia	868	FSM		
Morocco	686	MAR	212	9.4
Myanmar	518	MMR		
Namibia	728	NAM	264	26.8
Nepal	558	NPL		
Nicaragua	278	NIC		
Pakistan	564	PAK	92	12.2

Country	World Economic Outlook code	International Organization of Standardization code	International phone code (Global Entrepreneurship Monitor countries)	Average Total Entrepreneurial Activity index (#/100)
São Tomé and Principe	716	STP		
Solomon Islands	813	SLB		
Tajikistan	923	TJK		
Timor-Leste	537	TLS		
Vanuatu	846	VUT	678	54.7
Viet Nam	582	VNM	84	15.4
Zambia	754	ZMB	260	38.9
Zimbabwe	698	ZWE		
Agricultural				
Afghanistan	512	AFG		
Benin	638	BEN		
Burkina Faso	748	BFA	226	29.8
Burundi	618	BDI		
Central African Republic	626	CAF		
Chad	628	TCD		
Comoros	632	COM		
Congo (Democrat Republic of)	636	COD		
Cote d'Ivoire	662	CIV		
Djibouti	611	DJI		
Eritrea	643	ERI		

Country	World Economic Outlook code	International Organization of Standardization code	International phone code (Global Entrepreneurship Monitor countries)	Average Total Entrepreneurial Activity index (#/100)
Ethiopia	644	ETH	251	15.2
Gambia	648	GMB		
Guinea	656	GIN		
Guinea-Bissau	654	GNB		
Haiti	263	HTI		
Lesotho	666	LSO		
Liberia	668	LBR		
Madagascar	674	MDG	261	22.2
Malawi	676	MWI	265	32.3
Mali	678	MLI		
Mauritania	682	MRT		
Mozambique	688	MOZ		
Niger	692	NER		
Nigeria	694	NGA	234	39.3
Papua New Guinea	853	PNG		
Rwanda	714	RWA		
Senegal	722	SEN	221	39.3
Sierra Leone	724	SLE		
South Sudan	733	SSD		
Sudan	732	SDN		
Syria	463	SYR	963	8.4

Country	World Economic Outlook code	International Organization of Standardization code	International phone code (Global Entrepreneurship Monitor countries)	Average Total Entrepreneurial Activity index (#/100)
Tanzania	738	TZA		
Togo	742	TGO		
Uganda	746	UGA	256	32.1
Yemen	474	YEM	967	21.9
Not included				
Kosovo	967	KOS	383	5.2
Palestine (West Bank/Gaza)	275	PSE	970	9.8
Puerto Rico	359	PRI	787	8.5
Taiwan	528	TWN	886	8.4

Note: The five categories are based on the four levels of human development presented in the 2019 United Nations Human Development Report (United Nations, 2019b). The labels are changed to reflect the major focus of the economic structure. The very high-level category is bifurcated by identifying very high-level economies where over 70% of employment is considered service (not agricultural or industrial) and more than 20% of the adult population has post-secondary (vocational, trade, college, graduate, professional, etc.) educational experience in 2015 (Barro and Lee, 2016).

provides the average value of the prevalence of business creation for each country in the GEM data set.

NOTES

1. A summary of the GEM methodology is available in Reynolds et al. (2005) and the background of the project in Reynolds (2017). An overview of the research program and current details are available on the project website (www .gemconsortium.org).
2. These were simplified versions of procedures developed to identify cohorts of nascent entrepreneurs for the Panel Study of Entrepreneurial Dynamics program (Reynolds and Curtin, 2010).
3. The index is now sometimes referred to as the "early-stage entrepreneurial activity" index.
4. About 5% of the individuals are active in both stages of the firm creation process, managing a new firm and starting another venture. They are counted only once in developing the TEA index.
5. Reynolds (2014, appendix A).
6. Reynolds (2021). As the 1998 and 1999 interview schedules were preliminary pretests, full harmonization is only possible for data collected from the year 2000 to 2017.
7. Reynolds (2014).
8. Alvarez et al. (2014); Amorós et al. (2013); Bergmann et al. (2014).

Appendix B   Economic development: Cross-stage descriptions

A wide range of descriptions from a variety of sources was required for this assessment. In every case the average values for each stage of development reflects those countries with harmonized data. While in most cases it involves all Knowledge-Service economies, for less developed categories, where countries may not have fully developed national statistical agencies, it usually involves a representative sub-sample.

Descriptions of the five stages of development are provided in seven categories, as follows:

1. Economic overview.
2. Government emphasis and citizen attitudes.
3. Citizen status.
4. Entrepreneurial context.
5. Financial support.
6. Business creator characteristics.
7. New venture characteristics.

The sources of all data are provided in the notes associated with each measure or index. All data for the last two categories is based on the GEM database; selected GEM items are included in other tables under relevant topics.

There is no single source of harmonized data on the educational attainment of national populations. The most comprehensive effort to assemble demographic data from disparate national surveys has been completed by Barro and Lee (2016). Similar procedures were implemented in the GEM initiative to provide harmonized comparisons on adult educational attainment. The results are broadly similar, despite some variations in details.

Entrepreneurship and economic development

Table B.1   Economic development: economic overview

	Agricultural	Agricultural-Industrial	Service-Industrial	Progressive Service-Industrial	Knowledge-Service
Number of countries (n = 185)[1]	36	35	54	34	26
Total population: 2018, millions (total = 7,539)[2]	923	2,240	2,486	593	939
Share of global population	12%	30%	38%	8%	13%
GDP per capita (PPP): 2018 ($1,000)[3]	$2.1	$6.2	$13.1	$34.2	$48.2
Persons living on $1.90/day or less (percent)[4]	45%	17%	3%		
Persons in severe multidimensional poverty (percent)	37%	10%	1%		
Income inequality[5]					
Income share, low 40%: 2010–2017	17%	16%	16%	19%	20%
Income share, middle 50%: 2010–2017	51%	51%	52%	54%	55%
Income share, top 10%: 2010–2017	32%	33%	32%	27%	25%
GINI income inequality index: 2010–2017	40.6	42.2	40.8	34.4	32.4
Sector emphasis (% employment)[6]					
Agricultural	51%	38%	20%	6%	3%
Mining	2%	1%	1%	1%	
Manufacturing	6%	10%	12%	14%	11%
Utilities		1%	1%	2%	1%
Construction	4%	6%	8%	11%	7%
Trade (wholesale, retail)	17%	16%	16%	14%	14%
Transportation, communication	3%	5%	7%	8%	9%

	Agricultural	Agricultural-Industrial	Service-Industrial	Progressive Service-Industrial	Knowledge-Service
Accommodations, food service, bars	2%	3%	5%	5%	6%
Other services	6%	7%	7%	8%	6%
Finance, insurance		1%	2%	2%	4%
Real estate, business/admin services	2%	3%	4%	8%	12%
Public administration	2%	4%	7%	8%	6%
Education	3%	4%	6%	7%	8%
Health, social services	1%	2%	4%	6%	12%
Total	99%	101%	100%	100%	99%
Major sectors (% employment)					
Agricultural	51%	38%	20%	6%	3%
Industrial	12%	18%	22%	28%	19%
Consumer oriented	28%	30%	35%	35%	35%
Knowledge based	9%	14%	23%	31%	43%
Total	100%	100%	100%	100%	100%
Percent of non-agricultural informal jobs[7]	84%	68%	45%	33%	

Entrepreneurship and economic development

	Agricultural	Agricultural-Industrial	Service-Industrial	Progressive Service-Industrial	Knowledge-Service
Employment sources[8]					
Unregistered firms					
Self-employed (1 job)	50%	58%	13%	7%	
Micro-enterprise (2–9 jobs)	33%	18%	15%	6%	
Small enterprises (10–49 jobs)	1%	1%	10%	2%	
Medium, large enterprises (50+ jobs)	1%	1%	7%	3%	
Total unregistered firms	85%	78%	45%	18%	
Registered firms					
Self-employed (1 job)	4%	3%	3%	5%	
Micro-enterprises (2–9 jobs)	4%	5%	7%	16%	
Small enterprises (10–49 jobs)	2%	5%	9%	22%	
Medium, large enterprises (50+ jobs)	5%	8%	36%	39%	
Total registered firms	15%	21%	55%	82%	

Note: PPP = purchasing power parity; [1] country counts are reduced for some characteristics reflecting missing data; [2] United Nations (2019b, table 7); [3] International Finance Corporation (2019b); [4] United Nations (2019b, table 6), averages for 31 Agricultural, 28 Agricultural-Industrial, and 28 Service-Industrial economies; [5] United Nations (2019b, table 3); [6] International Labour Organization (2019), data for 2018; [7] United Nations (2019b, table 11), years 2011–2018, total n = 61, no data on Knowledge-Service economies; [8] International Labour Organization (2019), published averages (appendix 1) based on data from 25 Agricultural, 49 Agricultural-Industrial, 45 Service-Industrial, and 37 Progressive Service-Industrial and Knowledge-based economies, United States not included in the database.

Table B.2   *Economic development: government emphasis and citizen attitudes*

	Agricultural	Agricultural-Industrial	Service-Industrial	Progressive Service-Industrial	Knowledge-Service
Government operations					
Government expenditure as % of annual GDP[1]	23 %	30 %	30 %	37 %	40 %
Health and education expenses as % of GDP[2]	10%	9%	10%	11%	15%
Social protection programs as % of GDP (2007)[3]	1%	3%	5%	8%	12%
Military expenses as % of GDP[4]	1.6%	1.6%	2.1%	2.3%	1.7%
Gross domestic product/person ($ 2018)[5]	$2,100	$6,200	$13,100	$34,200	$48,200
Total gov spending/person ($ 2018)[6]	$490	$1,789	$3,759	$13,079	$18,921
Gov goods/service spending/person ($ 2018)[7]	$320	$1,117	$1,860	$6,323	$8,831
Total research and development spending/person ($ 2018)[8]	$6	$16	$56	$294	$1,018
Health spending/person (2018)[9]	$116	$317	$841	$2,008	$4,435
Education spending/person (2018)[10]	$73	$246	$583	$1,480	$2,612
Social protection programs/person (2007)[11]	$8	$102	$466	$2,184	$5,121
Military spending/person ($ 2018)[12]	$35	$105	$255	$940	$767
Citizen reactions, attitudes[13]					
Overall life satisfaction: 10-point scale	4.2	5.0	5.4	6.1	6.8
Confidence in national government: % yes	59%	62%	44%	40%	50%
Confidence in judicial system: % yes	51%	68%	42%	43%	62%
Feel safe outside at night: % yes	52%	58%	60%	67%	78%

	Agricultural	Agricultural-Industrial	Service-Industrial	Progressive Service-Industrial	Knowledge-Service
Satisfied with local community: % yes	64%	78%	75%	81%	87%
Satisfied with standard of living: % yes	44%	69%	61%	69%	81%
Satisfied with freedom of choice: % yes	65%	79%	78%	77%	83%
Satisfied with educational quality: % yes	49%	69%	61%	61%	69%
Satisfied with health-care quality: % yes	42%	60%	53%	63%	74%
Consider local labor market good: % yes	41%	42%	33%	38%	49%
National value structure[14]					
Authority: traditional (−1) vs secular-rational (+1)	−0.60	−0.43	−0.21	0.41	0.54
Individual well-being: survival (−1) vs self-expressive (+1)	−0.26	−0.39	−0.27	−0.04	0.77
Authority: secular-rational	9%	14%	25%	50%	57%
Authority: intermediate	35%	39%	35%	33%	29%
Authority: traditional	56%	47%	40%	17%	13%
Total	100%	100%	100%	100%	99%

	Agricultural	Agricultural-Industrial	Service-Industrial	Progressive Service-Industrial	Knowledge-Service
Individual well-being: self-expression	18%	15%	20%	31%	63%
Individual well-being: intermediate	41%	37%	38%	35%	25%
Individual well-being: survival	41%	48%	42%	34%	13%
Total	100%	100%	100%	100%	101%

Note: [1] United Nations (2019b, table 10); [2] United Nations (2019b, dashboard 5), computed from percentage of GDP spent on military in relation to spending on health and education; [3] International Food Policy Research Institute (2019), includes funding for sickness and disability, old age, survivors, family and children, unemployment, housing, social exclusion, social protection, and research and development on social protection, data are average values for 14 Agricultural, 20 Agricultural-Industrial, 37 Service-Industrial, 28 Progressive Service-Industrial, and 26 Knowledge-Service economies; [4] United Nations (2019b, dashboard 5); [5] International Finance Corporation (2019), purchasing power parity adjusted; [6] Miller et al. (2020), adjusted to reflect proportion of GDP actually spent, computed index squares this value to dramatize the impact of small increases in the absolute level of expenditures; [7] United Nations (2019b, table 10), 2013–2018 average, total government expenditure for goods and services including wages but excluding military capital formation expenditure; [8] United Nations (2019b, dashboard 5), percentage of GDP spend from public and private sources multiplied by GDP per person for 2018; [9] United Nations (2019b, table 8), percentage of GDP spend on health care multiplied by GDP per person for 2018; [10] United Nations (2019b, table 9), percentage of GDP spend on education multiplied by GDP per person for 2018; [11] International Food Policy Research Institute (2019), includes funding for sickness and disability, old age, survivors, family and children, unemployment, housing, social exclusion, social protection, and research and development on social protection, data are average values for 14 Agricultural, 20 Agricultural-Industrial, 37 Service-Industrial, 28 Progressive Service-Industrial, and 26 Knowledge-Service economies; [12] United Nations (2019b, dashboard 5), percentage of GDP spend on the military multiplied by GDP per person for 2018; [13] United Nations (2019b, table 14), for "feel safe outside at night" and "satisfied with freedom of choice" the values are the average of responses for men and women; [14] Inglehart et al.'s (2020) pooled time-series data is the source of values for waves 1 to 6, available data from wave 7 harmonized and added from Haerpfer et al. (2020), average values for each country averaged across all waves with available data, development-stage averages reflect values available for 20 Knowledge-Service, 22 Progressive Service-Industrial, 30 Service-Industrial, 11 Agricultural-Industrial, and nine Agricultural economies.

Table B.3　　*Economic development: citizen status*

	Agricultural	Agricultural-Industrial	Service-Industrial	Progressive Service-Industrial	Knowledge-Service
United Nations Human Development Index[1]	0.48	0.62	0.74	0.84	0.92
Major components[1]					
Life expectancy at birth (years): 2018	62.2	68.5	74.0	77.3	82.0
Adult mean years of education	9.2	11.5	13.6	15.4	17.3
GNIPC: 2011 ($1,000, PPP)	$2.0	$5.8	$12.6	$33.9	$46.5
Population age structure[2]					
% population 0–15 years old	43%	29%	23%	20%	16%
% population 15–64 years old	54%	65%	68%	67%	65%
% adults 65 years and older	3%	6%	9%	13%	19%
Total	100%	100%	100%	100%	100%
Educational attainment[3]					
Literate adults, % of population: 2018	51%	78%	94%	97%	98%
% labor force w/ secondary, advanced education	18%	34%	56%	75%	84%
% adults with no education: 2015[4]	45%	20%	6%	4%	2%
% adults with primary experience: 2015	33%	34%	25%	14%	9%
% adults with secondary experience: 2015	19%	40%	54%	63%	53%
% adults with post-secondary education: 2015	3%	6%	16%	19%	37%
Women: 25+ with high school+ education	17%	42%	70%	82%	89%
Men: 25+ with high school+ education	29%	48%	71%	83%	91%

	Agricultural	Agricultural-Industrial	Service-Industrial	Progressive Service-Industrial	Knowledge-Service
Labor force activity and characteristics[5]					
Adults: 15+ employed, % of population: 2018	62%	60%	54%	59%	59%
Adults: 15+ in labor force, % of population: 2018	65%	64%	59%	62%	62%
Women: 15+ in labor force	58%	52%	46%	51%	57%
Men: 15+ in labor force	73%	76%	72%	72%	68%
Ratio of high-skilled to low-skilled jobs	1.4	1.1	2.9	3.2	6.2
Percentage working-poor adults (<$3.60/day)	66%	30%	8%		
Retirement security[6]					
Percentage eligible adults with pension	13%	37%	60%	80%	92%

Note: PPP = purchasing power parity; GNIPC = gross national income per capita, includes income from overseas operations from domestic businesses; [1] United Nations (2019b, table 1); [2] United Nations (2019b); [3] unless noted otherwise, from United Nations (2019b, tables 5 and 9); [4] from Barro and Lee (2016), the original source of all educational attainment estimates in United Nations (2019b), values are averages across 25 Agricultural, 25 Agricultural-Industrial, 37 Service-Industrial, 28 Progressive Service-Industrial, and 26 Knowledge-Service economies; [5] United Nations (2019b, tables 5 and 11); [6] United Nations (2019b, table 11).

Table B.4   Economic development: entrepreneurial context

	Agricultural	Agricultural-Industrial	Service-Industrial	Progressive Service-Industrial	Knowledge-Service
Business, property rights registration[1]					
Business registration: no. of procedures	7.3	8.6	7.6	7.0	4.3
Business registration: days to complete	22.3	30.0	26.7	15.8	7.1
Business registration: costs ($ 2018, PPP)	$1,210	$2,417	$2,317	$2,025	$1,219
Business registration: cost % of annual income	63%	34%	20%	6%	3%
Business registration: % with capital required	44%	34%	18%	41%	38%
Business registration: capital req % of GDPPC	53%	35%	17%	15%	14%
Property registration: no. of procedures	6.1	6.3	6.6	5.0	5.1
Property registration: days to complete	72	73	39	35	22
Property registration: % of property cost	8.0%	6.1%	5.7%	3.0%	4.8%
Land rights administration quality: index	7.2	10.5	14.1	19.9	23.4
Land rights administration coverage: index	0.5	1.2	2.2	4.9	6.5
Physical property rights recognition index	5.3	5.7	6.3	6.7	7.7
Intellect property rights recognition index	4.5	4.4	4.7	5.9	7.8
Entrepreneurial climate index[2]	1.2	0.2	0.3	-.3	-.5
Business creation good career choice: % yes	84%	71%	75%	64%	57%
New firm creation leads to status: % yes	86%	75%	74%	67%	68%
Media coverage of new businesses: % yes	72%	62%	65%	58%	59%
Strong support (yes to all three)	59%	41%	44%	34%	29%

	Agricultural	Agricultural-Industrial	Service-Industrial	Progressive Service-Industrial	Knowledge-Service
Readiness for entrepreneurship index[3]	1.1	0.7	0.3	–.4	–.5
See good business opportunities: % yes	59%	59%	48%	37%	38%
Know an active entrepreneur: % yes	60%	54%	46%	40%	38%
Has skill, knowledge to start a business: % yes	75%	63%	62%	51%	44%
High readiness (yes to all three)	38%	31%	22%	16%	13%
Fear of failure discourages business creation: % yes	27%	37%	34%	41%	40%

Note: PPP = purchasing power parity; GDPPC = gross domestic production per person, refers only to production of goods and services within the country; [1] World Bank (2020); [2] Reynolds (2021), data from GEM data set, entrepreneurial climate index based on average normalized values of the three components, reflects cultural and social support for business creation activity, mean values for nine Agricultural, 13 Agricultural-Industrial, 32 Service-Industrial, 25 Progressive Service-Industrial, and 26 Knowledge-Service economies, 105 countries representing a human population of 6.6 billion as of 2018; [3] Reynolds (2021), data from GEM data set, readiness for entrepreneurial index based on average normalized values of the three components, reflects the potential of adults in the population for participation in business creation, mean values for nine Agricultural, 13 Agricultural-Industrial, 32 Service-Industrial, 25 Progressive Service-Industrial, and 26 Knowledge-Service economies, 105 countries representing a human population of 6.6 billion as of 2018.

Table B.5   *Economic development: financial support*

	Agricultural	Agricultural-Industrial	Service-Industrial	Progressive Service-Industrial	Knowledge-Service
Sources of financial support					
Domestic financial inst credit/person[1]	$612	$2,988	$9,714	$29,517	$78,511
Informal investors					
Prevalence (#/100)[2]	10	10	6	5	4
Recipients of informal investors support:[3]					
• Family member	49%	45%	48%	46%	38%
• Relatives	22%	19%	15%	11%	7%
• Work colleagues	3%	6%	6%	7%	9%
• Friends, neighbors	22%	26%	27%	28%	31%
• Strangers with good ideas	3%	3%	3%	6%	11%
• Others	1%	1%	1%	2%	4%
Total	100%	100%	100%	100%	100%
Financial inclusion indices[4]					
Government and policy coordination and support	56	59	60	68	
Stability and integrity of financial services	59	62	67	72	
Regulation of products and outlets	56	55	65	69	
Consumer protection, privacy enforcement	48	53	67	84	
Facilitating infrastructure, policy support	50	59	70	75	

	Agricultural	Agricultural-Industrial	Service-Industrial	Progressive Service-Industrial	Knowledge-Service
Financial inclusion participation[5]					
Borrowers/1,000 15–64 years old	13	46	61	14	
Percent female borrowers	53%	67%	61%	56%	
Percent rural borrowers	41%	47%	48%	34%	
Loans outstanding/1,000 15–64 years old	16	47	64	17	
Outstanding loan balance, average (US$)	$900	$1,624	$2,009	$3,571	
Loans with payments 90 days overdue	7.8%	4.7%	4.8%	4.1%	
Connected potential[6]					
Internet access (% of population)	18%	33%	58%	81%	89%
Mobile phone subscribers (#/100 population)	70	97	114	136	126
Government spending on communication ($/100)[7]	$3	$8	$10	$23	$17
Government spending on communications: % total	0.76%	0.66%	0.31%	0.23%	0.12%

Note: [1] United Nations (2019b, table 10); [2] Reynolds (2021), country values averaged across all years with data, mean values for nine Agricultural, 13 Agricultural-Industrial, 32 Service-Industrial, 25 Progressive Service-Industrial, and 26 Knowledge-Service economies, 105 countries representing a human population of 6.6 billion as of 2018; [3] based on the most recent informal investment by representative samples of 6,100 informal investors in nine Agricultural economies, 8,300 in 12 Agricultural-Industrial economies, 27,800 in 32 Service-Industrial economies, 30,900 in 25 Progressive Service-Industrial economies, and 40,400 in 26 Knowledge-Service economies (Reynolds, 2021); [4] Economist Intelligence Unit (2020), 12 Agricultural economies (Congo (Democratic Republic of), Cote d'Ivoire, Ethiopia, Haiti, Madagascar, Mozambique, Nigeria, Rwanda, Senegal, Sierra Leone, Tanzania, Uganda), 15 Agricultural-Industrial economies (Bangladesh, Cambodia, Cameroon, El Salvador, Ghana, Guatemala, Honduras, India, Kenya, Morocco, Myanmar, Nepal, Nicaragua, Pakistan, Viet Nam), 23 Service-Industrial economies (Bolivia, Brazil, China, Colombia, Costa Rica, Dominican Republic, Ecuador, Egypt, Indonesia, Jamaica, Jordan, Lebanon, Mexico, Panama, Paraguay, Peru, Philippines, South Africa, Sri Lanka, Thailand, Trinidad and Tobago, Tunisia, Venezuela), five Progressive Service-Industrial economies (Argentina, Chile, Russia, Turkey, Uruguay); [5] data assembled by MIX (2019) from questionnaires completed by 762 financial service providers across 91 countries in 2016 and 2017 emphasizing serving low- and middle-income individuals, data from 24 Agricultural economies (Afghanistan, Benin, Burkina Faso, Burundi, Comoros, Congo (Democratic Republic of), Cote d'Ivoire, Ethiopia, Haiti, Liberia, Madagascar, Malawi, Mali, Mozambique, Nigeria, Papua New Guinea, Rwanda, Senegal, Sierra Leone, Syria, Tanzania, Togo, Uganda, and Yemen), 25 Agricultural-Industrial economies (Angola, Bangladesh, Cambodia, Cameroon, El Salvador, Ghana, Guatemala, Guyana,

Honduras, India, Iraq, Kenya, Kyrgyzstan, Laos, Morocco, Myanmar, Nepal, Nicaragua, Pakistan, Solomon Islands, Tajikistan, Timor-Leste, Viet Nam, Zambia, and Zimbabwe), 30 Service-Industrial economies (Armenia, Azerbaijan, Bolivia, Bosnia and Herzegovina, Brazil, China, Columbia, Dominican Republic, Ecuador, Egypt, Fiji, Georgia, Indonesia, Jamaica, Jordan, Lebanon, Macedonia (North), Mexico, Moldova, Mongolia, Panama, Paraguay, Peru, Philippines, Samoa, Serbia, South Africa, Tonga, Tunisia, and Uzbekistan), 8 Progressive Service-Industrial economies (Argentina, Belarus, Bulgaria, Chile, Kazakhstan, Kosovo, Romania, and Russia), as it was not clear if changes in the number of financial service providers from 2016 to 2017 reflected organizational terminations or non-response from some institutions, data to represent the country was taken from the year with the greatest number of total borrowers; [6] United Nations (2019b, table 13); [7] International Food Policy Research Institute (2019), reflects government financial support for 2007, data are average values for five Agricultural, 12 Agricultural-Industrial, 16 Service-Industrial, 21 Progressive Service-Industrial, and 18 Knowledge-Service economies.

Table B.6 Economic development: business creator characteristics

	Agricultural	Agricultural-Industrial	Service-Industrial	Progressive Service-Industrial	Knowledge-Service
Number of countries	9	13	32	25	26
Business creation (#/100): 10 %-tile[1]	15	11	9	5	5
Business creation (#/100): average	27	24	17	10	8
Business creation (#/100): 90 %-tile	39	39	28	15	12
Nascent entrepreneur	79,000	126,000	161,000	21,000	33,000
New business owner-manager	60,000	77,000	163,000	13,000	18,000
Total business creation active	139,000	203,000	324,000	34,000	51,000
Proportion of global total (751,000,000)	18%	27%	43%	5%	7%
Business creation: opportunity (#/100)	18	15	11	7	6
Business creation: best choice (#/100)	8	8	5	2	1
High-potential business creators (#/100)[2]	0.92	0.41	0.43	0.46	0.24
Male business creation (#/100)	30	27	19	13	10
Female business creation (#/100)	24	21	14	8	6

Entrepreneurship and economic development

	Agricultural	Agricultural-Industrial	Service-Industrial	Progressive Service-Industrial	Knowledge-Service
Proportion all active					
Men: 18–64 years old	53%	58%	59%	64%	65%
Women: 18–64 years old	47%	42%	41%	36%	35%
Men: 18–24 years old	14%	12%	11%	9%	7%
Men: 25–34 years old	18%	20%	20%	21%	19%
Men: 35–44 years old	10%	14%	15%	17%	18%
Men: 45–54 years old	7%	8%	9%	12%	14%
Men: 55–64 years old	4%	4%	4%	5%	7%
Women: 18–24 years old	12%	9%	7%	5%	3%
Women: 25–34 years old	16%	14%	13%	12%	10%
Women: 35–44 years old	10%	10%	11%	9%	10%
Women: 45–54 years old	6%	6%	7%	7%	8%
Women: 55–64 years old	3%	3%	3%	3%	4%
Household income					
Highest third: prevalence (#/100)	30	28	20	14	10
Middle third: prevalence (#/100)	28	25	17	9	8
Lowest third: prevalence (#/100)	25	20	14	7	6
Highest third: proportion all active	42%	38%	39%	46%	44%
Middle third: proportion all active	29%	34%	33%	30%	33%
Lowest third: proportion all active	29%	28%	28%	24%	23%
Highest third: daily personal income[3]	$13.20	$36.40	$83.00	$201.00	$297.00
Middle third: daily personal income	$6.60	$18.20	$41.50	$100.50	$148.50

	Agricultural	Agricultural-Industrial	Service-Industrial	Progressive Service-Industrial	Knowledge-Service
Lowest third: daily personal income	$3.30	$9.10	$20.75	$50.25	$74.25
Household size: average 2018[4]	5.4	4.7	3.9	3.1	2.5
Education: prevalence (#/100 adults)[5]					
Graduate experience	27	29	20	15	11
College, post-high school	27	27	19	12	9
High school degree	27	25	17	10	7
Pre-high school	26	25	16	8	6
None	23	22	14	7	5
Education: proportion all active					
Graduate experience	1%	2%	6%	11%	16%
College, Post-high school	14%	18%	27%	32%	40%
High school degree	25%	29%	37%	36%	30%
Pre-high school degree	26%	34%	20%	17%	12%
None	34%	18%	10%	3%	1%
Total	100%	99%	100%	99%	99%
HUMAN CAPITAL: Prevalence (#/100 adults)					
Highest	30	29	21	14	11
High	28	27	19	12	9
Intermediate	30	27	17	10	8
Low	27	24	15	8	6
Lowest	22	20	13	6	4

Entrepreneurship and economic development

	Agricultural	Agricultural-Industrial	Service-Industrial	Progressive Service-Industrial	Knowledge-Service
HUMAN CAPITAL: Proportion all active					
Highest	7%	12%	17%	26%	30%
High	13%	16%	24%	26%	28%
Intermediate	37%	27%	26%	25%	25%
Low	23%	26%	20%	15%	12%
Lowest	20%	18%	12%	7%	5%
Total	100%	99%	99%	99%	100%
Labor force activity: pre-profit only					
Prevalence (#/100)					
Full-time work	20	20	14	9	6
Part-time work	13	16	11	7	4
Homemaker	7	8	5	3	3
Student	6	6	5	3	2
Retired, disabled)	9	10	5	1	1
Not working	13	12	8	5	5

	Agricultural	Agricultural-Industrial	Service-Industrial	Progressive Service-Industrial	Knowledge-Service
Proportion all active					
Full-time work	77%	73%	70%	79%	77%
Part-time work	5%	7%	8%	6%	9%
Homemaker	5%	7%	6%	3%	2%
Student	4%	3%	3%	3%	3%
Retired, disabled		1%	2%	2%	2%
Not working	8%	8%	11%	7%	7%
Total	99%	99%	100%	100%	100%

Note: [1] The tenth and ninetieth percentiles are utilized to exclude extreme cases that may reflect failure to completely harmonize all features of the data collection; [2] active business creators expecting ten or more employees in five years and some or major impacts on the markets in which they will compete; [3] figures based on 2018 annual household incomes, adjusted for purchasing power parity for 2011 (International Finance Corporation, 2019a), examination of several national household income distributions suggested that the median value for the lowest third would be about half the overall median and the median value for the highest third would be twice the national median, figures converted to daily income to provide a better measure of the immediate situation confronted by typical individuals; [4] United Nations (2019a), based on most recent data available from 31 Agricultural, 27 Agricultural-Industrial, 38 Service-Industrial, 25 Progressive Service-Industrial, and 23 Knowledge-Service economies; [5] based on harmonized GEM data files that emphasize those involved in business creation (Reynolds, 2021), there may be some variation in coding and coverage with the harmonized files assembled by Barro and Lee (2016).

Table B.7   *Economic development: new venture characteristics*

	Agricultural	Agricultural-Industrial	Service-Industrial	Progressive Service-Industrial	Knowledge-Service
Number of countries	9	13	32	25	26
Pre-profit venture counts	46,000	126,000	112,000	14,000	15,000
New firm venture counts	38,000	101,000	78,000	8,000	10,000
Total early-stage venture counts	84,000	227,000	190,000	22,000	25,000
Sector emphasis					
Agricultural	17%	9%	10%	6%	5%
Mining	<1%	<1%	<1%	<1%	<1%
Manufacturing	7%	10%	10%	10%	7%
Utilities	<1%	<1%	<1%	1%	1%
Construction	1%	2%	3%	7%	7%
Trade (wholesale, retail)	51%	56%	42%	30%	22%
Transportation, communication	2%	4%	5%	7%	7%
Accommodation, food service, bars	7%	8%	11%	8%	7%
Other consumer services	7%	6%	8%	10%	11%
Finance, insurance	1%	1%	1%	2%	2%
Real estate, business/admin services	4%	3%	7%	15%	22%
Public administration	<1%	<1%	<1%	<1%	<1%
Education	1%	1%	1%	2%	3%
Health, social services		1%	1%	2%	5%
Total	98%	101%	99%	100%	99%

	Agricultural	Agricultural-Industrial	Service-Industrial	Progressive Service-Industrial	Knowledge-Service
Major sectors (% ventures)					
Agricultural	17%	9%	10%	6%	5%
Industrial	9%	12%	15%	18%	15%
Consumer oriented	68%	73%	66%	55%	48%
Knowledge based	6%	5%	10%	22%	32%
Total	100%	99%	101%	101%	100%
Sector emphasis (% jobs)					
Agriculture	18%	10%	10%	5%	5%
Mining	<1%	<1%	1%	<1%	<1%
Manufacturing	7%	11%	10%	11%	8%
Utilities	<1%	<1%	<1%	<1%	1%
Construction	1%	2%	4%	9%	9%
Trade (wholesale, retail)	46%	52%	39%	29%	21%
Transportation, communication	3%	4%	6%	9%	7%
Accommodations, food service, bars	7%	8%	10%	7%	7%
Other consumer services	6%	6%	9%	8%	10%
Finance, insurance	<1%	<1%	1%	3%	2%
Real estate, business/admin services	6%	3%	7%	14%	22%
Public administration	<1%	<1%	<1%	<1%	<1%
Education	3%	1%	1%	1%	3%
Health, social services	1%	1%	1%	2%	4%
Total	98%	98%	999%	98%	99%

Entrepreneurship and economic development

	Agricultural	Agricultural-Industrial	Service-Industrial	Progressive Service-Industrial	Knowledge-Service
Major sectors (% jobs)[1]					
Agriculture	18%	10%	10%	5%	5%
Industrial	9%	14%	16%	21%	17%
Consumer oriented	62%	71%	65%	53%	46%
Knowledge base	10%	6%	10%	21%	32%
Total	100%	101%	101%	100%	100%
Job creation (five-year projections)					
None	15%	22%	15%	11%	19%
1–9 jobs	65%	62%	62%	54%	53%
10–49 jobs	17%	14%	19%	27%	22%
50 or more jobs	3%	2%	4%	8%	6%
Job creation total	100%	100%	100%	100%	100%
Market impact					
Major expansion	3%	3%	3%	3%	3%
Some expansion	20%	16%	18%	14%	10%
Little expansion	23%	26%	25%	29%	31%
No expansion	54%	55%	53%	54%	56%
Market impact total	100%	100%	99%	100%	100%

	Agricultural	Agricultural-Industrial	Service-Industrial	Progressive Service-Industrial	Knowledge-Service
Export potential (ventures by % external customers)					
76–100	3%	4%	4%	8%	9%
51–75	3%	4%	4%	6%	6%
26–50	3%	5%	5%	7%	7%
1–25	3%	6%	6%	9%	9%
None	88%	81%	81%	70%	69%
Export potential total	100%	100%	100%	100%	100%

Note: Reynolds (2021), mean values for nine Agricultural, 13 Agricultural-Industrial, 32 Service-Industrial, 25 Progressive Service-Industrial, and 26 Knowledge-Service economies, 105 countries representing a human population of 6.6 billion as of 2018; [1] based on counts of team owners plus employees and sole contractors for each start-up venture and new firm, firms with multiple owners down-weighted to adjust for overrepresentation in the samples, proportions computed for each year with complete data, then averaged across survey years for each country, averaged across countries at each stage of economic development.

References

Alvarez, C., D. Urbano, and J. E. Amorós. (2014). GEM Research: Achievements and Challenges. *Small Business Economics*, 42(3): 445–465.

Amorós, J. E., N. Bosma, and J. Levie. (2013). Ten Years of Global Entrepreneurship Monitor: Accomplishments and Prospects. *International Journal of Entrepreneurial Venturing*, 5(2): 120–152.

Barnett, H. G. (1963). *Being a Palauan*. New York: Holt, Rinehart, and Winston.

Barro, R. J. and J. W. Lee. (2016). Dataset of educational attainment. February. www .barronlee.com. Accessed May 30, 2020.

Beach, Hugh. (1981). *Reindeer-Herd Management in Transition: The Case of Gtuorpon Saameby in Northern Sweden*. Stockholm: Almqvist and Wiskell International.

Beals, Ralph L. (1966). *Community in Transition: Nayon-Ecuador*. Los Angeles, CA: University of California.

Bergmann, Heiko, Susan Mueller, and Thomas Schrettle. (2014). The Use of Global Entrepreneurship Data in Academic Research: A Critical Inventory and Future Potentials. *International Journal of Entrepreneurial Venturing*, 6(3): 242–276.

Bety. (2011). Hopes and Fears: Returning from Europe to Nigeria to Start Up a Small-Scale Business. https://aaeafrica.org/home/profile-2/admin/. Accessed June 12, 2021.

Blumberg, Rae Lesser. (1995). Gender, Microenterprise, Performance and Power: Case Studies from the Dominican Republic, Ecuador, Guatemala and Swaziland. In Christine Bose and Edna Acosta-Belen (eds), *Women in the Development Process in Latin America: From Structural Subordination to Empowerment*. Philadelphia, PA: Temple University Press, pp. 194–226.

Bogaraz-Tan, Vladimir Germanovich (Bogaras, Waldemar). (1904–1909). *The Chukchee: Material Culture* (Part 1), *Religion* (Part 2), *Social Organization* (Part 3). Leiden: E.J. Brill.

Bradfield, Maitland. (1971). *The Changing Pattern of Hopi Agriculture*. London: Royal Anthropological Institute.

Bradfield, Maitland. (1973). *A Natural History of Associations: A Study in the Meaning of Community*. New York: International Universities Press.

Clark, Gracia. (1994). *Onions Are My Husband: Survival and Accumulation by West African Market Women*. Chicago, IL: University of Chicago Press.

Cohen, David W. and E.S. Atiendo Odhiambo. (1989). *Siaya: The Historical Anthropology of an African Landscape*. Nairobi: Heinemann Kenya.

Colson, Elizabeth. (1971). *The Social Consequences of Resettlement: The Impact of the Kariba Resettlement upon the Gwembe Tonga*. Manchester: Manchester University Press.

Convergences. (2018). *Microfinance Barometer 2019*. Paris: Convergences.

Crocombe, R.G. (1967). *Four Orokaiva Cash Croppers*. Canberra: Australian National University.

Crownpoint Rug Auction. (2021). Crownpoint Navajo Rug Auction. https://crownpointrunauction.com. Accessed March 21, 2021.

Curtin, Richard T. and Paul D. Reynolds. (2018). *Panel Study of Entrepreneurial Dynamics, PSED II, United States, 2005–2011.* Ann Arbor, MI: Inter-University Consortium for Political and Social Research. https://doi.org/10.3886/ICPSR37202.v1.

De Soto, Hernando. (1989). *The Other Path: The Invisible Revolution in the Third World.* New York: Harper and Row.

De Soto, Hernando. (2000). *The Mystery of Capital.* New York: Basic Books.

EIU (Economist Intelligence Unit). (2020). *Global Microscope 2020: The Role of Financial Inclusion in the COVID-19 Response.* New York: Economist Intelligence Unit.

Gilbreath, Kent. (1977). *Red Capitalism: An Analysis of the Navajo Economy.* Norman, OK: University of Oklahoma Press.

Gutierrez de Pineda, Virginia and Sydney Jamie Muirden. (1948). *Social Organization in La Guajira.* New Haven, CT: Human Relation Area Files.

Haerpfer, C., R. Inglehart, A. Moreno, C. Welzel, K. Kizilova, J. Diez-Medrano et al. (eds). (2020). *World Values Survey: Round Seven – Country-Pooled Datafile.* Madrid and Vienna: JD Systems Institute and WVSA Secretariat.

Hansen, Suzy. (2012). How Zara Grew into the World's Largest Fashion Retailer. *New York Times Magazine*, November 9.

Heiberg, Marianne. (1989). *The Making of the Basque Nation.* Cambridge: Cambridge University Press.

Heinen, H. Dieter. (1973). *Adaptive Changes in a Tribal Economy: A Case Study of the Winikina-Waro.* Ann Arbor, MI: University Microfilms.

Hogland, Eric J. (1989). The Society and Its Environment. In Helen Chapin Metz (ed.) *Iran: A Country Study.* Washington, DC: U.S. Government Printing Office, pp. 71–136, 315–317.

Holloman, Regina. (1969). *Development Change in San Blas.* Ann Arbor, MI: University Microfilms.

Human Relations Area Files. (2020). *eHRAF User Guide.* New Haven, CT: Yale University.

IKEA International A/S. (2020). Company Profile, Information, Business Description, History, Background Information on IKEA International A/S. http://www.referenceforbusiness.com/history2/37/IKEA-International. Accessed November 9, 2020.

Inglehart, R., C. Haerpfer, A. Moreno, C. Welzel, K. Kizilova, J. Diez-Medrano et al. (eds). (2020). *World Values Survey: All Rounds – Country-Pooled Datafile.* Madrid and Vienna: JD Systems Institute and WVSA Secretariat.

Ingold, Tim. (1976). *The Skolt Lapps Today.* London: Cambridge University Press.

International Finance Corporation. (2019a). *World Economic Outlook Database April 2019.* Washington, DC: International Monetary Fund.

International Finance Corporation. (2019b). *World Economic Outlook Database October 2019.* Washington, DC: International Monetary Fund.

International Food Policy Research Institute. (2019). *A Database User Manual for (SPEED) Statistics on Public Expenditures for Economic Development.* Washington, DC: International Food Policy Research Institute.

International Labour Organization. (2019). *Small Matters: Global Evidence on the Contributions to Employment by the Self-Employed, Micro-Enterprises and SMEs.* Geneva: International Labor Organization.

International Labour Organization. (2020). ILOSTAT database. https://ilostat.ilo.org/data/. Accessed May 28, 2020.

Jefremovas, Villia. (1991). Loose Women, Virtuous Wives, and Timid Virgins: Gender and the Control of Resources in Rwanda. *Canadian Journal of African Studies*, 25(3): 378–395.

Johnson, Basil. (1988). *Indian School Days*. Toronto, Canada: Key Porter.

Kato, Atsushi and Eriko Miyake. (2015). *Habitus That Leads Mama to Entrepreneurs: The Case Studies of Three Japanese Women Entrepreneurs*. Washington, DC: International Council for Small Business.

Khuwinphan, Pricha. (1980). *Marketing in North-Central Thailand: A Study of Socio-Economic Organization in a Thai Market Town*. Bangkok: Chulalongkorn University Social Research Institute.

Kidd, Stephen W. (1999). *Love and Hate among the People without Things: The Social and Economic Relations of the Enxet People of Paraguay*. Dissertation: University of St. Andrews.

Koop, Sabine, Tamara de Reu, and Michael Frese. (2000). Sociodemographic Factors, Entrepreneurial Orientation, Personal Initiative, and Environmental Problems in Uganda. In M. Frese (ed.), *Success and Failure of Microbusinesses Owners in Africa: A Psychological Approach*. Westport, CT: Quorum Books, pp. 55–76.

Kopytoff, Igor. (1965). The Suku of Southwestern Congo. In J.L. Gibbs, Jr. (ed.), *Peoples of Africa*. New York: Holt, Rinehart and Winston, pp. 441–477.

Kopytoff, Igor. (1971). The Suku of the Congo: An Ethnographic Test of Hus's Hypotheses. In F.L.K. Hsu (ed.), *Kinship and Culture*. Chicago, IL: Aldine, pp.69–86.

Lewis, Robert. (2019). IKEA. Encyclopedia Britannica. www.britannica.com/topic/IKEA. Accessed November 9, 2020.

Lloyd, Peter Cutt. (1965). The Yoruba of Nigeria. In J.L. Gibbs, Jr. (ed.), *Peoples of Africa*. New York: Holt, Rinehart and Winston, pp. 549–582.

Mamo, Dwayne (ed.). (2020). *The Indigenous World 2020*. Copenhagen: International Work Group for Indigenous Affairs.

Miller, Terry, Anthony B. Kim, and James M. Roberts. (2020). *2020 Index of Economic Freedom*. Washington, DC: The Heritage Foundation.

MIX. (2019). *Global Outreach and Financial Performance Benchmark Report: 2017–2018*. Washington, DC: MIX Headquarters.

Morrissey, Janet. (2015). Mixing Cuisines, Mexicue Moves beyond the Food Truck. *New York Times*. https://nyti.ms/1JGNkDv. Accessed November 27, 2021.

Navajo Rug Appraisal Co. (2021). The Crownpoint Navajo Rug Auction. www.navajorunrepair.com. Accessed March 20, 2021.

Noon, Nuriyah Noriah. (1989). A Case Study of the Malaysian Small-Scale Enterprise Nursery Schemes. Retrospective Theses and Dissertations. 9229. https://lib.ddr.iastateedu/rtd/9227.

Nueno, Jose Luis, Miguel Bazan, and Silvia Rodriguez. (2011). AJE: Taking On Bigger Rivals. *Financial Times*. www.ft.cm/content/462d0482-0577-11e1-8eaa-00144feabdc0. Accessed June 13, 2021.

Osella, Filippo and Caroline Osella. (2000). *Social Mobility in Kerala: Modernity and Identity in Conflict*. Sterling, VA: Pluto Press.

Parkin, David J. (1978). *The Cultural Definition of Political Response: Lineal Destiny among the Luo*. New York: Academic Press.

Polgreen, Lydia. (2011). Scaling Caste Walls with Capitalism's Ladder in India. *New York Times*, December 22, p. A1.

Reynolds, Paul D. (1998). Business Volatility: Source or Symptom of Economic Growth? In Zolton J. Acs, Bo Carlsson, and Charlie Karlsson (eds), *Entrepreneurship, Small and Medium-Sized Enterprises, and the Macro-Economy*. Cambridge: Cambridge University Press.

Reynolds, Paul D. (2012). *Firm Creation in the Business Life Course: MENA Countries in the Global Context*. Report submitted to International Development Research Center, Ottawa and Organisation for Economic Co-operation and Development, Paris.

Reynolds, Paul D. (2014). Business Creation Stability: Why is it so Hard to Increase Entrepreneurship? *Foundations and Trends in Entrepreneurship*, 10(5–6): 321–475.

Reynolds, Paul D. (2017). Global Entrepreneurship Monitor (GEM) Program: Development, Focus, and Impact. In Raymond J. Aldag (ed.), *Oxford Research Encyclopedias: Business and Management*. New York: Oxford University Press, to be available at www.business.oxfordre.com.

Reynolds, Paul D. (2018). *Business Creation: Ten Factors for Entrepreneurial Success*. Cheltenham, UK and Northampton, MA, USA: Edward Elgar Publishing.

Reynolds, Paul D. (2020). *The Truth about Entrepreneurship: Policy Making and Business Creation*. Cheltenham, UK and Northampton, MA, USA: Edward Elgar Publishing.

Reynolds, Paul D. (2021). *Global Entrepreneurship Monitor: Adult Population Survey Data Sets: 1998–2017*. Ann Arbor, MI: Inter-University Consortium for Political and Social Research. https://doi.org/10.3886/ICPSR20320.V5.

Reynolds, Paul D. and Richard T. Curtin. (2009a). Business Creation in the United States: Entry, Startup Activities, and the Launch of New Ventures. In U.S. Small Business Administration (ed.), *The Small Business Economy: A Report to the President 2008*. Washington, DC: U.S. Government Printing Office, pp. 165–240.

Reynolds, Paul D. and Richard T. Curtin (eds). (2009b). *New Firm Creation in the U.S.: Initial Explorations with the PSED II Data Set*. New York: Springer.

Reynolds, Paul D. and Richard T. Curtin (eds). (2010). *New Firm Creation: An International Overview*. New York: Springer.

Reynolds, Paul D. and Richard T. Curtin (eds). (2011). *New Firm Creation: An International Overview*. New York: Springer.

Reynolds, Paul D., Sammis White et al. (1993). *Wisconsin Entrepreneurial Climate Study*. Milwaukee, WI: Marquette University Center for the Study of Entrepreneurship. DOI: 10.13140/rg.2.2101489.09444.

Reynolds, Paul, Niels Bosma, Erkko Autio, Steve Hunt, Natalie De Bono, Isabel Servais, Paloma Lopez-Garcia, and Nancy Chin. (2005). Global Entrepreneurship Monitor: Data Collection Design and Implementation: 1998–2003. *Small Business Economics*, 24: 205–231.

Reynolds, Paul D., Diana Hechavarria, Li Tian, Mikael Samuelsson, and Per Davidsson. (2016). *Panel Study of Entrepreneurial Dynamics: A Five Cohort Outcomes Harmonized Data Set*. Research Gate. DOI: 10.13140/RG.2.1.2561.7682.

Rosen, Lawrence. (2010). Understanding Corruption. *The American Interest*, 5(4): 78–82.

Seliverstova, Nataliya and Aleksandra Somkova (2018). Female Entrepreneurship in Russia: Women Wanted! Thesis: Linnaeus University.

Smith, David Merrill. (1995). Death of a Patriarch. *Anthropology and Humanism*, 20(2): 124–132.

Starr, June. (1978). *Dispute and Settlement in Rural Turkey: An Ethnography of Law*. Leiden: E.J. Brill.

Suarez, Maria Matilde. (1971). *Nieuwe West_Indische Gids*, Vol. 48. Gravenhage: Martinus Nijhoff, pp. 56–122.

Tikkanen, Amy. (2020). Ingvar Kamprad. *Encyclopedia Britannica*. www.britannica
.com/bibliographjy/Ingvar-Kamprad. Accessed November 9, 2020.
Tschopik, Harry, Jr. (1951). *The Aymara of Chucuito, Peru*. New York: American
Museum of Natural History.
United Nations. (2019a). *Database on Household Size and Composition: 2019*. New
York: United Nations Department of Economic and Social Affairs.
United Nations. (2019b). *Human Development Report: 2019*. New York: United
Nations Development Programme.
U.S. Department of the Interior. (2014). *2013 American Indian Population and Labor
Force Report*. Washington, DC: U.S. Department of the Interior.
Watson, Lawrence Craig. (1968). *Guajiro Personality and Urbanization*. Los Angeles,
CA: University of California.
Wikipedia. (2020). IKEA. https://en.wikipedia.org/wiki/IKEA. Accessed November
9, 2020.
Wikipedia. (2021a). Amancio Ortega. https://en.wikipedia.org/w/index,php?title=
Amancio_Ortega&oldid=1281234701. Accessed June 16, 2021.
Wikipedia. (2021b). Kola Real. https://en.wikipedia.org/wiki/Kola_Real. Accessed
June 13, 2021.
Wikipedia. (2021c). Zara. https://en.wikipedia.org/w/index.php?title-Zara_(retailer)&
oldid=1028529928. Accessed June 13, 2021.
World Bank. (2020). *Doing Business 2020*. Washington, DC: World Bank. DOI:
10.1596/978-1-4648-1440-2.
World Bank Group. (2015). *Our People, Our Resources*. Washington, DC: World
Bank.
Wyckoff, Lydia L. (1986). *Third Mesa Hopi Ceramics: A Study of the Ceramic
Domain*. Ann Arbor, MI: University Microfilms.
Yeh, Emily T. (2004). Property Relations in Tibet since Decollectivisation and the
Question of Fuzziness. *Conservation and Society*, 2(1): 108–131.
Yunus, Muhammad. (1998). Poverty Alleviation: Is Economics any Help? Lessons
from the Grameen Bank Experience. *Journal of International Affairs*, 52(1): 47–65.

Index